Hard
Bargaining
in
Sumatra

Southeast Asia

POLITICS, MEANING, AND MEMORY

Rita Smith Kipp and David Chandler

SERIES EDITORS

Hard Bargaining in Sumatra

Western Travelers and Toba Bataks

in the Marketplace of Souvenirs

ANDREW CAUSEY

UNIVERSITY OF HAWAI‘I PRESS   *Honolulu*

Illustrations in this volume were supported in part by a grant from Columbia College Chicago.

Library of Congress Cataloging-in-Publication Data

Causey, Andrew.

Hard bargaining in Sumatra : western travelers and Toba Bataks in the marketplace of souvenirs / Andrew Causey.

p. cm — (Southeast Asia)

Includes bibliographical references and index.

ISBN 0–8248–2626–4 (alk. paper) — ISBN 0–8248–2747–3 (pbk. : paper)

1. Toba-Batak (Indonesian people)—Social conditions. 2. Toba-Batak (Indonesian people)—Economic conditions. 3. Wood-carving, Toba-Batak—Indonesia—Samosir Island. 4. Culture and tourism—Indonesia—Samosir Island. 5. Souvenirs (Keepsakes)—Indonesia—Samosir Island. 6. Samosir Island—(Indonesia)—Economic conditions. 7. Samosir Island (Indonesia)—Social life and customs. I. Title. II. Series.

DS632.T62 C38 2003

381'.45745'089992—dc21

2003009994

Designed by Rich Hendel

Printed by The Maple-Vail Book Manufacturing Group

CONTENTS

Color plates follow page 118.

ACKNOWLEDGMENTS

Luckily for me, writing a book is more like molding clay than carving wood: words, like clay, are continually added and subtracted, a little more here, a lot less there; in carving, decisions to saw and shape wood must be final, for there is no putting back the wood once it is gone.

For help in forming this work I want to thank Ward Keeler, who mentored me in Southeast Asian studies; Katie Stewart, who taught me about tales and the telling of them; and Steve Feld, who guided me to discover cadence and rhythm in the everyday. I would also like to thank the following people for helping me know what words to put where, which to cut, and when to add: Deborah Kapchan, the late Linda Schele, Joel Sherzer, Keila Diehl, David Henderson, Calla Jacobson, and David Samuels for their thoughtful comments on early drafts of this work, and Kathleen Adams, Kenneth George, and Susan Rodgers for their insights on later drafts. Many of the issues discussed in this work were aided by conversations with other scholars and friends. For their patience in listening to my long-winded stories, and their raised eyebrows about my half-baked ideas, I would like to thank the following people: Sandra Niessan, Mary Steedly, Rita Kipp, Ed Bruner, Sally Ness, Anthony Reid, Bob Fernea, Elizabeth J. Fernea, Victoria Beard, Jill Forshee, Lynne Milgram, Elizabeth Keating, Emily Sokoloff, Begonia Aretxaga, Lynn Denton, Carla Reiter, Tad Tuleja, Katrin Fleisig, Carol Cannon, Diane April, Red Wassenich, Karen Pavelka, Jim Stroud, Cathy Henderson, Kathleen Hoski, Barbara Baskin, Leslie Morris, Frances Terry, Jane Henrici, and Penny van Horn, an artist and friend who sometimes saw more clearly than I could myself. Two people who instructed me when I was at my most recalcitrant deserve special thanks: Jerry Epstein, who helped me to think logically, and the late Bonnie Kingsley, who encouraged me to explore my intuitions.

Parts of this book were partially worked out in previous publications, sometimes with conclusions that differ from what is found here, and sometimes with more in-depth examinations and details than what is included here. Sections of Chapter 5 are found in "Stealing a Good Idea: Innovation and Competition among Toba Batak Woodcarvers," published in *Museum Anthropology,* 1999, and in "The Folder in the Drawer of the Sky Blue Lemari: a Toba Batak Carver's Secrets," which appeared in *Crossroads: an Interdisciplinary Journal of Southeast Asian Studies,* 2000. Parts of Chapter 6 also appear in "Making an Orang Malu: Aesthetic and Economic Dialogues between Western Tourists and Toba Bataks in the Souvenir Marketplace," published in *Converging Interests: Traders, Travelers, and Tourists in Southeast Asia,* edited by J. Forshee, et al., University of California Press, 1999, and in "The Singasinga Table Lamp and the Toba Batak's Art of Conflation," which appeared in the *Journal of American Folklore,* 1999.

I would also like to thank all the editors at the University of Hawai'i Press who made this work more readable.

My research would have been impossible without the help of many institutions and individuals in Indonesia. My thanks to the Indonesian Institute of Sciences (LIPI) and to the Committee for Area Development Planning, Medan (BPPD) for permission to do my fieldwork in North Sumatra. I would like to especially thank Dr. Usman Pelly at IKIP Medan for his sponsorship of my work, and Dr. A. Dahana and Nellie Polhaupessy for the many times they came to my assistance. My research was made possible by grants from Fulbright IIE and the Social Science Research Council; the financial assistance of these funding agencies is greatly appreciated. For their help in administering the Fulbright IIE grant, I would like to thank Marty Adler, Donna Woodward, and Sikap Sebayang. Finally, at Columbia College Chicago, I would like to thank Provost Steve Kapelke for the financial assistance to make this book more visually appealing, with additional thanks to Dean Cheryl Johnson-Odim, who enabled me to spend many hours of quality time with the manuscript of this book.

My sincere gratitude goes to my Toba Batak friends on Samosir, without whose hospitality and knowledge I could not have written this book: Bapak and Ibu Pardamean Marpaung (br. Singaga) and children for opening their home to me as if I were a family member; Bapak and Ibu Maricce Sidabutar (br. Marpaung), Nenek Aprianto Siadari, Bapak and Ibu Aprianto Sitorus (br. Samosir), Junna Samosir, Bapak and Ibu Dede Sinaga (br. Manurung), Bapak and Ibu Bonggas (br. Sinaga), Mr. and Mrs. Dome (br. Samosir), Bapak and Ibu Dasni Harianja (br. Siallagan), Bapak and Ibu Fernando Siallagan, and Bapak and Ibu Lindung Siallagan (br. Parhusip), for their infinite patience and endless humor. Thanks to them all for sharing their stories with me. I would also like to thank the owners and employees of the hotels, Mr. Mas, Sony, and Barbara, for all of their help with my questionnaire and the many, many cups of coffee they provided for me.

My greatest thanks go to my mother, Catherine Lees Causey, and to my four siblings and their families, for the years of financial, moral, and emotional support they have given me while I worked on this book, and to Mike Arnold, for his endless capacity to be supportive and understanding while I wrestled with it.

* * *

Figure 2 is from Jonathan Swift's *Travel into several remote nations of the world,* 1792. All other photographs were taken by the author.

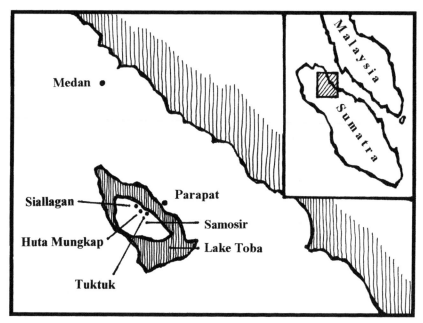

Sumatra and Samosir Island

Introduction

"Tunggu Dulu Tesnya…": Stories from the Fancy Mat

My carving teacher, his wife, and their children were seated on the brightly colored woven mat, and they asked me to tell them how I first came to visit Samosir Island. They had heard the story before, but wanted to hear it again to savor the images of confusion, of delight, of anger. So I told them the story again, starting at the very beginning.

I first came to North Sumatra, Indonesia, as a tourist in 1989. Like many others, I had worked at a job I didn't really like in order to save enough money to make the trip. And like many others, I was ill-prepared for the journey: I did not speak the language, I had an unclear itinerary, and knew very little about the cultures I was going to visit. Nevertheless, the trip from Los Angeles to Medan is a long one, and it gave me plenty of time to read through the two guidebooks I was carrying. The glossy color photographs I saw reaffirmed one thing for me—I would visit the huge crater lake, Toba, and the mountain island that rose up from its midst. This was the land of the Toba Bataks, the people (as I read in the book) who had been isolated from the world for centuries, and who were rumored to have once been cannibals.

I knew a little about the Toba Bataks before I began my journey, but not very much. I had seen examples of their carvings at a museum and was drawn to the simplicity of their lines and the strength of their forms. After touring the gallery, I had a great desire to possess such carvings of my own: lustrous black figures worn smooth by decades of use. The guidebook told me that artisans were still producing traditional objects, but I imagined myself cherishing something ancient, polished with eons of sweat and smoke. In a pinch, I told myself, I would be content with something new.

Once on Sumatran soil, I felt dazed and unfocused. I had done a terrible job of memorizing the simple phrases outlined in the guidebook, and the blur of words, magnified by the stifling heat of the coastal city of Medan, made me feel defensive and confused. Still, the people I met were earnestly friendly and tried to talk to me using English words, which calmed me. When I finally arrived at the lakeside tourist town Parapat, I was beginning to feel comfortable with my situation. Traveling alone in a strange country, I convinced myself, would provide for me a kind of emancipation, for I would find an inner strength that would allow me not only to take care of myself but to *grow*.

I spent a week on Samosir, the island in the lake, finding ways to communicate with local people, photographing their grandly decorated homes and verdant fields, and exploring the tourist marketplaces. I found a few souvenirs to buy in the stalls, but was disappointed that all the real antiques seemed to be gone. On the day before I was to leave Samosir and travel to the island of Java, I made one last search for the dark, burnished objects I desired. I was poking around behind leather bags and below racks of hanging T-shirts when a smiling vendor came up to me, saying in heavily accented English, "You want antiques?" There was no time left for me to be distant or vague with her in the hope that my casual attitude would help in the bargaining session. With wild eyes, I told her, yes, I was looking for antiques, at which point she escorted me to a traditional home not far from the market.

Despite the fact that it was a clear sunny day, it was very dark inside the old house, for it was brightened only by a small open window. "Wait here," she said, "I will get my husband. He has antiques; he will sell you antiques." As I waited in the dark, I squinted my eyes to better see where I was. The room was wide and spacious, with no furnishings except the woven mat on which I was sitting. I reached my hand out to feel the cool floor, consisting of huge worn planks that glowed dully with the reflected light from the window. As my eyes adjusted to the dark, I began to see that every wall was hung with carvings. There were water-buffalo horns with masklike stoppers. There were black walking sticks decorated with creatures standing on one anothers' backs. There were ornate sheathed knives and staring human figures, elegant covered vessels and oblong mandolins. And all of them sang to me of their wonderful age—I had found the antiques!

A middle-aged man entered the main room from behind a curtain, introduced himself to me in English, and sat down on the mat with me. He told me that he had been gathering these objects for years. Although they were his own private collection, he said he would be willing to sell one or two of them because he saw I had an interest in the culture of his ancestors. He showed me many things and told me the stories that explained how they had been used and why they were rare. His wife brought hot tea for us to drink as we chatted, but I do not know how long we sat there talking. I selected an object from his collection that I was intimately drawn to: a carved box with a saddle-shaped lid. He wanted a great deal of money for this antique, but we negotiated and compromised, and he lovingly wrapped the carving in paper. It was a high price to pay, but I now owned one of the glossy old objects with which I had become obsessed. As I left the old house, he invited me to come visit him again whenever I returned.

I had no time to gloat over my new possession, for the ferry to the mainland was ready to go. I crammed the box in my backpack and raced off to the dock. In Parapat, I rushed to catch the bus to the airport in Medan, and in a few hours I was in Java. Compared to the bright clear light and the cool fresh breezes of North Sumatra's mountains, Jakarta was an insult to the senses. All I could find was a poorly ventilated cell in a shabby hotel, and all I wanted was to return to Lake Toba. I opened my bag, pining for the highlands, and found my antique. Now I could admire it, could feel the shine of its aged patina, could revel in the intricacy of its design. Ahhhh, the box was beautiful. In addition to the elaborate interlocking surface details, it had the head of a delightful snakelike creature at one end of the lid. It smelled musky from the centuries of tobacco that had been stored in it. I turned the box over to see if there were figures or engravings on the bottom, but there was nothing. "What's this stuff?" I asked myself as I prodded my fingernail into a crevice. It was brown and came loose as I picked at it. "Huh. I guess it's dirt," I thought, trying to reassure myself. But when I took the box over to the bare bulb sticking out of the hotel room's wall, I saw that the wood underneath the substance was nearly white with fresh little splinters sticking up.

Frantically, I looked at the other cracks and fissures. There too was the dark substance. If I picked it and rubbed it between my fingers, it stained them; it had a distinct petroleum-based scent. I knew now that I had been had.

My antique was a fake. I had bought something worth *nothing*. I fumed, then put the box and the lid down carelessly on the cot and left the room to find a beer and some solace or distraction. How could I have been so foolish? How could I not have seen that I was being set up? How had my eye for the real, my taste for the venerable, if nothing else my penuriousness . . . how could they all have failed me? The box went to the bottom of my bag for the rest of the trip. I was angry at it and at the people who had made it, and I did not really care whether I was careful with it or not.

I bought many other things on my trip—batik sarongs, grimacing masks, and ballpoint pens made to look like Javanese puppets—but when I unpacked them all once I was home again, the Batak carving was still my favorite. Back home, it did not seem to matter so much that the box was masquerading as an heirloom from the time of the Batak ancestors, for I now began to see in it an integrity of character and honesty of design that could not be masked with shoe polish.

Partoho, Ito, and their seven children all stared at me long after the story had ended. Ito clicked her tongue, saying: "They cheated you and you still came back here. You were drawn back here to do your research years later for a *reason*." She nodded her head at me as if we both accepted the inevitability of fate.

"Maybe," Partoho added. "But I hope you didn't return to get your money back from the man in the old house, because he moved to Medan long ago, and no one has heard from him since!" He turned to me to say, "You'll have to keep that box, Andru. Too bad for you!" Ito let out an exasperated sigh at her husband's little joke, then rose to heat up some more tea.

I had only been back in the cozy home of Partoho and Ito for an hour and we had already recovered our comfortable pattern of conversation. I had been gone from the village Huta Mungkap, where Ito and her husband Partoho lived, for four months and was now returning to finish my fieldwork. As I stepped off the boat, Ito stopped in the path when she saw me coming toward her house. She was covering her laughing mouth, and as I got closer I could hear her saying, *"Aduh! Lihatlah! Lihat Andru yang GEMUK seperti bosnya!"* ("Wow! Just look! Look at Andrew who is FAT like a boss!"). She called out to Partoho and her children that a "big boss" was coming down the path. They all stood exactly where they were, smiling and asking how I could have put on so much weight (ten pounds) in so little time, telling me that if I was to live in Huta Mungkap again, I must go back to eating "farmer food": rice and fish and chili sauce. "You'll look like a Batak farmer again in no time," she told me.

Partoho invited me into the house where we could sit down, have a glass of hot sugared tea and a *kretek* (I: clove cigarette), and talk. Sharp words were spoken to a pair of children who were lounging in front of the black-and-white television set trying to make sense out of an undubbed American cartoon as it slowly flipped on the dim screen. They snapped the machine off and rolled out the family's fancy mat. This heavy plastic mat, saved for special occasions, was woven with yellow scrolls on a field of crimson red and was placed ceremoniously on top of the worn everyday mat on the living-room floor. I was invited to sit down, as usual, to Partoho's right with my back to the wall (so I could face the television). Ito sat on his left. The two girls were busy in the kitchen making tea, but the boys all flopped down on the mat in an arc to my right. The two oldest sons, both past high school age, were sitting closest to me making small talk, but the younger ones sat around me in a ring, smiling and gaping as they had a good, long look.

I started to tell them a funny story about changing planes in Jakarta, but Ito put her hand on my wrist, saying, *"Tunggu dulu tesnya . . ."* ("Wait a second for the tea . . ."). She frowned toward the kitchen doorway and told the girls to hurry up. (An unspoken rule dictated that we could only chatter about truly minor topics—"the boat arrived on time," "the weather is nice and clear," nothing that would evoke a "story" or an extended narrative—until the tea was placed in front of each person.) The youngest girl brought in the enameled metal tray heavy with clear, golden tumblers that softly jittered against each other and placed it in front of Partoho. We waited quietly as she kneeled and put each person's glass in front of him or her, then found a place in the ring of family members on the mat. Partoho hushed the group and made a brief prayer in both Toba Batak and Indonesian thanking God for my safe return, and wishing us good health, prosperity, and success in all of our endeavors. There was a brief pause. Then the conversation burst into full bloom. Did you find a job when you were in America? Did you see that the village road was paved? Tell us what you ate there to become so fat! Are the neighbors still fighting? Tell us again about the first time you came to Samosir!

This circle of domestic conversation, which flourishes in the place where private and public overlap, which embraces both familiars and outsiders, and which shunts between chatter, gossip, and intricate stories, is what best characterizes the nature of my fieldwork among Toba Bataks living on Samosir Island—the way I sat talking and learning with the people of Huta Mungkap village. My experiences sitting in Batak homes engaging in conversation is not so different from the experiences of other researchers, of course. Kathleen Stewart describes how Appalachians use stories to help create the world they experience; this narrated "space at the side of the road" is like a "scenic re-presentation of the force of a lyric image with the power to give pause to the straight line of narrative ordering of events from beginning to end . . ." (1996:34). The narratives that unfold on the fancy mats of Samosir are not so different, because they too use the artful play of talk to both guide and deter truth's rigidity.

Many of these rounds of talking took place in the home of my carving teacher, Partoho, and his wife, Ito (plate 1), whose living-room television seemed always to be quietly murmuring to the semiattentive audience of seven children and their school friends who wandered in and out the front door. After a meal, dishes would be picked up, and the rice crumbs on the floor and mat would be swept out the door for the chickens. The topaz-colored glasses would soon appear, filled with the hot sugar water they call *tes* (TB: tea), and clove smoke would rise up around the single electric light bulb and then farther up, to the open beams of the roof already black with sooty cobwebs and dust. Because they live very close to the stone-cobbled path that connects the lakeshore (dotted with tourist hotels and Batak bathing spots) with the main asphalt road that cuts through the center of Huta Mungkap and circles the island, there is a steady flow of people passing by Partoho and Ito's house day and night: neighbors going home weighted down with galvanized tubs of damp laundry balanced on their heads; cousins returning from the vegetable market on the mainland; and a variety of westerners searching for places to stay, laughing loudly on rented bicycles, or slipping quietly past the house carrying mysterious packages. On occasion, some of these passersby (usually Bataks) stopped by the house after dinner to talk. While everyone in the room would politely engage in topics having to do with the weather, the church, or the local news, it was only when a "story" began to be told that the unanimous demeanor of the listeners, except for the youngest of children, was one of rapt attention.

The narratives told at these times usually concerned recent personal experiences composed in a familiar, almost formulaic, structure. If the story was a success (that is, if it was greeted by the listeners with sounds of amazement or disbelief), it was quite often told all over again, recapturing details in greater depth and color. These story tellings, the major component of the domestic circles of talk, would commonly extend into the quietest hours of evening, when even the high schoolers had fallen asleep, the tea had gone cold, and the ashtrays were brimming with cigarette butts and clove ashes.

On this particular late afternoon, as it was the day of my return, Ito wanted to review not only how I had first come to Samosir in 1989 but also how she and I had originally met twelve months before. She told the story of how she had "found" me wandering around in the tourist marketplace in the neighboring town of Siallagan: "I thought you were a tourist buying carvings, and you looked so RICH! Remember? I called you over and asked you in English where you were staying, right? And, remember, you started speaking Indonesian and said you were staying at a *losmen* (I: home-stay hotel) in Huta Mungkap. . . . Think of that! Huta Mungkap, my very own village, and your *losmen* right next door to my house! 'How lucky we all are,' I thought, 'to be so close.'" I told Ito that I remembered our first meeting too, but added that the details of my coming to Huta Mungkap were more complicated, that the way it all happened was much more interesting. They smiled and settled themselves down for a meaty narrative:

When I landed in Medan, I asked a taxi driver, a Batak man, as it turned out, to take me to the cheapest hotel. He brought me to a glittering glass and chrome high rise. "Too expensive!" I bleated, but he told me he knew the manager, who would give me a discount.

The sparkling panes of mirrored glass on the building turned out to be a facade covering up a crumbling colonial ruin from the 1930s whose thick concrete walls enclosed dark, shadowy cubicles. It was being renovated from the front to the rear, and the rooms at the back were indeed very cheap, but also unventilated and swarming with mosquitoes. The most affordable restaurant in the area was across the street at another dilapidated hotel whose own modern facade, I guessed, was planned but not yet built. I ate at this place each day that I was forced to be in Medan obtaining my letters of permission to do research in the province of North Sumatra. Because of this, I got to know the waiters and cooks fairly well. It was here that I first began to hear about Pak Wil.[1]

Pak Wil, they told me, is an old Dutchman who had come to retire in Sumatra. "He is very old and gray, but strong enough to lift a man off the ground and throw him!" they said. "Pak Wil was the soldier who captured our first president, Sukarno, when he was considered to be an outlaw by the returning Dutch colonial government —he found Sukarno hiding in the hills above Lake Toba and took him and his entourage to jail," I was told, "and he can speak Indonesian fluently." When they found out I was going to Lake Toba in the mountains west of Medan to do research on the Toba Batak culture, they said, "Pak Wil is already there." I was both curious and annoyed about this "Pak Wil" who seemed to be one step ahead of me, but I gave him little thought, knowing that the lake was so huge that we would never meet.

I got all of my government permits finished in less than a week and left the sweltering miasma that suffocates Medan. Seated in a crowded van that passed through, first, palm oil plantations, then coffee and chocolate plantations, and finally rubber tree plantations, it was several hours before I felt any drop in the temperature. By the time I got to Parapat, the main resort on the edge of the lake, the mountain air had been blowing in through a crack in the window for an hour, so I felt washed free of the hot breath of the lowlands. The bus driver left me and my awkward backpack and bags at an inexpensive *losmen* on one of the main roads in the town. It was already late in the afternoon, so many of the rooms were taken. There was only one still empty, near the shared bathroom, which the housemaid told me had been vacated only a day before by Pak Wil. "Is he still around?" I asked. "Will I meet him?" I was told that he had left to go live on Samosir, the huge mountainous island in the center of the lake. The vague twinge of annoyance returned when I heard this: I was planning to move to Samosir myself as soon as I received my local permits.

I had selected Samosir rather than Parapat as my field site because I had come to investigate how Western tourism was changing the way Toba Batak wood carvings are made, and the small towns on the east coast of the island are where westerners tended to go. Nevertheless, I decided to make the best of my forced stay on the mainland by seeing what kind of objects the souvenir shops lining the streets had for sale. Most of the stores (which seemed to exude out of the bottom floors of the town's buildings, spreading their wares onto the sidewalk, up the facade, and out onto bamboo poles that wavered above the street) sold the same sorts of things: postcards, leather bags, beaded pouches, palm-frond hats, T-shirts, and ornate black carvings. When I asked the shop owners where they got their carvings, some tried to convince me that they made them all themselves; others admitted that all Toba Batak carvings come from Samosir. They stopped short of telling me the exact locations of the towns that made the tall figural staffs and the embellished water buffalo horns in case I was a wealthy trader trying to cut them out of a potential deal.

I traveled back and forth across the giant mountain lake several times, trying to figure out where I should live: would it be Tuktuk, the place where all the tourist accommodations were, or in one of the two larger towns, Tomok and Ambarita, where the tourist "sights" are? On my fourth day of wandering around the center of tourism, I met a very bright and outgoing young Batak woman wearing red lipstick and red shoes who sat near me in order to practice her English. I told her what my project was: that I was looking for a village where wood carvers lived, someplace that was close to the tourist center but not swallowed up by it. She thought about it for a minute but finally said she could offer no suggestions as she was not from the area. She then added this: "If you want to stay at a place that is clean and quiet, just follow along with me to the *losmen* where my

friend Pak Wil is staying. I think you might like it." The attraction
of coincidence was too great for me to resist, so I joined her on her
journey to Huta Mungkap.

Pak Wil eyed me suspiciously the first few times I met him. He was
much as he had been described to me: a tall, powerfully built man
with white hair, easily angered, and slightly taciturn. He looked at
me with piercing blue eyes when we ate breakfast at the same table
the first time and, speaking Indonesian with a voice like a shiv,
demanded to know why I was asking him so many questions. I stam-
mered a little, and this seemed to make him more angry. He said (in
English now): "You came to talk with tourists? Then go talk to *them*,
not me! I'm no tourist." I was a little surprised at his outburst but
just met his glower with a stare, waiting a few seconds before saying,
"So you're a Batak then?" His face froze in its glower, then melted
into a pool of charm as he shouted, "HA ha-HAA!" while clapping his
hands with crazy glee at my insolence. He switched to Indonesian
again, saying "We will drink *kamput* (I: a kind of distilled liquor)
tonight and have a long chat!" He got up from the table to leave
smiling and pointed at me, squinting with one eye as if I were a
naughty child.

I met him in the evening at the same table: he had already started
in on the rot-gut liquor and beckoned me to join him. "The Bataks,"
he started (in English, to avoid insulting the hotel workers as much
as if he had used Indonesian), "are stupid, ignorant people. I was
here in Lake Toba after the war, fighting to keep our colony. You
heard that I helped capture Sukarno? It's true! I have pictures to
prove it. Well, I lived here at the lake for over a year and came to
love the place and vowed I would come back to stay. During that
year, I discovered how stupid and bullheaded the Batak people are,
how they are so tangled up in their *adat* (I: customary laws and
traditions) that they can't progress, how they are too dumb to know
when to leave their antique culture behind so they can improve their
lives; but I also discovered then that I love them. I came back here
to help them, but they won't listen to me! I want to retire here, but
how can I live with such backward people who won't listen to reason? I love the women here, but I want to punch the old-fashioned
men and boys. I love this place, the lake, the island, the mountains,

but where can I live? Is there a place here where I can live out my life without drowning in *adat?!*" His narrative went on like this for several hours, the words becoming more and more disjointed as he spoke them (and as I heard them). We finished off the bottle of burning resin.

It was only many months later, after Pak Wil (in the manner of one who has truly succumbed to bittersweet love) had boomeranged between the lake and the mainland, finally finding a plot of land near Parapat on which to build his retirement house, that I began to hear echoes of his confusing diatribe in the words of Western tourists. Like Pak Wil, many had come to Samosir loaded with preconceived notions of who the Toba Bataks might be, and what the lake and island meant to them. While Pak Wil had returned for what he hoped would be the rest of his life, these other westerners came for only temporary glimpses of something beautiful, interesting, or different. For them, confused interactions with the local people would be only momentary, and only in the controlled atmosphere of tourist hotels, restaurants, and shops. I wondered how many of the westerners with whom I spoke would return to the area someday—which of them, like Pak Wil, would be pulled back by some ineffable desire to reconnect with Toba Bataks in order to—to what? To begin understanding where their incomprehension had begun?

I stopped my story here because it was late and I was weary; I had run out of words. The two eldest boys walked me back to the hotel, where I sat on the porch looking out over the lake, thinking. I thought about Pak Wil returning to Lake Toba. Was I just like him? Why had I returned?

Well, for one reason, I returned to Huta Mungkap because I still had a lot of research to do. As it turned out, my decision to disembark from the ship in order to meet Pak Wil had landed me in an ideal fieldwork site. Huta Mungkap is a village of about 150 people, halfway between Tuktuk (where all the tourist hotels are) and Siallagan (the village near Ambarita where one of the tourist "sights" is located). For the first few weeks I stayed in the hotel, I considered Huta Mungkap merely as a convenient place from which to search for my ideal: a carving village that was slightly isolated from the crush of tourism. It was only when I met Ito in the marketplace in Siallagan, and was later invited back to her house to meet Partoho and his brother-in-law Nalom, that I realized how serendip-

FIGURE 1. *Huta Mungkap has no center*

itous my move had been: Huta Mungkap is one of only a handful of towns in the area where so many full-time carvers live, and is unusual among that handful for being able to claim three master carvers in addition to eight part-time carvers.

Huta Mungkap didn't look the way I expected a Toba Batak village would: it had only two or three of the huge wooden *adat* houses whose tall peaked roofs and stilt foundations are pictured in postcards and guide-books (plate 2). In fact, Huta Mungkap didn't look much like any kind of a village at all, Toba Batak or otherwise. Most of the houses were nestled down by the lake, away from the main paved road, and there was no "center" (figure 1). Except for a few carvers' shops, a couple of houses, two small *kedai* (I: small roadside shops), and three restaurants that tried to attract Western tourists, all that could be seen of the town from the road were plowed fields.

The village had not always been so dispersed. In the old days, before the Japanese forced them to build the road in the 1940s, and before the first tourists had come to the island in the 1960s, Huta Mungkap had been up on the hill that overlooks the present town. Along with three other smaller villages, Huta Mungkap had thrived on the hill for thirteen generations, protected by thick stone walls topped with a kind of bamboo that grows dense and thorny. After Indonesia gained its independence in 1945, the Toba Bataks living in these villages no longer felt threatened by colonizers and invaders, and so moved down to the shore to be closer to the lake waters. The move from hill to shore did not happen all at once: Partoho grew up on the hill in the early 1960s, and the last house was finally dismantled and reconstructed near the lake fifteen years later.

I rented the only empty house in the village, a rambling concrete villa whose ocher-colored walls had been slowly decaying for years. I was slightly outside the cozy confines of Huta Mungkap proper, which isolated me from some village events but gave me a great deal of privacy. This house was a palace by local standards, and was surrounded by a voluptuous garden of glossy rhubarb-colored philodendrons and goliath begonias whose pale lavender flowers lasted only a day. Not far behind the house was a forested hill where one of the old villages had been located. Here were towering hardwood trees, bushy thickets, and grass clumps, all pulsing with brown moths as large as my hand, and orange dragonflies. In the early morning, as I drank my coffee on the back porch, I would see small, quiet birds, sleek with dew, as they crept in the hedges picking among the gray berries hanging there, and in the mid-afternoon, when the whistles and shrill squeals of the bugs were at their most piercing, golden finches would dart zigzags between the branches of the giant trees. Woven through and around all this color and noise was the syncopation of the tiny woodpeckers called *apok,* whose regular, monotone notes calling back and forth to each other provided the village with an everyday tempo that was always slightly off the beat.

My house was a haven of solitude, for people in the village rarely came to visit even when I invited them. They gave all sorts of polite reasons for this, some people saying that, because I had no wife to make tea, they did not want to trouble me, and others implying that an evening walk, such as a visit to my house would entail, across the dry fields, under the giant trees, and past the cracked boulders (all places where spirits might hover), was too great a risk for a local person to take. The long evenings alone in my house, from which I could see the twinkling lights of the village homes, were difficult to endure.

It was because of this that I began visiting the homes of people such as Partoho and Ito, risking the danger of passing the spirits in hollow tree trunks to have some company. I happily sat on their plastic mats in their *ruang tamu* (I: guest rooms) listening to village rumors, scandals, and histories above the television chatter. Here, in these in-between places that are not really part of the intimacy of the "inside" family rooms and not completely part of the formal and structured "outside" of the public spaces, jokes are made, recipes are shared, rules of etiquette, and thoughts about aesthetics are discussed; it is also where long-winded narratives like this one are told.

This book is about tourists and artisans, wood carvings and marketplaces. It is about how the tourists and artisans interact, about how the carvings are made, how they are sold, and how they are collected. It poses questions that are at once simplistic and philosophical: Who is who? What is what? Where is there? In many ways, the book is about inaccurate assumptions and mistaken identities, and about the subsequent confusions and revelations that unfold when the errors are revealed. But it is also about how places that attract tourism allow individuals (both tourists and nontourists) to behave atypically.

As an ethnography about the Toba Bataks, this book tells about the lives of certain individuals, at a particular time and through a particular perspective. Using a series of stories about my experiences with woodcarvers and tourists, I will try to evoke for the reader what life is like in a small North Sumatran village that is the focus of tourist attention. In doing so, I hope to evoke the flavor of the narratives I heard so often while sitting on the woven mats of my Toba Batak friends, where occurrences were retold, not to establish some aspect of factual reality, but to re-create an experience in order to let the mundane become momentarily plump with significance, and to reveal connections and relevancies that in any other context might seem extravagant or farfetched. Unlike the Balinese sitting rooms described by Unni Wikan (1990:41), in which a visitor might feel uncomfortable and suspicious, Toba Batak sitting rooms are places where visitors can speak their minds, and where conversations and ideas flow freely. I tell these stories in an effort to illuminate some of the ordinary aspects of living on Samosir Island, occasionally allowing myself the luxury of pausing over vignettes or details that might seem extraneous. Here, basking in what I saw as Samosir's character, the seemingly insignificant moments are allowed to sing their implications to the fullest.

The shape of some of these stories is intended to mimic the narrative form I came to understand as being most typically Toba Batak: that is, beginning with several sentences that state the context of the story (and the speaker's intentions in telling it), which are repeated a second time using parallel words or synonyms; progressing to a presentation of the story itself, including all pertinent and unusual details, and stressing peak events two (sometimes three) times using phrases of equal or similar meaning; continuing on until the crux of the tale is uttered abruptly; and ending with a brief reiteration of the introduction followed by several sentences noting in different ways that the narration is an accurate portrayal of the way things happened (cf. Rodgers 1995: 16–18). The stories I am referring to here are not the formal retellings of previously told tales (such as Mary Steedly describes among the Karo Batak [1993:203]), but are rather narratives that individuals tell of recently lived experiences.

My intention is to provide a collection of narrative accounts written in a way that cleaves as closely as possible to an oral style. Although I am writing the stories in English, I try to maintain a sense of the cadence and lilt of Batak-inflected Indonesian. I do this not only to emphasize the character and importance of Toba Batak story-telling traditions but also to allow myself the creative freedom I find necessary to portray my experiences among the Toba Bataks meaningfully. Many of the stories here contain statements or dialogues presented in quotation marks. These quoted sections rarely represent mechanically recorded utterances (the story in Chapter 6 being the primary exception), for I found in my research that the appearance of a tape recorder stifled more talk than it inspired: the machine itself became the object of conversation, the small flickering lights and soft purring of the mechanism constantly making people forget what they were just about to say. In this work, quotation marks indicate stories and conversations as they were reconstructed and written down in my field notes shortly after they were uttered. All conversations with local people were carried out in the Indonesian language rather than in Toba Batak, a language in which I lacked fluency (see Chapter 3); all conversations with westerners were carried out in English.

As with many Batak stories, mine play fast and loose with some of the "facts." Here, time is compressed, characters renamed, and venues shifted slightly as needed, not only in an effort to make the stories more compelling, but also to evoke the ambience of Huta Mungkap most vividly. All personal names have been changed, as has the name of the village where the research was done, in order to preserve the privacy of those with whom I spoke; no other place-names are pseudonyms. I try to highlight the humorous aspects of events in these stories in order to mirror the Toba Bataks' own propensity toward wordplay and comedy in everyday conversation—a characteristic which neither the Bataks nor the anthropologists that work with them have yet fully addressed.[2]

During the fifteen months of my fieldwork on Samosir (1994–1995), I talked with westerners from a variety of nations about their reasons for coming to the area, and their reasons for purchasing carved wood souvenirs. I also spoke at length with Toba Batak vendors in the souvenir marketplace about their experiences with Western tourists, and how they managed to sell their carvings successfully, often despite their lack of proficiency in English. Finally, I talked extensively with Toba Batak woodcarvers, one of whom (Partoho) took me on as his apprentice.

By means of these conversations and the apprenticeship, I began to understand how Toba Batak wood-carvers and vendors perceive Samosir both as a home and as a tourist site, how they create ways to understand themselves and Western tourists, and how they try both to preserve and to rejuvenate their wood-carving traditions. I also began to understand how Western tourists imagine the terrain through which they are moving, how they compose notions of self- (and other) identities, and the means by which they judge and select carved wood souvenirs.

The challenge I face here is how to illustrate the Toba Bataks and the Western tourists, their touristic encounters and the effects of those encounters, and my relationship to it all, without relying on one single totalizing framework—of dominant and resistant, of us and them, or of them and other—the use of which might clarify certain relationships, but only at the cost of masking others. My effort has been to describe touristic situations on Samosir Island in such a way that the individual participants and their diverse cultural contexts are fairly and clearly represented.

If there is any continuous thread that connects the stories in this work, it might be a curiosity about such things as how people identify difference or how they distinguish categories. That is, throughout this work the reader will be provoked to think about the way in which certain categories are discerned and particular types are differentiated, the way in which variations are bounded and congruities marked. The focus here is how two specific groups, Western tourists and Toba Bataks, construct and define boundaries (for people, places, and objects), and then act on those constructions and definitions.[3] To make the situation more clear, a few words must to be said here to illuminate some of the limits of my field-work experiences and to clarify how this book is written.

TALKING WITH THE TOBA BATAKS

Many Toba Bataks did not know how to interact with me because they did not know where to place me socially; they wanted to identify the name of a position with which to connect me, but found it difficult to say exactly who I was. I was excluded altogether from the most basic Toba Batak social system because I had no clan name.[4] Furthermore, I had only an ambiguous connection to another of the important classifiers, occupation. Where did I belong in their social system? It is possible that my background as a one-time professional cartoonist and illustrator helped me in forming some relationships with Toba Batak individuals: I think Partoho would have been less willing to teach me carving if he had not seen my artistic abilities; my standing with certain adolescent boys seems to have improved when they saw I could draw caricatures. Even though I drew pictures to entertain my local friends in the *kedai* on various occasions, people did not think of me as *seniman* (I: "artist").

It was obvious that I was an outsider, a westerner, and a male, and these characteristics excluded me from certain interactions and conversations (such as with unmarried females). But there were other issues as well. The Toba Bataks do not consider it peculiar for a Western male in his late twenties or early thirties to be unmarried, but when one reaches the late thirties there must be some explanation for this state of affairs.[5] I showed no interest in chasing after the local or Western tourist females, and furthermore showed no interest in talking about such pursuits, so some Bataks toyed with the idea (which they discussed very diplomatically and, so they thought, out of my earshot) that I might be a weird form of *banchi* (I: transvestite, or hermaphrodite).

Others saw a certain purity of intent in my actions and coupled this with my extended education to propose that I was some sort of *pendeta* (I: pastor or priest). When I offered to teach English at the local high school without pay, many saw me fitting into the social category of instructor. Despite the fact that my employment at the high school lasted only three or four months, my social standing as "teacher" remained for the duration of my fieldwork.[6] Because of this, many of the Bataks I knew on a daily basis referred to me as Pak Guru (I: Mr. Teacher), a designation I accepted with pleasure, considering the alternatives. The primary consequence of this social designation is that topics having to do with sex or sexual desire and bodily functions were usually not discussed in front of me, nor was I privy to any kind of explicit information on these subjects should I ask.

TALKING WITH WESTERN TOURISTS

I was amazed at how difficult it was to interact with Western travelers on Samosir. At home, I have no trouble striking up conversations with strangers on public transportation and love nothing more than to share stories with a chatty group of friends over rounds of intoxicating beverages. But as a researcher I discovered that breezy or spontaneous conversational interludes with other outsiders were hard to find. I did talk with travelers from a variety of Western nations, of course, finding opportunities to converse with others walking along the road, visiting the marketplaces, or riding the ferries. More often, the chats occurred in the restaurants and *kedai* that cater to visitors. My interactions with westerners were usually cordial, but there were also times when conversations wobbled and sputtered, then ended prematurely. Looking back, it seems that these chats often failed when I asked the respondents to shift from providing me with their observations of the new cultural surroundings to sharing information derived from introspection of their personal motivations and desires.

Another part of the problem may have been, as it was with the Bataks, my social identity. Although I do not know for sure, I think many Western visitors saw me as an anomaly. I clearly was not a "real" traveler like them. I lived full-time in the area and talked with the locals. I also dressed more like an elderly package tourist than a young backpacker, and I asked too many nosy questions about purchases, tastes, and preconceptions. I was not a real traveler, but "researcher" did not seem believable either. After all, who ever heard of studying Western tourists? Overall, I found travelers to be wary of other westerners who were not like them. They seemed especially suspicious of those who did not seem to fit into a particular category (such as "traveler," "tourist," or "spouse of a Batak," for example), so people such as myself and Pak Wil tended to be avoided.

It is unfair to suggest that the travelers who avoided my company and questions did so for the same reasons, however. One European woman did not hesitate to state frankly her dislike of Americans, giving this as the reason she would not speak to me. Several people kindly apologized for not participating, saying that they were on vacation and just wanted to rest quietly, not to think or reflect. Some young women clearly felt uncomfortable speaking to a strange man; still others were simply reluctant to talk because they did not wish to discuss their buying preferences and selections.

USING QUESTIONNAIRES

Because my personal rapport with Western tourists was inadequate to allow me access to their perceptions of Samosir Island and of the Toba Bataks and their carvings, I decided after six months to begin gathering information by means of a questionnaire. One hundred and seventy-five copies of the questionnaire were taken to seven tourist hotels and a coffeehouse. Despite the fact that all of the managers at these businesses initially showed interest in the project and agreed to participate, after several months it became clear that six had neglected to hand out the forms, or had lost them altogether.

The questionnaires that were returned uncompleted were taken to the remaining two participating hotels. At one of these hotels, the forms were left out on a restaurant counter, necessitating tourist initiative for their completion. At the other hotel, workers agreed to assist me by encouraging guests to complete the questionnaire as they waited for their food to be prepared. I eventually received completed forms from one hundred and nineteen individuals, the majority of whom took the time to answer all or most of the questions, despite the unintended difficulty of the English language used. When the responses to the questionnaires were compiled, I noticed that there were gaps in the scope of the questionnaire and in the completeness of the answers. This prompted me to examine the data cautiously: rather than considering it as an autonomous body of information, it was used to support statements recorded in tourist interviews or hypotheses based on observations of tourists.

After I handed out the tourist questionnaire, I decided to compose another one (in Indonesian) for the Toba Bataks in the area. I did this because I realized that some individuals (especially young or unmarried women) did not feel comfortable with the typical interview situation, and because, upon seeing the questionnaire for westerners, several Bataks asked me why I did not seem interested in their opinions on the tourism issue.[7] The information provided in this questionnaire augmented data I collected in interviews and conversations.

THE CONTEXT OF THE TIMES

Something brief should be said about the broader world in which my fieldwork was conducted. Sometimes in this book, the stories I tell might give an impression of timelessness, or might suggest that everything is, was, and will be fine on Samosir Island. There was, in fact, an aspect of such an attitude in the tourist center while I lived there. Because Lake Toba is such an out-of-the-way place, the daily happenings of the political world, whether it was at the provincial, national, or international level, did not tend to have much salience in the lives of the rural Toba Bataks, and not very much more in the lives of the travelers who passed through the area. Toba Bataks seemed only lightly touched by such "outside" concerns perhaps because they directly impacted their lives so little: people living on the island live, with minor exceptions, very close to poverty whether economic times are booming or waning.

Nevertheless, certain actions of the provincial and national government did have some impact. President Suharto's New Order government promoted ethnic diversity as a way to increase tourism throughout the archipelago, but did so in such a way that a group's ethnic identity never overwhelmed their national identity (Kipp 1996:110). This national interest in the development of tourism may have assisted in the building or improving of airports, bridges, docks, and roads, all of which make travel to Batakland much more comfortable and easy for tourists. Tourism is no doubt also made more probable by the government's fairly lenient transit visa, with which most outsiders can stay in the country for up to two months at a time.

Actual promotions of tourism by the government were not extensive: pamphlets distributed nationally almost always include mention of Lake Toba, but the material culture of the area is usually represented only by weavings, not carvings.[8] In addition, the government supports "Lake Toba Fest," a celebration of the variety in Batak culture, including parades of national dress, poetry readings, exhibitions of local produce and manufacture, and carving contests. It is not clear whom the sponsors intend to attract to the festival, but my experience is that it draws mostly a local, rather than international, audience. In general, it seems, the government's best assistance to the Lake Toba area is to leave it alone, letting Batak entrepreneurs control the destiny of its development. Local people occasionally complained that the government did not do more to promote their area and their cultures, but they also feared the possible effects of provincial edicts (see Chapter 2). In the end, Samosir Island, an out-of-the-way place in more ways than one, seemed to feel only residual ripples of the waves of change enacted in Medan and Jakarta.

STRUCTURE OF THE BOOK

For those interested, the first chapter provides a theoretical road map for beginning to understand some of the issues I raise in the book. Here, I outline some of the discussions that swirl around subjects such as "place," "home," "identity," "value," and "art." As an overview of themes that have been of interest to scholars sometimes for decades, the discussions here are only introductory. The reader is encouraged to further investigate these topics by seeking out the works referred to throughout the chapter, and also in the endnotes.

Chapter 2 concerns Lake Toba and Samosir Island as places where meaning is layered many times over. These are places that are dually claimed, both by tourists as a "vacationland" and by Toba Bataks as a homeland, and the chapter tries to untangle how such places can be shared through ongoing negotiations, and how they are described, represented, and used by each group.

Chapter 3 deals with notions of identity. Many of us simply assume we know who we are, so what is there to think about? As this chapter tries to show, developing identity is a deeply complex process that combines introspection, self-affiliation, and descriptions and assumptions by outsiders. One of the important points to consider here is the extent to which one's identity is negotiable.

Chapter 4 describes the life of a Toba Batak carver and family. As an outsider looking into such a life, it may seem like an ideal pastoral world where traditions are paramount and worries are few. In actuality, the situation described shows how difficult it can be to balance creativity and innovation with practicality and clever bargaining.

Chapter 5 deals with the ways in which values and meanings of Toba Batak carvings are created and negotiated by carvers, vendors, and Western buyers. At issue here are questions about the divisions between "art" and craft, about the meaning of monetary and spiritual investments, and also about how discernments between real and not real are made.

Chapter 6 discusses spaces of interaction for Toba Bataks and Western travelers. Touristic places are not simply the same as all other places on earth. There is a quality to the spaces where travelers and local people come together that seems to permit a broader range of activities, where individuals are allowed to explore the range of possible behaviors, than is ordinarily found outside the tourism context. One such place, the marketplace of souvenirs on Samosir Island, is discussed in detail in order to begin understanding the character of such in-between places.

Chapter 7 focuses on the ways Toba Batak carvers try to excel in the marketplace by making a variety of carvings, from replicas of antiques to daring innovations. Under consideration here is not only the extent to which Western travelers are implicated in the change of the Toba Bataks' art traditions, but also the ability of carvers to understand and satisfy the tastes and desires of Western buyers.

I

Orienting the View

The reader might wonder how I chose which stories to tell in this book. They were not picked simply because they best explained my version of the events that happened on Samosir Island, but also because they can be read as allegories resonating with broader issues of interest to anthropologists, art historians, and artists: How do individuals distinguish themselves from others? How does that identification change in different situations? What does it mean to go to a place? What does it mean to call a place "home"? Why do people buy things when they travel? How do they select what to buy? Are the things they buy authentic? Can traditions be preserved? How do art forms change, and what does it mean to innovate? The answers to some of these questions may seem obvious at first glance; but they, and others like them, are confounding in their complexity. Stories excel at bringing life to events and situations, but they are not always so successful at explaining their meanings. Oftentimes, stories have difficulty addressing the question "why?"

It is for this reason that I have opted to orient the reader theoretically right from the start. The first section of this chapter reviews some issues related to personal identification: how tourists, and the groups they travel to visit, are defined and talked about. The second section concerns the importance of place: how a location is claimed and how it is experienced. The final section relates to material objects: what it is authentic, what is art, and why some people consume. I suspect that some readers will be tempted to skip these sections, and I welcome them to do so if they wish. My aim is to let the narratives in other chapters take precedence over the theoretical discussions and references[1] because I want to stress to the reader that the lives and cultures of Toba Bataks and Western tourists make less sense when thought of metaphorically (as "texts" to be "read" for example) than they do when understood narratively, as tales to be heard. Still, I feel obligated to point out to the reader that both the stories and the theories that inform them are like cords whose braiding connects the strands to each other at the same time as it strengthens them.

LOCATIONS: WHERE IS THERE?

If we are to talk about tourism, it is difficult to avoid a discussion of place.[2] Tourism is, after all, primarily concerned with people moving from one place to another. This section will address the notions "place" and "home" as they pertain to tourism. The discussions here can be used as a framework for descriptions in the following chapters that concern both the Toba Bataks' conception of their ancestral homeland and their reactions to the constant flow of visitors who regard their territory as a recreation area, and Western tourists' conceptions of the destinations they construct as different, exotic, or "out-of-the-way."[3]

A Concept of Place

In a purely philosophical view, it might be said that the character of a place (you might say its "personality") comes from its contact with human subjects.[4] The nature of the contact is of great concern here because, in the context of tourism, places are dually claimed: temporarily by tourists and continuously by the indigenous people.[5] That is, interactions between a tourist and a local person occur in a place where both parties *assume* a right to be. Is the connection with a given place of equal intensity for both parties? Surely, the relationship some people have to a place is more compelling than it is for others.

It is perhaps this point exactly that underlies various land rights issues and disagreements over tourism development,[6] where groups argue for their rights to places not *necessarily* because of religious meaning or economic importance, but because of a more encompassing bond founded on a feeling of oneness with the place.[7] In an example such as this, the implicit assumption is that they are referring not just to any lands but rather to *their* lands, places whose significances are socially shared and enduring. The point is not about "ownership" of place, but rather about rights and obligations to place.[8] Clearly, this is an issue of some importance in the context of tourism, for many tourists presume a right to travel (given adequate finances and governmental permissions) to a location without the accompanying responsibilities to either the place or the people who live there.[9]

Perhaps the question concerning obligations to a place would be less serious if the majority of tourists were even aware that these *are* issues to consider. Most research about what motivates tourists to travel, however, indicates that few tourists have thought very seriously about the responsibilities travel demands of them.[10] Instead, it seems that the majority of tourists are blissfully unaware of their relationship to their vacation destination. They are traveling for other reasons: to see something different, to relax, to experience something "more authentic," or simply to get away from home.[11]

Notions of Home

When we talk about tourism (as opposed to some other forms of travel, such as nomadism), we assume a single starting point, a "home" (a broader term could also be used here: home-base, homeland) that is departed from and then returned to.[12] Although it is spoken of in general in the context of tourism, home always implies a specific tourist-central position,[13] and always assumes an idealized (if not archetypal) place—that is, the "home."[14] Thus, not only does the term "home" subtly imply that all tourists' homes are somehow comparable, it also excludes the people living at the tourist site altogether, leaving them out of the action that constitutes tourism and implying that where they are, home is not.[15]

This may seem to be a minor point, but it is one worth exploring. Tourism, especially cultural tourism (that is, tourism inspired by an interest in seeing other cultures), implies that one moves away from the familiar and domestic toward the different, unusual, and in some cases exotic. For this reason, a travel destination tends to be thought of by tourists as some kind of "not-home," even though it is home to the people living there. The significance of the latter's homes (homelands), should not be discounted, for even though they may engage in movements and travels, most of these groups who are the focus of tourist attention are such precisely because they live in a particular "place" that can be visited.

That is why a thorough discussion of the action of tourism must simultaneously embrace the home that is traveled away from and returned to, and the home that is traveled to, that is, the home of the group being visited. Tourism as an action cannot be essentialized simply to mean the act of traveling (i.e., moving through space) when it involves interactions with these people, without severely limiting its discursive value. For this reason, the fact that the "tourism" is often defined in reference to "the tourist" is not incidental. It points to a critical supposition: it is *tourists* who perform the act of tourism, not the others.[16]

The issue of what constitutes "home" in the tourism context is not merely an interesting point of discussion. It is one that has very real ramifications when tourism planners, taking stock of what they can market and how, begin to redefine homes as sites and hamlets as nameless way stations on otherwise vacant beaches that can easily be displaced by large tourist developments.[17] What qualifies as "home" and what does not are clearly arbitrary designations, and made at the discretion of economically powerful individuals.

Here I shall attempt to address notions of home equitably by suggesting that to be a Toba Batak is to recognize Samosir Island as "home," at the same time realizing that a tourist's idea of tourism is founded on a concept of "home" that is specifically *not* Samosir Island. In doing so, I hope to resist the trap of privileging tourist over local when considering the acts, the "process," of tourism. I am consciously downplaying attention to tourism's physical moves from place to place in order to focus on those events of stasis that punctuate the travel and during which time the tourist and the local interact.[18]

The Touristic Place

So, how can we understand a place that is simultaneously home and not-home, that is at the same time common and exotic, familiar yet strange? How can we describe places that are both in between these oppositional pairs and encompassing of them? One of the things I grappled with most in studying tourism on Samosir Island was why individuals (both Western visitors and Toba Bataks) acted in ways that appeared to me to be atypical when they were in these in-between places. I watched as travelers who spoke no Indonesian rented ill-maintained motorcycles to drive (map-less) on the steep dirt roads of the countryside; I saw others who jostled past old women in marketplaces with no apologies or argued loudly in restaurants while ordering. I also watched young Toba Batak men fondling and kissing their Western girlfriends in front of their elders on the ferries returning to Samosir Island and teens playfully slapping travelers as they rode by on their bicycles, not to mention female vendors physically pulling and dragging male travelers into their stalls to make a sale. In other circumstances, it seemed to me that these actions would probably be seen as wildly aberrant behavior.

It was as if all of these people were freed from the bonds of their cultural rules, and thus freed, were acting out previously unexamined desires and urges. The behavior I saw was not like the unbridled expressions of passions and emotions that one might see in a carnival setting (like Mardi Gras, for example), for it was not frenetic or spontaneous. Rather, what I saw were people exploring, or testing, possible ways of being that were outside their ordinary cultural rules but were allowed, even sanctioned, because the locale of their actions and interactions was an in-between space.[19] There was a flavor of exhilaration in their actions and interactions, an exuberance that seemed to allow them new access to expansive self-presentation and encouraged them to express new performative selves. Somehow, it seems, the touristic place—the place that is both home and not-home—was a kind of neutral zone, where cultural rules were partially suspended so that fantasies and urges could be acted out.[20] Miriam Kahn, researching cultural tourism in Tahiti, discusses a similar concept of an in-between place, following Lefebvre by calling it a "thirdspace" (2000:7). In her work, she proposes viewing places like Tahiti as complex spaces that are "generated within historical and spatial dimensions, both real and imagined, immediate and mediated. Various notions of place, often at battle with each other, nonetheless involve, underpin, presuppose, respond to, and generate one another" (2000:8). This conception of the space where cultural tourism happens, like that presented here and elsewhere (MacCannell 1992; Bruner 1996), investigates actions that occur between two positionings, in Kahn's formulation, a contestational dialectic between the physical/perceived and the mental/conceived.

Another way we might understand the in-betweenness of the touristic space is to see it as a kind of utopia. Not a utopia per se, but utopia-like, or to use Louis Marin's term, "utopic."[21] Marin (1984) describes utopic spaces as neutral gaps between two opposed points (in this case, between the regulated world of perceived reality and the world of pure fantasy and desire) where individuals can playfully explore possible ways of being that eventually contribute to their own growth or change. An important component of Marin's model of utopic spaces is that they are narrativized—

that is, described and discussed by those taking part in them (1984: 198–201). The stories told about behaviors in utopic spaces have several functions: they help individuals define what it is they have experienced; they allow introspection on events that have passed; and they help to map the boundaries of what is possible in future interactions. [22]

The stories found in this book are retellings of narratives from a utopic space: the touristic place. Because the touristic place is so varied on Samosir Island—including not only tourist sights, hotels, and restaurants, but also treks across the island, trips across the lake, and jaunts to the countryside—the possibilities of utopic narratives are almost limitless. While the stories I provide here may make reference to a number of sites within the touristic place, the focus is on the souvenir marketplace. In some ways, the souvenir marketplace is the utopic space par excellence, for in it one can see individuals exploring the formation of self and other identities, the boundaries of place and home, as well as the meanings of such notions as "traditional," "authentic," and "innovative."

IDENTIFICATIONS: WHO IS WHO?

Travel, at the very moment it happens, necessitates a change in status for those who participate in it: a worker moving slowly along the freeway is a commuter; a vendor who travels door to door is a peddler. This is not so different in the kind of travel called tourism: change of status occurs when tourists and those people who are the focus of tourist attention begin to redefine themselves, when they attempt to communicate that definition to others, and when they discern (or in some cases construct) identities for others.

Tourism and Its Participants

When the focus of tourist interest is a cultural group perceived to be different from that of the tourist, it is often referred to as cultural tourism. [23] In the context of cultural tourism research, three active participants can be identified: the tourist, the group that is the focus of the tourist's attention, and the academic investigator. [24] Attempts at defining "the tourist" have been the subject of several academic works, whose final conclusions are often based on statistical analyses of visitor arrival information, on general objective observations, or on suppositions of the kind of experiences the tourist seeks to gain (that is, "tourist motivation").[25] The research results show that there is no one type of tourist, and no one sort of motivation.

The Tourist as "Traveler" A commonly used definition of "tourist" is "a temporarily leisured person who voluntarily visits a place away from home for the purpose of experiencing a change" (Smith 1989:2). Tourists can be a varied lot. In the Lake Toba area, one can find tourists who are local (from Sumatra), domestic (from other areas of Indonesia), Southeast Asian (people from nearby countries, such as Malaysia or Singapore), and international (people from countries beyond the regional confines of Asia). Because my primary interest pertains to Toba Batak wood carvings sold as mementos in the marketplace, and because the vast majority of people who buy the carvings are from Europe, North America, Australia, and New Zealand (comprising much of the cultural area often referred to as "the West"), I will focus on those individuals in this book. To be more specific, this work discusses a subset of the group called "Western tourists": those who refer to themselves as "travelers" (the term I will usually use to refer to them).

Travelers make a point of distinguishing themselves from those individuals who join package tours, carry suitcases, ride in taxis or rented cars, and stay in hotels that have room service—people they refer to derisively as "tourists."[26] In my conversations with them, travelers generally indicated that they had a very strong sympathy for indigenous groups and their traditions, that they made a conscious effort to accept cultural differences, that they were serious about learning from other cultural groups, that they were angry about environmental degradation, and that they were making less of an impact on both environments and local cultures than were "tourists"; in general, "travelers" tend to sneer at what they consider to be the superficiality of tourists' experiences.[27] All travelers on Samosir Island, regardless of their mother tongue, use English to communicate with those not from their own country, even though sometimes their command of English is limited to dealing with basic necessities. Only on rare occasions are travelers able to speak Indonesian.

In the most general terms, the traveler can be briefly described as follows: a twenty-something individual from Europe, North America, Australia, or New Zealand traveling for an extended period of time on limited funds, carrying all necessary possessions in a backpack, and interested in abandoning certain perceived characteristics of Western culture (such as materialism and alienation) in favor of experiencing something more "real" in a place different from home. What motivates these individuals to travel?

There is no one answer. While one author may say that, in general, tourists travel because of interconnected desires (to change the environment, to engage in new experiences and interact with new individuals, to rest and relax, and to find some form of self-fulfillment or self-realization),[28] another author may say that tourists are on a search for the "authentic" (in particular, an authentic other) because they are alienated from their own superficial cultures (MacCannell 1976:240).[29] Still other authors suggest that travelers use their overseas experiences as a way to impress others with their worldliness (and perhaps their wealth) (Munt 1994). Tourists may travel for all of these reasons or none of them (it truly depends on the individual).

The "Tourate" One of the problems with how tourism has been discussed in anthropological investigations until recently is that it tended to be defined in terms of the tourist: that is, tourism is what tourists do. Lately, however, researchers have begun to look at the groups who are the focus of cultural tourism as active participants in the construction of touristic encounters, rather than as passive servants catering to the tourists' demands.[30] Although this shift from describing the groups who are the object of tourist attention as having some degree of agency is a positive one, there is still a problem of terminology in these discussions. Whereas the definition of the category "tourist" has been the subject of many articles, those people who are the focus of the tourists' interests are often discussed in general terms, as "locals," as "natives," or as "residents" (see Cohen 1984, Van den Berghe 1992, and Draper and Kariel 1990, respectively). Previously, these groups were referred to as "hosts," a term whose use several researchers have argued against for some time because it is essentially a euphemism that masks, not only the fact that tourists and "hosts" do not have equal access to power in the relationship (Bruner 1991:241), but also that in many cases the people being referred to by the term many have no say in whether they are to partake in tourism or not (DeKadt 1979:9).

When a more specific reference to the group is made, it is usually to an ethnic or national affiliation: "the Balinese," "the Gambians," "the Toraja," and so on (see Picard 1990, Farver 1984, Volkman 1990, respectively). In this work, I will also follow this course of action when making specific reference to the people living on Samosir Island, using at times "the local people," "the Toba Bataks" or "the Bataks," and the like for clarity's sake, but not without first examining the issue more closely.

In tourism research, the term "tourist" or "traveler" is used to talk about people on excursions in general. If the subject is a specific group of tourists, then adjectives are added to specify them: for example, "German package tourist." This straightforward system is obviously useful in such discussions as it can identify, with more or less precision, a particular social subcategory within a group. Unfortunately, this system is not often used when talking about groups who are the focus of tourist interest. As was shown above, these groups are dealt with as if they were a uniform entity.

On Samosir Island, it became clear very quickly that to talk about "the Toba Bataks" in terms of tourism was imprecise, because only a small number of people living on the island were actually involved, directly or indirectly, with tourism. How can I make it clear who I am talking about? I think it is necessary to coin a term which recognizes that the individuals who interact with tourists are, in the context of cultural tourism, a subgroup of their culture. I am not the first to make this distinction. Bruner (1991) briefly uses the term "visitee" and Van den Berghe (1992; 1994) the term "touree" for the ethnic group that is visited. Although these are more accurate than host and some of the other terms that have been used over the years, they nevertheless do not indicate that the ethnic group being referred to has agency in touristic encounters, suggesting rather that the group is passive when gazed upon (cf. Urry 1990). For this reason, I will refer to them as the "tourate." This word not only contextualizes the group in terms of the action (tourism), but also indicates that its members simultaneously have some degree of agency in that action and are changed by it.[31]

So who are the Bataks? A brief introduction will suffice here. The Bataks are one of Indonesia's largest ethnic groups, perhaps numbering as many as 4.3 to 4.8 million people.[32] There are said to be six subgroups within the ethnic designation Batak: Toba, Karo, Dairi (or Pak Pak), Simalungun, Angkola, and Mandailing.[33] The Toba subgroup is often said to be the most *asli* (I: original) of the Bataks, and they are often the unmarked group: it is not uncommon to hear other subgroups (such as the Karo) distinguish themselves from the "Bataks," meaning the Toba Bataks (see also Kipp 1996:161).[34] People living on Samosir Island will often make a similar assumption, stating that "We Batak do x, but the Dairi people do y." Defining the boundaries of Batak ethnic identity is clearly problematic, since it is continuously being negotiated and contested by the various subgroups at the same time it is being constructed by and with outsiders such as Western tourists and anthropologists. Nevertheless, by identifying a subset boundary, that of the Toba Batak "tourate," I hope both to specify the group with whom I worked as well as to disrupt notions that "the Batak" correlates with some discrete social entity.

The Tourism Researcher Often, the academic researcher concerned with tourism is not considered to be an integral participant in touristic encounters.[35] Because of the way my work with Western travelers and Toba Bataks unfolded, however, I often found myself in the middle: translating the language of conversations and explaining (to the extent I was able) one group's culture to the other. Because one of my working assumptions in interactions of this sort is that there is no such thing as a truly impartial mediator, I see myself as a dual accomplice.[36] As researcher, I am deeply implicated in the information I present here, since, via my own various identities as ethnographer, translator, mediator, friend, suspect, teacher, artist, joker, advisor, or questioner, I inserted myself between, and wove myself around, the interactions I had come to study. I was an avid participant and a persistent observer, and for this reason I am unable to pretend that my portrayals in this work are exclusive of my own personality, for my presence may have affected the ways in which interactions unfolded.

Mistaken Identities

What might be clear at this point is that because those participating in tourism (tourists, tourates, researcher) are actively constructing their identities as their interactions with others unfold, and because the interactions are usually conducted without the benefit of a language spoken and understood with equal fluency by all parties, there are numerous opportunities for mistaking identities: not simply misunderstanding the identity of the other, but sometimes of the self as well.

In the case of the Toba Batak tourates, it is often easy to lump all tourists, travelers, and foreign researchers into one undifferentiated group, *orang barat* (I: westerner) or *orang putih* (I: white person), to refer generally to individuals whose ancestors originated in Europe, because their culture is believed to be shared. Sometimes, the tourates' stereotype will coincide with a westerner's own construction of identity but with a different perspective (for instance, the tourist may consider backpacking through Asia to be daring with a positive slant [adventurous], whereas the Toba Bataks may look at it as daring with a negative slant [foolhardy]). At other times their perceptions of westerners can be preposterous, such as the popular belief that all westerners are prompt or that all live in concrete houses. Similarly, some tourists may perceive the Toba Bataks simplistically, imagining them as "primitive" or "animist" rather than modernizing Christians. Other tourists may see the Bataks as a collateral part of an exotic backdrop—as "incidental others"—in front of whom they can act out their exhilarated fantasies and dreams.

Part of this book is concerned with exploring how the participants in cultural tourism are able to sustain interactions with each other despite their differences, and how their perceptions of themselves and the others change.[37] In looking for a model to understand these interactions, we might consider Gregory Bateson's (1981) discussion of what he calls complementary schismogenesis. He says that two groups interacting will react and counterreact such that there will be "a tendency towards progressive change" (that is, differences will tend to intensify) *unless* "other factors are present to restrain the excesses of (the particular behaviors)" (Bateson 1981:176). In the case of tourists and Batak tourate, the "complementary schismogenesis" is kept from veering off into the excesses of behavior that might undermine the interactions (such as overbearing arrogance on the part of the tourists and xenophobia or disgust on the part of the Bataks) by what Bateson says are the social circumstances that hold the two parties together—that is, "some form of common interest, (or) mutual dependence" (183).[38]

Using Bateson's model, I suggest that at least one of the contexts that allow and encourage interactions between tourists and Toba Bataks is found in the marketplace, where Bataks provide objects and narratives that seem to satisfy westerners' desire for the "primitive," and tourists furnish the curiosity and capital for the Bataks to continue providing it. In looking at the marketplaces on Samosir Island in this way, we shall be trying to understand the actual process by which tourists and tourates interact so that the desires of both parties are somehow satisfied.

MATERIAL OBJECTS: TAKING THINGS HOME

One goal of the touristic encounter is the fulfillment of material desires —that is, the accumulation of things of value and worth. For the tourist, this is often expressed in the desire to possess meaningful objects from the foreign lands through which they are traveling; for the tourate, the goal is often to acquire money by selling objects representative of their material culture.

On Samosir Island, tourists find a wide array of wood carvings ranging from quickly made human figures to elaborately engraved water-buffalo horns. Western tourists come to Samosir Island expecting to find art that is representative of the local culture, a mental image of which seems to be based on their own assumptions about what they might find in rural Asia,[39] but also on what they read in tourist guidebooks, which describe the carvings as "traditional" and "magical."[40] Information about the carvings that they glean in the marketplace from Toba Batak vendors tends to corroborate these descriptions. Because many travelers seem to be seeking out "authentic" experiences, it seems logical to say that the objects they bring back home with them would reinforce this aim. Purchasing carvings at the point of manufacture is one way to obtain authenticity, but another way is to choose objects that seem to preserve ancestral traditions. It is not surprising then, that I found that Western travelers tended to look for "authentic," "traditional," and "primitive" carvings.[41]

One of the fascinating things about wood carving on Samosir Island is that Western tourists' desire for "tradition" and "authenticity" have encouraged the Toba Batak carvers to continue to make and sell objects based on the forms developed by their distant animist ancestors, despite the fact that they are all Christian and come from families who converted to Christianity by the 1930s. At the same time, however, the carvers are also creating innovations: objects that resemble the antiques but that manipulate the old forms or designs in novel ways. It is interesting that these innovations are sold by Toba Batak vendors using the same kind of descriptive words and stories that they use for "traditional" objects. In fact, most vendors refer to the whole range of contemporary carvings with the words *tradisi* (I: traditional) and *antik* (I: antique); they do not conceptually separate them from objects actually made in the past. Tourists, seeking representative icons of place or proofs of their travels, purchase both the innovative and the traditional forms, largely unaware that there is any difference. To make sense out of this state of affairs, it might help to look at some of the ways in which these terms are used, and what they are intended to mean.

Tradition and Innovation

Ordinarily, when the term "tradition" is used, many of us understand this to refer to a set of beliefs derived from past social experiences and actions that are accepted through consensus over time and reaffirmed in the present. Implicit here is that reference is being made to something that is bounded and unchanging, transmitted from past individuals to present individuals in an uninterrupted line. This is a common definition of the term, but soon after it is uttered, its slipperiness becomes obvious: At what point does something become traditional? On whose word do we depend to know whether something is traditional or not? Do traditions change? Addressing these questions is essential if we are to understand the term's social function and its intimate connections (particularly, although not only, in the West) with concepts such as innovation, authenticity, taste, and value.

Edward Shils (1971) posits that tradition is not monolithic and unchanging, but rather, because it is a body of beliefs transmitted in some form by individuals through time, has the capacity for modification by means of innovation. Shils' reinterpretation of the concept "tradition" stresses its flexibility for incorporating change by noting that innovations can be conscious or unconscious (1971:128),[42] and that they can be minute and incremental or more novel and rapid (1971:144). One of the important aspects of his theory is that it strategically places individuals existing in the present as being simultaneously dependent on past traditions and at the very nexus of the transformation of tradition. In the context of cultural tourism, tradition's flexibility is seen not only in modifications from internal innovation but also in its ability to integrate influences and innovations from outside the culture.

In cultural tourism, the focus of tourist interest is cultural difference. Individuals are traveling to other places to experience ways of living and being in the world that are unlike their own ways of living and being; the two cultures are assumed to have boundaries that separate them from each other. The process of distinguishing boundaries of differentness tends to define cultures or traditions as discrete entities, and it is this process that facilitates the "consumption" of cultures by tourists. In some ways, you could say that the traditions are being bought by tourists like any other commodity: tourists purchase access to another culture in order to "consume" its differentness (its unique foods, performances, and arts). Over time, this externally constructed version of what differentness means may be integrated internally in the culture, which Shils calls the "modification of already existing traditions" (1971:144), either consciously or unconsciously. This change is often identified as innovation.

While changes appear to be directed by Western culture in this application of the theory, the interaction between the two cultures is not simply a case of a dominant group instituting change in a subordinate one. It is, instead, an interplay (albeit enacted on unequal footing) between the two: the changes or influences may be initiated by the tourist, but they are actively integrated by the tourate. One might wonder, how can Western cultural influences be integrated into the tourates' culture without the two of them eventually becoming indistinguishable from each other? Perhaps it is that the outside influences are only ever integrated to the extent that they are accepted as being "possible" within the tourates' traditions.[43] That is, perhaps the tourates will only incorporate outside influences if and when they seem to "fit" with their existing traditions. As a consequence of considering tradition to be a set of actions and beliefs that change over time in response to both outside and inside influences, we are forced to rethink what "authentic" means.

Authenticity

Dean MacCannell describes the drive of the (specifically Western) tourist to experience authenticity as being fueled by the fragmentation and alienation of modern society (1976:146). He notes that tourists are looking for "immediacy" and "presence" in other places because they may find them lacking in the displaced and mediated relationships they have with their own society. As he sees it, "modern man has been condemned to look elsewhere, everywhere, for his authenticity, to see if he can catch a glimpse of it reflected in the simplicity, poverty, chastity or purity of others" (1976:41).

Oddly enough, the places sought out by tourists as being authentic are precisely those which have been previously marked as being so: guidebooks give directions on how to find the best examples of traditional houses, and other tourists pass on information about the most untouched villages. Jonathan Culler (1981) talks about the inherent paradox in this situation: if tourists are looking for something they can believe is "authentic" (by which is often meant "unspoiled"), they will feel unfulfilled when it is marked as such because the very act of marking it has mediated their experience, making it seem ordinary or banal. So where is the real authentic? Some authors have suggested that it may not exist,[44] while others have proposed that it will be realized only when it is seen or experienced in tandem with its perceived opposite (which itself has, paradoxically, its own realness), the "inauthentic," or fake.[45] These two theories—the one proposing that there is no authentic, and the other that everything is perhaps equally authentic—may not be sufficient to explain the complexity of the term.[46]

Observations in the everyday world indicate that there is an authentic for many people (among them tourists), and that it is a knowable and real concept, not just a theoretical issue. John Frow suggests that, in general, the authentic is identified in reference, not to the inauthentic, but in reference to a collection of "typicalities" (1991:126), or what might be called "style."[47] A buyer apparently finds satisfaction in the "authentic" thing or experience because it is felt to be unique or original, it has cultural or historical integrity, or, in reference to material objects, it shows fine workmanship or attention to detail.[48] But these features are often not enough to ensure that an object will pass the inspection of selective Western buyers, for as Sandra Niessen states, "The West has required non-Western arts to be nonfashion- and nonmarket-oriented in order to be traditional and authentic and thus worthy of preservation and scrutiny" (1999:175). In fact, this is one of the conundrums that face Toba Batak carvers: how to satisfy Western buyers' desires for objects with perceived cultural integrity when at the same time selling them in a marketplace setting.

What does "authentic" mean in the context of the souvenir marketplace on Samosir Island? Well, I suppose the term must refer to how travelers themselves discern and evaluate the objects they see and buy based on a favorable comparison to what are perceived to be cultural "typical-ities." How travelers come to know the typicalities of Toba Batak art is not exactly clear, but they seem to educate themselves by means of prior texts (guidebooks, museum catalogs, ethnographies), narratives (stories told by other tourists or by Toba Batak vendors), and intuitive notions such as "real" or "traditional." Because the attributes of authenticity can be so varied, and the sources of authority so numerous, we find it to be, like the term "traditional," a category of perception that is both evolving and negotiable.

Art and Souvenirs

Many tourists who travel away from that which is familiar to them eventually obtain some kind of keepsake or memorial of their trip. These objects—be they postcards, key chains, seashells, pot shards, weavings, or carvings—are commonly referred to as souvenirs, but this term is fairly imprecise, as it can be made to carry the weight of such dissimilar things as vials of water from Lourdes, cartoon pencil erasers from Disney World, and of course Toba Batak carvings from Samosir Island. The meanings of these objects can be vastly different, and yet English offers us few words with which to categorize them all, except for "souvenir." On the one hand, it does not seem really appropriate to force such various objects and essences (the sacred, the banal, the idiosyncratic, the iconic) all under the jurisdiction of one term, even for the sake of a general discussion. On the other hand, most readers understand from their own experience that sou-venirs can have many shapes and many meanings. In this work I shall try to get around the simplifications that the term "souvenir" entails by refer-ring to the things tourists bring home as "touristic objects," but I ask the reader's indulgence when I lapse into using the more common term.

At the outset, one might wonder why people bring things home at all, and it should be no surprise that there are dozens of overlapping and intertwined reasons that help us to understand this behavior. One might be that touristic objects are in some way aesthetically, or sensually, pleas-ing to those who obtain them. Another might be that many westerners come from societies that encourage consumerism, so that the buying and possessing of objects (at home or abroad) is a strong culturally encouraged desire. Some have said that tourists obtain touristic objects as proof (both to themselves and to others) of their experiences in "extraordinary" places, or as evidence of their increased status as world travelers.[49] Others have suggested that people desire to obtain objects because they believe these things can change or affect their lifestyle, or that these new possessions can actually transform them, perhaps spiritually.[50] Speaking specifically about souvenirs, Susan Stewart proposes that people wish to possess them as "traces" of experiences that are not repeatable (1984:135). Because the souvenir evokes an ongoing narrative (where it came from, what it means), she maintains, it allows the experience to be consumed perpetually, and may enable the possessor to reconnect with the larger social body by sharing souvenir-inspired narratives.

Given that any of these motivations may be operative when a traveler is selecting a meaningful touristic object, the dilemma may not be deciding whether the thing is authentic or traditional but whether it is craft—or "art." This is because, for some people, an object that can be designated as art has more value (either economic, spiritual, or aesthetic) than one that is considered to be craft work (Metcalf 1997). Making the distinction between the two is often difficult, but a few of the generally accepted characteristics of art are uniqueness, cultural integrity, and sometimes age.[51]

The value of uniqueness may be particular to the West, and comes in part from the conception of the artist as an individual personality (Janson 1970:305) and the subsequent appreciation for such things as signature (Appadurai 1986:45). Perhaps the contemporary appreciation of uniqueness in a work of art is associated with an aversion to consuming things produced in mass quantities, things that many other people will own. While more meaning is often attached to objects that are unusual because their narratives can be heard above the clamor of ordinary things, the value of rarity or scarcity derives from the fact that consumption is differential: only certain people have the means to own rare things (Belk 1987: 172). In the case of objects from groups outside the West, scarcity often comes from the belief that traditions have disappeared or, in extreme cases, that the cultures producing them have "died" (Errington 1998).

The evaluation of whether something has cultural or historical integrity (that is, whether it corresponds to a body of typicalities and is not anomalous [Baugh 1988:483]) is another way in which art is discerned and valued. Here, the concern of art's value is connected to its adherence to a perceived history or tradition of manufacture, what is sometimes referred to as national or regional "style." This characteristic of art evaluation may seem to be in conflict with that of uniqueness described above, but this only underlines the arbitrary nature of the process of making discernments and valuations of art.

Closely allied with these two valuations is that of "age." Age can imply a direct connection with a continuously valued tradition (Tambiah 1979: 123), or it can represent the actual physical manifestation of something valued and preserved through time (Geary 1995). In either case, the evaluation of age validates historical connections to tradition while legitimizing the importance or value of the aesthetic production by its very existence despite the rigors of time, and one of the visible features of an aged object is its venerable surface—polished, worn, encrusted, oxidized, burnished—its patina.[52]

An important issue to consider at this juncture is who decides whether a thing is art or craft, for as Ruth Phillips and Christopher Steiner observe, "Distinctions between categories of art, artifact, and commodity are projections of individual experience that reveal, in the end, far more about those who collect objects than those who produce them" (1999:19). While it is true that there are times when the buyers of touristic objects are responsible for the final judgment about their possessions, there are other times when a more formal verification is performed by individuals vested with consensually accepted authority (curators, connoisseurs, collectors, and the like), either through verbal declaration or written certification. The statements made by such individuals can help to define values for art objects, but it is also vital to remember both that the valuations can be ignored, amended, and contested, and that the opinion of the authority verifying something as "art" can be accepted without the institutional affiliations or credentials buyers usually require: Errington shows how the J. Peterman company shifted Thai baskets from being functional objects to art simply through creative narrative (1998:151).

Other cultures, like the West, may distinguish among different groups of aesthetic productions as well, but they do not necessarily imply judgments of value. The Toba Bataks whom I met, using the Indonesian words *seni* (I: art) and *kerajinan tangan* (I: handicrafts; lit: "hand's diligence"), discern differences such as the West makes between art and craft, but the usage is varied and contextual. Sometimes *seni* is used to imply uniqueness; other times it refers simply to intricacy of manufacture; there are still other times when the same object is referred to as *seni* and *kerajinan tangan* in the same conversation. Here, I make no distinction between art and craft when referring to Toba Batak wood carvings, except when

I am describing how Western tourists discuss these objects, because what this book seeks to explore are the specific ways in which culturally constructed tools of discernment are implicated in the desire to consume and create touristic objects.

This chapter has tried to address some of the issues that arise in the context of cultural tourism. It may seem overly fussy to wonder what "home" means, or how a person's identity is constructed, or why we buy souvenirs when we travel, but as soon as the surface is scratched it becomes clear that there is still much to consider. What I have attempted to do here is to uncover some of the assumptions that are made about place, identity, value, and consumption, and the theories that are developed to make some sense of them, in an effort to provide a way of thinking about the events that are described in the chapters that follow.

2

Locating Lake Toba

      I can hear the boat before I can see it, the noise of its guttural diesel engine blending with local pop music blaring over the overwrought speakers mounted on the passenger canopy. It is Saturday morning, the day of the big vegetable market in Parapat on the mainland, and I have somehow missed the first (the fast) boat. It is frustrating to ride the second boat because it stops at every little inlet and tourist hotel; the only advantage is that it is less crowded. The engine idles as it drifts closer to the stone and concrete dock on which I wait, and within seconds the wiry deckhands with their unbuttoned secondhand shirts have leapt down to pull the ropes, hauling the boat close enough for me and the others to board. There are just about as many local Toba Bataks getting on today as there are Western travelers, and, as usual, many of the former head down to the benches in the hold while all of the latter head up to the metal seats on the canopied roof. I follow the tourists and the handful of Batak men who want to smoke their *kreteks* outdoors. I like it up on top because I can feel the deep, cold air on my cheeks as we scud across the waves and can see clearly the views of Samosir Island as it recedes, and of Parapat as it comes into view.

      The Toba Batak women tend to sit in the body of the boat, if possible, when crossing the lake. On market days, they sit very close to one another on the wooden benches that line the hold and on plastic mats they have laid down on the inside deck; they are protected from the wind and spray by tarps that are lashed down over the windows. Here in the hold they tell each other stories, discuss the latest vegetable and fish prices, and perform the final preparations on the produce they are carrying to market to make them more salable, trimming off withered stems and ragged leaves.

      Even when they are not going to market, however, many Batak passengers sit down below, whether the day is balmy or cold. While waiting for the boat one day with my middle-aged friend Gobara, I asked her why this was. Her eyes frowned with concern as she told me: "It's not good to sit up on top. You need to be careful—*masuk angin!*" (I: "the wind enters").[1] She went on to tell me that the wind can enter the body (especially through one's mouth and nostrils, but also through the extremities like fingers and toes, causing them to become cold) and create all kinds of health problems, from aches in the forehead and neck to nausea and flatulence. She paused a moment then added, "It's also better to sit down below when crossing the lake because it's safer."

Like most other Toba Bataks I met on Samosir Island, Gobara believes that the giant lake, which is practically at her doorstep, and whose waters she uses every day for drinking, cooking, bathing, and washing dishes and clothes, must be understood and respected. At most places along the island's shore, Toba Bataks know that the lake can almost be taken for granted: it fulfills all routine uses and is also a perfect place for children to play and tourists to swim. People talk about how pure the water is, and how refreshing; some even go so far as to say that regular swimming or bathing in its waters is health-giving. But Toba Bataks also realize that there is more to know about the lake. One must also know its dangers.

Gobara tells me that while most of the shore is safe, indeed unremarkable, there are a few treacherous places. Such a place is only yards from one of the most expensive tourist hotels on the island. I was told that within the last several years three people had mysteriously drowned there, physically pulled to the bottom, they said, by something like (yet not) a powerful hand.[2] At places like this, people who are excellent swimmers are pulled down as easily as those who are inexperienced, and Chinese[3] are as liable to drown as Toba Bataks, though no westerner has yet succumbed. Gobara said: "Those people get pulled down into the lake because they are not respectful. People don't respect the lake anymore. Sometimes they urinate in it, or defecate in it. Other times they say impolite things, or wicked things. If they do these while they are near those dangerous spots, it's certain they will be dragged down and drowned." I asked her if it was the lake itself which pulled them down, to which she replied: "How is that possible? How can the lake itself drown anyone, eh? No, it is the people living in the lake who are pulling down the impolite and disrespectful ones."[4]

Partoho, Gobara's brother, was waiting with us, and he told me that once, in the most ancient days of the ancestors, there was a terrible storm that raged on and on. The rain fell heavier each day until finally it washed all the hillside villages into the lake in a torrent of mud and water. The people of those villages had no time to save themselves and, in essence, no time to die properly.[5] They "live" at the bottom of the lake still and will not molest humans above unless they are provoked by insults, bad behavior, or disrespect. If someone curses the lake or treats it poorly, that person will be pulled down, boat and all if need be. While some Toba Bataks attest to the truth of this story, others say that it is not the "people living in the lake" that cause trouble. Rather, it is the lake itself that is the agent of drownings. As one teenager told me: "People forget that they have to respect the lake and think they can do as they please to it. They forget that the lake is still alive."[6]

It is partly this desire to show respect to the lake that prompts many Toba Bataks to sit in the hold of the boat when they make the crossing to the mainland. A show of respect during the crossing, to the majority, includes such things as speaking in a low voice, speaking only about serious (as opposed to humorous) topics, and behaving with circumspect demeanor and behavior. In the hold, where the boat's huge engine shudders beneath the deck boards with an inescapable hammering and grinding, talk is often impossible, lending to the space an ambience appropriate for personal introspection and a feeling of "safety"—from the wind, and from the ever-present threat of being "pulled down" to the bottom of the lake.

But on this day I am on the tented roof with the noisy Western tourists and the deafening music. The air rushes past my ears and nose and lips, and my fingertips are cold, and I don't really care. I see Parapat's fancy hotels come into view, their rooms each sporting tall, peaked eaves in imitation of the Toba Bataks' traditional houses (plate 3). As we pull up to the dock, the passengers grow lively and begin racing to the prow of the boat so as to be among the first to jump back down to the firm, warm earth again, and go off in their various directions, whether it be to shop, sell, or take a bus to another destination. My own objective is the same each Saturday: to take the *oplet* (I: small public van) to the post office, to eat breakfast in a restaurant, and to do my week's grocery shopping.

There is no mail today, so I eat my meal alone in a huge airy hall owned by some Chinese-Indonesians. They don't turn their florescent lights on until the tour bus groups come through, so I sit by the plate-glass windows through which the light from outside comes in, soft and diffused. I sip the coffee I am brought, a rich and bitter silt, waiting for my weekly indulgence: egg on toast and cream of mushroom soup. Today, there is nothing to do while I wait but look out the windows at the shops and salespeople across the street. Although the restaurant is right on the Trans-Sumatra Highway—the tight two-lane road that is the main artery connecting the towns farthest north on the island with those farthest south—cars and trucks pass by only sporadically. I have eaten at this place many other times with no mail in hand, waiting and looking across the street at the cramped shops that cater to passing tourists, but only today do I find it odd that I have not seen a single tourist buy anything but potato chips or toilet paper at any of the shops, even though all sorts of T-shirts, beads, postcards, and wood carvings are offered.

One of the shops specializes in locally made oil-on-canvas paintings. From my seat in the restaurant I can see huge hybrid doves with long serrated tails doing some wide-eyed courtship dance on a misty forest floor and country scenes where oxen are pulling wooden carts on a dirt path skirting a field that is suffused with a kind of honey-yellow dawn light. By far the most common subjects for paintings are lake scenes. I am, after all, sitting adjacent to one of Sumatra's (well actually, one of Indonesia's) most dramatic and famous tourist spots, Lake Toba.

It is a little strange to be sitting at a restaurant table which is positioned in such a way that by glancing right out the plate-glass window I can see a glimpse of Samosir Island five miles away, steeply mountainous and rising gray-green out of shimmering, ultramarine Lake Toba, and by glancing left I can see a miniature rendition of a similar view painted naively in brilliant primary greens and blues (plate 4). Some of the paintings portray Samosir Island's sharp, forested spine as seen from the mainland, anchored with a dense and dark brushy undergrowth in the foreground. Others seem to look north up the coast of Samosir Island, as if the artist were bobbing quietly in a *parau* (TB: canoe) near the shore gazing especially hard at the glassy surface of the lake reflecting the turquoise sky. One painting I can see from my table takes me high above the tallest volcanic mountain and looks lovingly down on both lake and island: I am now level with the cumulus clouds thousands of feet up, although I can still spot a tiny home with its sway-backed roof perched on a hillside just above a peaceful inlet.

There are some days when I hate to look at these paintings—days when their strong acrylic hues speak only of imitation and falseness and when their hominess and sentimentality revolt me. I think: "What are these visual lies? Who could dare mix blues and greens with so little sympathy for nature and no awareness of the life of poverty here? How can they paint a world so plastic and sappy?" On these days I am very critical of the way the local environment is rendered: cliffs look like steam radiator heaters, mountains take on the perfect plastic symmetry of a steering wheel's grips, and clouds are portrayed as sickly, over-yeasted baked goods. Everything relating to nature in these pictures is sculpted and heavy, and everything is kelly green, turquoise blue, appliance white, and goldenrod yellow. It is hard for me to reconcile my own perceptions of the loveliness of the place, all its subtleties and atmospheric nuances, with these vaudevillian backdrops.

There are many other days, however, when I see these paintings as emblematic of the Toba Bataks' great love and longing for the land upon which they are living. What before seemed to me to be a disregard of the landscape's sublime variations of form and color now presents itself as a gauze thoughtfully placed before my eyes to divert my attention from nature's blemishes. On these days, the paintings are not visual lies, but rather the inventive perfections of the place, of "home." On these days, I do not see the Batak painter at work in the studio as a person conniving, but rather as a person lost in a concentrated reverie—one who seems utterly deaf to the clang of right now, and who is deeply involved in negotiating the physics of pigment and canvas with the sensual dreamic memory of the world around. What I see now are painters in love, caressing the taut fabric surface with brushes that are sensual extensions of their fingertips.

Too romantic? Perhaps. Although the Batak do love the soil and breath of their homeland, and although there may be those who manifest this love through their paintings, the fact is that these paintings are for sale. The cold, hard truth is that the manufacture of these painted scenes is a business, and every shop has scores of canvases displayed in bins, leaning against walls, and stacked in dark corners.[7]

I look at the painted lake scenes across the street today and wonder who buys them all. I know they must be selling, because I never see the same ones two weeks in a row and because the proprietor seems to glow with economic prosperity.

I have seen a purchase being made only three times: twice by what appeared to be young and wealthy Batak civil servants, and once by a visiting Malaysian wearing a sari. When I finished my breakfast, I decided to ask a few of the shop owners about their main customers. The answers I got varied only slightly in their caginess. I was told: "Oh, everyone likes these views of the lake. Everyone! We sell to the Taiwanese, the Japanese, the city Bataks, and we have lots of westerners—people just like you— who buy them to take home as souvenirs. Come on, have a look. . . ." The sales pitches that followed assured me the paintings were all original and hand-painted. It was difficult to extricate myself from the shops and continue on to the vegetable market, but I did manage to do so (and without a painting, too).

When my shopping was done, I returned to the pier near the market to wait for the boat home. On the ride back to Samosir Island, and then again on the walk from the island's shore to my house, I pondered the paintings and their place in the local imagination. I have seen these paintings in the houses of affluent locals as well as in the lobbies of the hotels. This puzzles me. Why are these paintings displayed by their owners in places so close to the lake itself? I think to myself that the paintings might act as signs instructing the visitor to turn around and look at the immensity of the real thing. But I really do not know why people living on the shoreline own paintings of the shoreline. I feel that if I pursue this topic, if I can just think of the right question to ask them, I will have opened a door to Toba Batak visual aesthetics, their conception of place, and perhaps, tangentially, a window onto their construction of self.

When I next see my friend Partoho the carver, I bring the subject up. He is sitting down on the smooth concrete threshold of his house, on the shady south side that is protected from the sun's heat by a large *kemiri*[8] tree. He is finishing off a carving by scraping the knife blade on the figure's flat planes to remove nicks and other cut marks.

I say: "You know those paintings they have for sale in Parapat, the views of the lake and island? What do you think of—?" He immediately interrupts me: "Yes! I love them. They are so beautiful. If I had the money, I would buy one—a big one—and put it up on the wall above the television so I could look at it any time I wanted." I am a little surprised at his bright answer and ask him which type he likes best, which one he would buy if he had the money. Would he like a sunset seascape? A view of a forest stream beside which a pair of deer look up in the filtered rays of sun? Or perhaps a view of the lake. "The lake," he says. I try to sell him on the huge doves or the wooden cart at dawn, but he will not be swayed. "I can see the seashore on the television if I need to. Those animals in the forest? The doves? The cart? Ah, not very interesting for me. But a beautiful view of Lake Toba? *That* I could look at everyday and enjoy."

I am ready for his answer. I point out that we are sitting on his stoop not fifty feet from the lake's edge where we can see Parapat's tiny pale houses and hotels clustered on the shore and clinging to the foothills. They are glinting copper and gold now, mirroring the last bright rays of the setting sun. Rising above the tiny sparkling dots are the dark forested hulks of mountains, eroded into soft shoulders that recede into overcast clouds whose misty edges look like torn silk. I say: "Why would you want a painting of the lake when you have this to look at? Why isn't this view enough?" He doesn't really understand my confusion, and answers me, saying, "One is a painting, one is nature. They are different, see?"

I try a different tactic. I direct his memory to the nearby tourist hotel, which has big windows looking out onto the lake and opposite which, on a whitewashed wall, is a painted version of the same kind of view. "Why would they put that painting up there?" I ask. He doesn't seem to see anything ironic in the juxtaposition of the two. He says very practically, "If someone is sitting at the table talking to a friend who is looking out toward the lake, this allows them both to enjoy a view." I ask if they are the same thing, and he tells me no, the painting is a different view of the land and lake. "So why not just turn around and look at the lake?" I ask.

He continues: "See, for a visitor, a tourist, the view of the lake is new, and the view of the painting is new—both are new sights which they will be happy to see. But for me, they are not the same thing at all. When I open the door of my house and see the lake, all I see is a place to bathe and a place to wash dishes, not a beautiful view. I grew up here seeing this same view, and I continue to see it every day. I don't enjoy seeing it any more. But if I could look up on my wall at night and see a painting of the lake—with a mountain, with a village on the edge of the water, a road coming around with a car on it, and maybe a *rumah adat* (I: traditional home) over to this side—that would be great! I wouldn't have to open the door to see it!" I ask, "So you want a painting of the lake so you don't have to have the sun to light it up?" "Yes," he says, "but also because it is a *new* view."

I remembered the time when he and Ito and I went to the top of the mountain to see the *datu* (TB: traditional healer; shaman). The path up the steep and crumbling cliffs was barely visible and, because I was physically unprepared for the exertion, I stumbled to the scrubby plateau ten minutes after they had arrived. As I stood there heaving to catch my breath, I saw Partoho standing near the edge transfixed by the view and murmuring with an almost hypnotic voice the place-names he could identify from that height.

Later, when we came down from the mountain and were making the long walk home at dusk, he looked across the lake's surface at a point where the mainland is much closer to the island than it is in Huta Mungkap and said, "Look at that, you can practically reach out and touch the other side!" He thrust his arm out as far as he could, holding himself back at the armpit, and pretended to stroke the cordillera as if it were a horse resting on the other side of a fence.

It is clear to me that Partoho really loves the beauty of the land here, and I am not insensitive to the fact that living in the same place for most of his life inures him to seeing "his" view new everyday. Still, I am interested in why he prefers painted views. I asked him if he is at all bothered that these scenes are not true to the nature of the area: that traditional villages are placed at the very edge of the shore, that houses never cast shadows. What he said to me is this: it is not important that a lake painting depict a real village on a hilltop, or that it convey a particular time of day accurately. What makes the painting beautiful is that it encompasses and combines all the nice things about Batakland—that's what he enjoys. It is "like" the real view, but it is different.

All this talk about why he can no longer "see" his view of the lake— why he prefers painted scenes, why their imaginativeness suits him—is making Partoho uncomfortable, and he starts shifting around on the floor mat as he lights one after another of his *kreteks,* sighing and looking annoyed. "Why do you have to ask all these questions? Don't you have paintings in Texas? Don't you have views of places? Tell me what you have on your wall at home." I mumbled a little as I told him that I have a view of the Texas hill country—oak trees surrounded by bluebonnets lit up by the hazy afternoon sun of summer—on my wall at home. "So!" he sputtered, "It's exactly the same then! Why are you asking me all these questions?" he continued: "It's not so strange: you like to see what you know, but you want someone to see it for you differently. You want their view of your homeland on the wall because then you can see it all the time. It's a picture of your home, but it's new. That's just how it is."

A JEWEL CALLED HOME

A few days after my conversation with Partoho about the paintings, I decided to walk over to Tuktuk, where many of the largest and most luxurious tourist hotels are crowded along the shoreline, in order to talk with tourists about their reasons for coming to the area. As I walked along the road, I marveled at how different a local Toba Batak's perception of the island and the lake must be from that of a Western tourist. The English language guidebooks say things like "The province of North Sumatra is home to many of Sumatra's most popular attractions, including the jewel in the crown, Lake Toba" (Turner et al. 1995:501). Yet, for Partoho, this place—the island, the lake—is simply home, not a "popular attraction," not a "jewel in the crown." I wondered, "What does it mean for a place to be someone's vacationland at the same time it is someone else's homeland?" For a visiting westerner, all of Lake Toba's vistas would be new and endlessly photographable, all the trees, the bird songs, the scents of the flowers, and flavors of the food would be strange and enticing. For the Toba Bataks, the same vistas, trees, songs, and smells, and tastes would be so familiar and meaning-filled that they would be indivisible from the very atmosphere of life. I could see why Partoho might pine for a "new" view.

I arrived at the most elegant hotel in Tuktuk parched, so found a table on the veranda overlooking the lake and ordered a cooling beverage. As I waited for the drink to arrive, I noticed that someone had left a straw hat and guidebook on the table. I saw no harm in glancing through the book, a recent edition by a popular travel author. I flipped to the section on the Batak area and read the familiar information that described Lake Toba, an oblong body of water in an ancient volcanic caldera (which is approximately 62 miles long and 20 miles wide), as Southeast Asia's largest lake. The text continued on, quoting geologists who stated that the volcanic eruption that had formed the lake's caldera approximately 73,000 years ago was one of the largest single explosions in geologic history, throwing up approximately 600–720 cubic miles of debris 16 miles into the atmosphere (Chesner et al. 1991). Some scientists, in fact, believe that the volcanic blast was so enormous that it speeded up the onset of the last ice age (Rampino and Self 1992). Sometime after the caldera had begun to fill with water, the story goes, pressure from below caused rock materials at the center to rise up, forming a 330-square-mile island that now towers 500 feet out of the middle of the lake (plate 5).[9] Over the eons, erosion and other geologic forces shifted the formations so that evidence of the original volcano remains in only a few places. One of these spots, called Pusuk Buhit (TB: Navel Hill) by the Toba Bataks, lies on the western shore of the lake adjacent to the island.

On the next page of the guidebook was a three-part schematic illustration describing the geological formation of the lake and Samosir Island; the image looked very familiar. I glanced over to the registration desk now and saw the same schematic images painted in giant scale on the hotel's walls. Once, when I asked Partoho about the lake's origins, hoping for a richly detailed myth, he directed me to this very mural, saying, with a sweep of his arm across the horizon, "They say everything you can see here used to be inside the volcano." Many other Toba Bataks also subscribe to the scientific explanation for the creation of the lake, such as is depicted in the mural. They repeat the information they have read or heard with great veracity and conviction.

There is another origin story of the lake and the Toba Batak homeland, however, and this one does not describe geographic measurements and ages. This other telling of how things began starts at a time when the earth was covered in water.[10] According to the old Toba Batak tales, the middle world (where people live today) was once nothing but a huge sea at the bottom of which lived a giant fish and a huge dragonlike monster. In the upper world lived a young woman, Si Deak Parujar, with her parents and other relatives in a village that looked just like that of the Toba Bataks: the houses, which bordered a central plaza, were large wooden arks on stilts and were protected from the rain by thatched, saddle-shaped roofs. When Si Deak Parujar got to a certain age, her parents promised her in marriage to her father's brother's son, a young man whose face was that of a hideous lizard. Rather than meet this horrible fate,[11] Si Deak Parujar made a plan for her escape. In the center of the plaza was a huge rock covering the hole that looked down into the watery middle world. Knowing that this opening was her only chance to flee, she hid a spindle of thread in her clothing, and on her wedding day, just as the percussion orchestra was about to play, she raced to the rock and pushed it aside.

Before she jumped, she thrust her spindle under the rock and slid down the thread to the dark and unknown ocean below.

As she swam hopelessly in the water, Si Deak lamented: "Why shouldn't I cry . . . ? I have been slapped by the water, tossed by the waves, bitten in the foot by the great crab" (Niessen 1985:39); she implored her grandfather, Ompung Mula Jadi na Bolon,[12] to help her. By various means, she did in fact receive some soil from her grandfather, which she painstakingly built up to form a place called Liman Island (most people I met insisted that the name of the place she created is Pusuk Buhit, mentioned above). After she subdued the huge fish and the monster that ruled over this watery world, the land became stable. Her grandfather gave her all kinds of seeds to plant, and knowledge of medicinal herbs and architecture.

Meanwhile, Si Deak's parents and the parents of the lizard man, Si Tuan Rumauhir,[13] were beside themselves with anger and shame about the runaway bride. After some time had passed, Ompung Mula Jadi ordered that his grandson, the lizard man, should be cut into small pieces and put into a section of bamboo which would be thrown down the same hole through which Si Deak Parujar had escaped. Si Tuan Rumauhir's parents did as they were told, and when the bamboo came crashing down to the newly formed land, it burst open, revealing Si Tuan now as a handsome young man. With this development, Si Deak agreed to live with her husband and they had several children. One of their sons, Si Raja Batak, is considered by the Toba Bataks to be their original ancestor.

It is by means of this myth that the Toba Bataks claim inalienable rights to their lands, for their ancestors not only settled the area—building houses and retaining walls, diverting water, and planting crops—they in fact *created* the land. In actuality, very few Batak people I met agreed on the details of this myth: most told me that Si Deak Parujar slipped down her thread and landed on already formed solid ground at Pusuk Buhit. For them this explanation may have more legitimacy because it is substantiated by the information contained on a bronze plaque set at the base of the mountain.[14]

All the Toba Bataks I met on the island know the story of Si Deak Parujar, but when I brought up the subject of the lake's origins, I invariably heard the scientific facts about the ancient volcano's explosion.[15] What I discovered, however, is that for most of these people the traditional myth and the scientific description do not conflict; rather, they are simply layered one on top of the other. Partoho once told me that "the Batak have always lived on this land," and went on to say that the ancestors escaped the eruption's earthquakes, smoke, and ash, and came back when the land was cool and calm again.[16]

Whether the Batak homeland was created by Si Deak Parujar or by the actions of volcanic activity, it is a rugged and isolated terrain. Access to these lands is difficult from any direction, for the mountains are steep and jagged, and natural routes are few. This is one reason why the Bataks remained little known to the outside world for so long, and perhaps one of the reasons some of the Batak subgroups were able to maintain their separation from much of the influence of the Muslim groups surrounding them: the Achenese to the north, the Minangkabau and Angkola Batak to the south, and the Malays to the east.

Many Toba Bataks still consider their land to be isolated. After all, even places well serviced by transportation, such as Tuktuk, are at least two and a half hours from the nearby towns; travel from a Batak rural village to the urban center, Medan, can take the better part of a day. While Samosir Island and the lands surrounding the lake may be considered to be the "center" (both geographically and spiritually) of Toba Batak culture,[17] for many, especially those who have emigrated to urban centers, to other islands, or to other countries, this "center" is a distant one (again, both geographically and spiritually).[18] It is an odd position for rural Toba Bataks living on Samosir Island—knowing that somehow they are living in a place that is central, but nevertheless feeling that they are out-of-the-way.[19]

Jill Forshee writes about tourism on Sumba Island, Indonesia: "At the least, foreign visitors inspire local people to reevaluate their beliefs and conventions, which fundamentally involve issues of place and mobility" (2001:159). The same holds for rural Toba Bataks, but there is an added dimension to their feeling of living in an out-of-the-way center. It is created, to a certain extent, by the vast numbers of family members who have emigrated outside the homeland, either to find better farmland or better work.[20] Many people leave for several years but return to live out their lives working in the homeland. Others leave and never come back, making lives for themselves in ethnically mixed cities of Indonesia, occasionally returning to their natal villages to retire. Still others return only in body, their mortal remains carried to the land of their ancestors to be buried in their homeland's soil, and later removed, in bone and tooth, to the family tomb.

Urban Bataks often have strong nostalgic emotions when the topic of Tano Batak (TB: Batakland) comes up, but their participation in the lives of rural relations (in the form of financial assistance, for example) is tenuous. While some homeland inhabitants are annoyed by this incongruity, others empathize with their urban relatives' attitudes. Partoho told me that he wanted all of his children to move to the big cities and make a lot of money so they would not have to live like he and Ito do (and so they can support him in his old age). When I mentioned that his second son was such an expert carver that it would be a shame for him to take up some other work, Partoho replied: "Sure, I need help with the carving, but he's too smart to just stay here. He'll go to Medan or Jakarta because there's nothing for him here—just farming."

For some, the feeling of isolation was a source of despair: I was often told that tourism was welcomed because it made locals feel like they were in the current of the global community. For others, though, isolation seemed to nurture, if not also guarantee, the maintenance of tradition. In fact, the longer I lived on Samosir Island, the more I began to hear subtle cues suggesting that the closer a place was to the interior, the more traditional it would be.

Where was this "interior"? Well, it is more of an imagined center than it is an actual geographical entity, but Toba Bataks (and some of the other subgroups as well) generally agree that Samosir Island is its nucleus. Government authorities in Medan would refer to Samosir Island as the "center of Batak culture," and the dialect spoken on the island is considered to be the most authentic. Sometimes, comments were made indicating to me that people thought of Samosir Island as a place removed or distinct. One day, I had plans to visit the distant village of Huta Gingang, the fieldwork site of the late anthropologist George Sherman. I asked Nalom, Gobara's husband, if he knew how to get there. He told me he had heard of it but needed to get his bearings on its location, so said to me, *"Nah, desa itu di Samosir atau Sumatra?"* ("Now then, is that village on Samosir or in Sumatra?"). He caught himself distinguishing his island home from the surrounding mainland, and looked at me chuckling sheepishly as he continued to give directions.

All indications point to Samosir Island (and the areas immediately to the west and south of it) as the conceptual center of traditionalism. Toba Bataks living on the island told me I should pay close attention to the formal ceremonies I would see on Samosir Island because this is where they are still done correctly, where the orations and music are still performed as they were in the old days. It was implied that because Samosir Island is geographically closer to the original earthly place, Pusuk Buhit, the culture found there is naturally closer to the ancestors' customs and language. Partoho told me that I should ask Gusting, the widowed neighbor of Gobara and Nalom, about certain old traditions, because her family "originated" on the island. I asked him why he couldn't tell me about these things, and he explained that his primary ancestor originally came from Balige (a town to the south on the mainland) where things are done a little differently. He said that even though his family had lived in Huta Mungkap for ten generations, he still felt on occasion like an outsider.

Later, I discovered that even the center, the Samosir Island nucleus, has an interior. I told Gusting one day that I was going to hike to the top of Samosir Island. She nodded her head at this and pronounced it to be a good endeavor, since I would finally meet up with the people whose families had never moved from their natal villages. When I got to the top, I met a distant cousin of Gusting's who, when asked about *"tradisi asli"* (I: original traditions), told me that he was just a novice at such things, and knew only the most simple of prayers. The people who *really* retain and practice the old ways, he told me, are the *datu* living farther inland in isolated villages.

Months later, I happened to meet such a *datu*. He was a very old man with a long braided ponytail that he kept coiled up in his black *peci* hat [21] who lived in a village of perhaps thirty people near the summit of the mountain. He told me with a mischievous grin that he really knew nothing at all about the old ways—but his dear old teacher, the one who had taught him to read and write in Batak script and who instructed him in the mysteries of traditional prognostication—now, there was a true Toba Batak! As you might guess, the *datu*'s teacher lived farther inland, and closer to Samosir Island's crest.

And so it went. By conceiving of the "more original" Toba Bataks receding always farther into the geographic interior or back in time, contemporary Toba Bataks always seemed to situate themselves in a comfortable middle ground, neither completely immersed in the old ways nor entirely engaged with modern ones. It is perhaps no accident that many Bataks overlay the traditional and scientific origin stories on top of each other, for they create a world that is both ancient and emerging, both modernizing and traditional.

A TENUOUS BOND

On a calm day in the middle of the week, I decided to visit an acquaintance in Parapat. Ferries rarely came to the dock near my house except on weekends, so I walked into the nearby town of Siallagan. I found a concrete bench in the shade near the dock (a rickety wooden structure at the bottom of the path that passes through the souvenir marketplace) and, after half an hour's wait, found myself staring out at the sunny glimmers and cloud shadows bobbing around on the undulating lake surface. The shine of the lake and the sparkle of the wet sand on the little beach under the dock seemed so continuous to me that there was no way to locate an edge or boundary between them, or to imagine that one was water and the other land. I began to think about how differently the local people talked about the lake, and how they often spoke of it as if it were a separate entity, not dependent on the mountains of stone and soil to hold it in its shape and place.

Even though it was a part of everyday life—a place to bathe, wash dishes, swim—many people spoke of the lake in sacred or spiritual terms, some even going so far as to say that the lake itself has a *roh* (I: spirit, soul). Although no one I knew ever mentioned the name of the lake's spirit, it is recorded in historical documents as Boru Saniang Naga (Miss Thin-as-a-Snake). Some say that her spirit interpenetrates all bodies of water, not just the lake, and that she has control over fish, waves, and diseases and mishaps associated with water (Joosten 1992:16).[22] Those who believe that there is a lake goddess talk about her as if her temper is unpredictable, and it is implied that one is never really sure how to placate her whims.

Despite this, the lake is considered a nurturing entity. Several people admonished me for never bathing in the lake and for swimming in it so infrequently. Ito told me that I was lucky not to be sick more often than I was, as I swam in the lake so seldom, and when I was doubled over with cramps she reminded me that my recovery would be much quicker if I would go and bathe in the lake's soothing waters.

The lake's waters were thought to be superior for drinking as well. Referring to the situation at my rental house, Gusting said to me one day: "Be careful, okay? Your water comes straight from the heavens, straight from the metal [i.e., the corrugated roof], straight from the reservoir [the concrete container in the bathroom used to store water], straight from the pail! All of them too cold! Watch out for your health! Now, if you were to use the lake water . . . that is a good thing!" The lake's waters were said to be warm and refreshing, and the implication was that they were some-how healthier to imbibe.

Not all Toba Bataks are in awe of the lake. Some respect and cherish it but do not consider it to have a spirit. Many of these people (some of whom live in the tourist center and others in the cities) see the lake mostly as a natural resource that can be exploited. These people, though a minority, tend to see the lake as "potential," either as a vast and renew-able source of hydroelectric energy[23] or as a focus of tourist interest for which plans of ever-increasing development are continually being pro-posed.

It seemed to me that I had been looking out over the water for a very long time; there was not the slightest sound to indicate that a ferry was on its way. I was annoyed that I had missed the boat again and was just about to give up and walk home when I was joined by a couple of bored vendors who offered to share their day-old newspaper with me. I hadn't read a paper in days, and this one came from Medan rather than Jakarta, so it contained many articles of local, rather than national, interest. One of the men read every headline aloud in a listless voice, but his friend soon spied an editorial that was critical of a governmental decree made some years before concerning the use of Lake Toba and its coastal lands. All three of us sat up with a little more attention to hear the details.

Among other things, we were told, the decree stated that all dwellings and hotels had to sit back from the shore at least fifty meters, a concept, noted the editorial, that would mean tearing down at least half the tour-ist hotels on Tuktuk and hundreds of local houses all around the lake.[24] I asked the men where the fifty-meter-line boundary would be in Sialla-gan, and one said: "Oh, all the shops and *kios* (I: stalls) from here to the ancient Stone Chairs would have to be pulled down! We would have to move." I asked him where he would move, knowing not only that level land on this side of the island was at a premium but that his family might not have rights to any of it.[25] He made some vague statement about "going someplace else."

He changed the subject very quickly, saying, "They want our land, you know, and if they want it, they just find a way to take it." He didn't need to tell me explicitly who "they" were; it was quite clear that he saw this regulation as a cloaked move by the government to obtain control over parts of the Toba Batak homeland. He seemed very melancholy at the prospect of leaving the land, and I thought I might now begin to hear some inspiring rhetoric about the importance of one's bond to the land, about the strength of the Bataks' commitment to the homeland, to the lands originally formed by the grandmother Si Deak Parujar and continuously cultivated since the days of the first Batak, Si Radja Batak— but he remained quiet. I asked him what he would do if the government told him for some reason that he had to leave, that all the Toba Bataks had to vacate Samosir Island forever. He was smiling wistfully now, but replied in an almost chipper voice: "Oh, well, we'd have to go! The government owns all the land and the water in Indonesia, you know.[26] So, we'd just have to go." I couldn't believe his answer and so turned to the second man, who had been quiet all this time, for clarification. He said: "He's right. There's no use fighting the government! We'd have to go if they said to, but they'd give us some other land to live on." When I pressed both men on the issue, they added that they might put up a small fight to keep their land, but would be prepared to move because they saw the national government as a force far beyond their means to resist, despite the fact that other local groups in the area already had had some success in maintaining control of hereditary lands.[27] The point was, the vendor said, if the government wanted land, they would just take the places where huge hotels could be built. "And for that, we must move," he said.

I heard other rural Toba Bataks talk this way too, but it always confused me because ordinarily the talk about the homeland was strong and impassioned. Later, I realized that the Toba Bataks' love of their land is a bittersweet one, for like many beautiful things it can be claimed but not possessed. This is not just because the nation-state has title to the homeland, but also because, in the eyes of the Toba Bataks, the land belongs at once to the ancestors, to the living, and to the descendants yet to come. It is a place where the soil must be caressed with a protective touch, and where the most tenacious ties are not those made in legal documents but those made through the layering and overlapping of verbal maps, through the framing of genealogical connections, through mellifluous oratories and sentimental songs. Perhaps this is what Partoho was trying to say to me when we talked about the paintings: that a recomposed landscape of home, a "new" view, is sometimes more compelling than an actual one; that the painter's mediation (like the narrations that overlap and over-map) communicates a more vital truth about the place "homeland" than does the most loving gaze alive.

THE PATTERN OF THE PLACE

As noted, some say that a group's connectedness to its homeland is created in part by the pattern, or history, of its contact with it. For the Toba Bataks, connections with their homeland are also forged through an intensive naming and mental mapping of geographical features, through the connections those features have to social relations and genealogy, through events from the past, and even through episodes of which few traces remain.[28]

Ito one day asked me if I would like to go with her to a three-day funeral party in the village called Goroga; she told me there would be for-mal *gondang* (TB: the traditional gong, drum, and oboe ensemble) as well as dancing, aspects of the culture she knew I had so far missed. I did not know this village, and as I knew I could not accompany her, asked how we could meet. First, she said, "Oh, Andru, it's easy. You just go down the road toward Lontung. . . ." I interrupted her to say that I didn't know where Lontung was either. "Ach!" she croaked. "Okay, do you know where Inang's sister lives? *NO? Buh!* Do I have to hold your hand and take you there?" She went on, naming off the local *marga* (TB: clan) names I might know, to no avail. She then asked me if I remembered the time when the cross-island *oplet,* laden with muddy passengers and hired field hands hauling their May harvest of rice in gunny bags stacked five high on the roof (and topped with daring young boys), had slid off the road two months ago. Yes, I remembered that the event had happened, I told her, but had no idea where.

She tried a different tack now, reminding me that I had once said I had taken a Sunday morning walk down a path behind the village Siallagan, a trail that was very damp, where the leaves of *baringin* trees[29] grew very densely, making the pathway dark like a cave. I vaguely remembered once briefly mentioning some such description but could not really recall how I had gotten to that place. Ito, now exasperated, looked to Partoho, who just shrugged his shoulders, saying, "Forget it. He'll never find Goroga." Ito was not dissuaded. Now she thought of a new way to describe the place. She said, "Do you know where those large *jambu*[30] trees are? The ones near the cold-water spring?" I looked at her sheepishly, trying to pretend I knew where she meant. She saw through my attempt, and barked, "Andru! You ate those *jambu* and said how much you liked them. Now suddenly you have forgotten them!" I reminded her that I ate them but I didn't pick them, so I had no idea where they came from, and she retorted: "Well, *that's* where they came from! Goroga! Okay, never mind. I can't tell you how to get there. You are lost before you have left. If you want to go to this party, you will just have to follow your nose to the *jambu* trees, and follow your ears to the *gondang!*"[31]

What became obvious to me the longer I lived in Huta Mungkap was that intimacy of one's connection with the homeland is commonly shown through acts of naming and mental mapping. During a conversation or a story-telling occasion, if a speaker happens to mention a place, it is fully appropriate for him or her to locate that place in a variety of ways, sometimes noting whose tomb stands nearby, other times whispering that the *begu* (TB: ghosts) of two murdered lovers still hover nearby. Someone listening might want to add their own details to this information, describing the tomb in greater detail perhaps, or noting the style of clothes worn by the ghosts. Others might offer observations or memories about the place, which might in turn trigger more responses. When the narrations and mappings and over-mappings used to define and color the place are finally exhausted, the speaker continues on with the story or conversation. It is in this way that places in the landscape of the Toba Batak homeland are portrayed and invigorated, not only keeping the locations vivid in the mind, but also cementing, through a layering of narrated experiences, the intense connections different individuals have had there.

The kind of knowledge that one might have about the homeland varies, of course, from person to person. Ito seemed to have memorized every fruiting tree within a fifteen-mile radius, while Nalom knew the location of every tree whose wood he could use for carving. Gusting knew the boundaries and ownership history of everyone's fields from Huta Mungkap to Siallagan, in addition to the disposition of every *marga's* tombs in the area. Partoho talked about the area in terms of how many male mourning doves might be found in a particular glen or meadow. Any of these bodies of information might surface during conversations, story tellings, and direction givings, creating dense oral sediments of a place by connecting it to other places, bonding it with other times, relating it to a particular assortment of individuals, and, perhaps most important, using it as a shared emotional tie. When I stood with Ito and Partoho at the top of the mountain that time, looking out over the long east coast of Samosir Island, Partoho was quietly naming the places he knew, not as one might read a list, but rather as one might sing a refrain. For him, the enjoyment of observing the view was, it seems, not in knowing the boundaries or separations between the parts, but in seeing the pattern of the wholeness of the place.

"LAKE TOBA IS A MUST-SEE"

It was mid-afternoon on a sweltering day in the dry season. I was slumped on a chair in the dark room that served as the lobby for a small tourist hotel in Medan. The heat and humidity had drained all my initiative to move. Two travelers were sitting at the dining table sweating profusely onto the plastic tablecloth, pouring over their tourist guidebooks. They seemed to be sharing a silent anger. Another traveler wandered down the stairs nearby, clad in a sarong and rubber flip-flops; the towel hanging over his shoulder indicated that he was padding toward the *mandi,* the bathing room. The seated travelers seemed to know him, and one stopped him on his way, asking, "We want to go to the mountains, but we don't want to go to Lake Toba . . . it's too crowded with *tourists.* Where should we go?" The man standing looked very deeply and seriously into the face of the questioner and his advice was succinct: "You *have* to go to Lake Toba—it's a must-see."[32] He continued to the *mandi,* and the two sitting at the table closed their books, apparently resigned to the fact that a visit to the lake was required.

There are many reasons why westerners might feel the urge, or the necessity, to visit Lake Toba once they have arrived in Sumatra. Many are drawn to the mountains by a simple desire to find relief from the oppressive mugginess of Southeast Asia's lowland jungles and coastal piedmonts. Others are attracted by complicated longings for an imagined world that might be somehow more real than the one they have experienced so far. For some, the "view" of the natural environment is the focus of their visit, while others are looking for an inexpensive place to relax and reenergize. Whatever their motivation to come to Lake Toba was, I always heard hints of an underlying reason as well. This more subtle motivation was rarely articulated. Rather, in my conversations with them, travelers would say things like, "Sumatra is one of those places I've always wanted to see—you know, jungles, mountains, wild animals, strange people. . . ." What I heard in these conversations was that the place "Sumatra" was alluring because they imagined it as untamed, undiscovered—"exotic."

"Sumatra"[33] seems to be among those places that the Western imagination reserves for the most distant margins it can conceive of—not as far, perhaps, as "Timbuktu" or "Siberia," but certainly as unfathomable as "Mongolia" or "The Amazon."[34] One might think such comments have a quaint, old-fashioned ring, and that they certainly could not have been uttered in the current Global Age. But the truth of the matter was made clear to me whenever I told nonanthropologists where I was going for my fieldwork: first I would see a flash of horror in the eyes, which quickly (politely) melted into a look of concern; this was followed by questions relating to the purity of the drinking water and the nature of the toilet accommodations. Some people would ask where I was going, would wait to hear me say "To Sumatra . . ." and would then state their recognition, "Oh, like Java!" making an immediate connection to their morning coffee, the drink that they have been convinced, by the weight of at least two centuries of romantic novels and dozens of advertising schemes, comes from "exotic" places.[35]

The construction of "Sumatra" in the Western imagination as one of the archetypes of a far-off exotic place is certainly not new. William Marsden noted that Sumatra was associated with the almost mythical countries of Taprobane and Ophir (1811:3),[36] and J. Leyden was convinced that the Bataks' lands were described by Herodotus as being a place of cannibals and gold and that he located as more distant than India (1811:202). Thus, despite the fact that numerous westerners visited the island between the thirteenth and seventeenth centuries (including Marco Polo), in the minds of mid-eighteenth-century Europeans, Sumatra was a place so far removed from their reality that Jonathan Swift's (1726) placement of his strange imaginary country Lilliput off its southwest coast seemed perfectly fitting (figure 2).

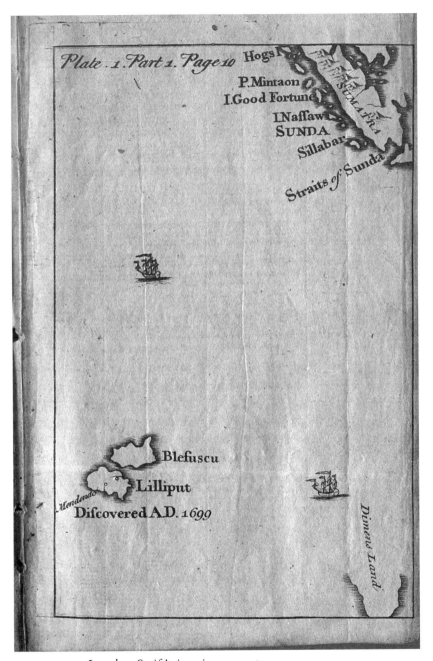

Plate. 1. Part 1. Page 10   Hogs
                    P. Mintaon
                    I. Good Fortune
                    I. Naffaw
                    SUNDA
                    Sillabar
                    Straits of Sunda

Blefuscu
Lilliput
Mendendo
Difcovered A.D. 1699

Dimens Land

FIGURE 2. *Jonathan Swift's imaginary country
Lilliput, which he placed off the coast of Sumatra*

If the notion of "Sumatra," a huge island with numerous trading ports on its coasts, seemed distant and foreign, imagine how much more exotic and unknown the *interior* (the Batak homeland) of the island must have seemed. In the mid- to late eighteenth century, westerners knew about Lake Toba only through rumors. It was only in the early nineteenth century that facts about the lake slowly began to be known. A British trader, John Anderson, probably getting his information from coastal Malay informants, wrote:

> [The lake] must be of a very great extent, as it is a day's sail across with a good breeze, the shore not being visible from the opposite side. The borders of the lake are reported to be in a high stage of cultivation. There is an island in the centre of it, where the edible birds' nests are procured. There are numerous villages, and an immense population of Battas, on its banks. Boats of considerable size navigate the lake, some of them having as many as fifty men in each.... (1971:202)

The size and mystery of the lake, added to a fascination with cannibalism, began to draw explorers to the interior. A German adventurer, Madam Ida Pfeiffer, for example, wrote:

> Mr. Hammers informed me that, scarcely two years ago, four men had been seized by the Battakers subject to the Dutch, and killed and *eaten.* All this did not deter me from my purpose; I was determined to penetrate if possible, through the great valley of *Silingdon,* as far as the lake *Eier-Pau* (Great Water),[37] which no European had hitherto seen, and of whose existence there was no other testimony than the stories of the natives. (1856:157)[38]

This desire to see or experience the previously unseen still motivates many contemporary tourists who come to North Sumatra. It compels them to scorn their guidebooks and drives them to hike off the recommended roads in order to penetrate farther into the interior. Some travelers have a gnawing urge to find "undiscovered" places where they will see, hear, taste, and feel things that are dramatically different than those they have yet known. Sometimes, they are aware all the while that such seemingly mythical locales are becoming scarcer and scarcer as the years pass, and that any well-documented place will become, in the words of one traveler on Samosir Island, "an overdeveloped tourist trap."[39]

Despite the concerns of various Western travelers, the Lake Toba area is not overrun with tourists, and recent history suggests that it will not be so in the future. Westerners began building small vacation homes and resorts as soon as they were able (a graded road was built by the Dutch colonial government using locally contracted laborers in 1917), and the natural splendors of the lake scenery and mountain air have been touted since that time. Nevertheless, considering the vast area of the Bataks' lands, the area is only slightly impacted by tourism. In fact, it is a paradox that the Indonesian economy (both local and national) depends heavily on international tourism yet one of its premier tourist destinations remains relatively undeveloped.

When I first arrived on Samosir Island, I wondered why there seemed to be fewer tourists there than in other areas of Indonesia, and why they all seemed to be of the "traveler" variety. Unlike Kuta Beach in Bali, or Yogyakarta in Java, there are no high-rise hotels or gated resorts in the Lake Toba area. Although there are a few starred hotels in Parapat, and one or two elegant ones on Samosir Island that cater to package tourists, there is nothing to compare with the highly developed and overpriced accommodations found on some other islands. Why is this so? It is very probable that the Toba Bataks' complicated land tenure laws have something to do with the level of development in the area, for I was told that outside investors must work with a Toba Batak partner, and that any lease or sale of land must have the approval of all adjacent neighbors.[40] It is not just this, however, that forms the character of Lake Toba's tourism development. Another part is played by what is called "tourist motivation," that is, the inner desires that prompt travelers to travel.

I noted that some Western travelers seem to come to the Lake Toba area because it is (to them) distant and exotic, and that these qualities promise to satisfy some urge to locate and experience dramatic difference. Many others, however, told me they came to see the "view." Now, it is well known to tourism developers that tourists motivated by their desire to see the landscape not only spend much less money per day but are also fewer in number than those who travel to experience, as Malcolm Crick calls them, the "Four S's"—sun, sex, sea, and sand (1989:308). While the climate in the Lake Toba area includes a good deal of sun, it also has tremendous rainstorms; while there may be the availability of sex for some, prostitution as such is almost unheard of; while the lake waters are usually ideal for swimming, the temperature can be quite cold; in addition, long stretches of white sand beaches with palm trees are rare. Perhaps because of these factors, the average stay at Lake Toba is four days, a fact that does not encourage large multinational corporations to invest there.

To say that Western visitors to Samosir Island and Lake Toba come primarily to see the view might be misleading. In fact, several travelers told me that they came to examine the status of the natural environment, apparently worried by numerous reports of rain-forest destruction. On one very miserable and rainy day, I was returning home from Parapat and happened to sit next to a strapping young German who told me with great concern in his voice that he had come to see the jungle. He gestured with his hand to encompass the lands of both the island and the mainland and said, in a voice filled with indignation, "Where is the rain forest? All I see are empty hills or tree farms!" Although his exaggeration made a dramatic point about the state of forest preservation in the world and echoed the fears of many other travelers, it may have reflected more about his assumptions of the way "Sumatra" should look than any historical reality: the earliest Western explorers to the area stated that the hills and mountains of the land were notable precisely because they were "perfectly free from wood" (Burton and Ward 1827:489).[41]

It is probably safe to say that no place on earth has one definitive description, meaning, or definition that is accepted by all those who experience it. Clearly, Lake Toba and Samosir Island are perceived differently by the various individuals who experience those places, whether they are Toba Bataks or Western travelers. It is fascinating to wonder how a place can be shared and enjoyed by such disparate groups of people.

A UTOPIC SPACE

What happens when the homeland of one group is also claimed as a vacationland of another group? What enables individuals of one group to recognize others' desires to express themselves in a place, and how are limits to that expression devised? In short, how do the two groups negotiate a way to share a space? In the case of tourism in the Lake Toba area, concessions seem to be made by the Toba Bataks more often than by Western travelers. This is because, in the context of international cultural tourism, Lake Toba and Samosir Island (not to mention "Toba Batak Culture") are commodities being proffered on the free market, and competition to please visitors is fierce. This is something about which both the Toba Batak tourate and the Western travelers are acutely aware. At a meeting that took place in Huta Mungkap just before I left the field, one of the men addressed me, saying: "Andru, soon you will return home. Help us. Help us by promoting this area. Help by saying this place is good so that people would rather come here [than go to another place]." Most of the Toba Batak tourate know full well that although their homeland is unique, there are still other lakes, other mountains, and other cultures with which they must compete in order to get Western tourists' money.

Western tourists are perhaps even more aware of their economic power. There were times when I spoke to travelers who told me with unrestrained annoyance that they should be accorded deferential treatment by local people because they were "giving" them money. In one instance, I found myself sitting at a table of Britons (a married couple and two young men traveling together) and one of them asked me what the Toba Bataks dislike about Western visitors. The most common complaint I had heard so far, I said, was their discomfort at seeing public displays of affection between members of the opposite sex. The married woman looked slightly haughty, as if her attitudes of propriety were being criticized, and said, "What? Am I not to give my little Nigel a tender peck now and again?" I may have made a mistake in responding that when one is in Rome, one should do as the Romans. Both she and her husband huffed and said: "Well, we've paid a good deal of money to get here *and* we're giving a good deal of money to the local people for our visit. You'd think they'd understand that *they* are the ones who are going to have to change a little if they want tourists' money!" One of the young men jumped in with his own brand of irritation, saying, "This is *some* place: you can't kiss your wife, but the guys are always trying to hold your hand!" [42] He concurred with Nigel's wife that, because he had chosen to spend his hard-earned cash in this place rather than some other, he was entitled to be treated in the way that was familiar to him (in this case, not to be touched by males).

Despite their irritations over the Bataks' seemingly odd attitudes and behaviors, I suspect that all of these travelers eventually managed to negotiate their ways of being: no doubt Nigel's wife was more circumspect in displaying her affections for as long as she was in the area; perhaps the young male lowered his barrier to Indonesian males slightly for the duration of his trip. Other travelers I met, in fact, seemed to revel in their chance to explore alternative ways of being, sometimes by amplifying their personalities and expressions of self, sometimes by trying the ways of the other.

The negotiations between Western travelers and Toba Bataks are ongoing and dependent on the particular individuals involved and the specific context within which they interact. That the negotiations occur with relative fluidity is perhaps evidence that cultural tourism is indeed a kind of utopic space: a place where different parties can, to a certain extent, investigate the possibilities that exist between their perception of reality and their desires, a place where they can act out one or many of the variety of their possible ways of being in the world. This is precisely because the space where most touristic encounters occur is geographically limited to the place I am calling the tourist center. Like a Venn diagram of two circles overlapping, the tourist center of Samosir Island is an in-between and neutral territory, a stage where explorations of the possible can be negotiated by the parties involved. Because the actual context of cultural tourism at Lake Toba is so clearly delineated, imaginative re-creation of the place by the Toba Batak tourate is possible because its construction is mostly narrative. That is, because tourism development has concentrated more on creating an image of the place in words and descriptions than it has on physically changing the environment and manipulating the culture, the Toba Batak tourate seem better able to "play along" with westerners who come to visit their homeland. If travelers desire to see "the largest lake in Southeast Asia" or "the largest volcanic caldera on earth," they may do so without impacting the Toba Bataks' concept of their homeland as "the land created by Si Deak Parujar"; if Western travelers consider Samosir Island a great place to relax and look at the view, they will without seriously infringing on the Toba Bataks' conception of the place as the center of cultural traditions.

For many westerners, Sumatra is one of the places at the very edge of their mental map of the world. Part of its draw is its perceived distance from known centers, a characteristic that lends it an exotic flavor for those seeking destinations they feel will be ever more removed from the global flow. Lake Toba and Samosir Island, in the interior of Sumatra, attract Western travelers because of their cool air and clear water but also because they are the homeland of the Toba Bataks, a culture about which the West has been curious for centuries.

Samosir Island is like many places where cultural tourism occurs, for it is a place whose meanings and uses are under constant negotiation by locals and outsiders. For Toba Bataks, Samosir Island is the eternal homeland and the lake is nurturing, some say sacred. For Western visitors, the island is a vacationland and the lake a beautiful tourist "sight." Fortunately for all, it seems, these interior places do not need to have single characters, but can be shared through ongoing, sometimes contentious, negotiations.

The cartoonish oil paintings of Lake Toba may represent the nature of Samosir Island's tourist center better than any documentary photograph ever could. Perhaps when Partoho told me that he could enjoy the painted view more than he could the real-life view, it was because he would be seeing something like what I am calling the utopic space: a place in between reality and desire, a place that is both home and not-home, and a place where things can be imaginatively re-created. Why do Western travelers avoid buying these paintings? It could be aesthetic dislike—they are not "realistic" enough. But it could also be because the views represent a vision of the re-created homeland that is distinctly Toba Batak, one that does not include outsiders or their tastes and desires. There is no way to know for sure, but I would guess that for Western travelers, the place "Lake Toba" is best represented by their own carefully framed documentary photographs or by the color postcards they buy, and that for the Toba Bataks, it is best revealed in the vivid and imagistic oil paintings.

3

Knowing Who Is Who

Ito was poised on the mat ready to begin. Smiling, she pulled her *sarong* (I: wrapped skirt) tightly around her waist, then moved her empty glass to the concrete floor near the wall behind her and leaned slightly forward as if to speak, but held her words in until she commanded the attention of everyone in the room.

She had just returned from the frontier—the border between the province of North Sumatra and that of Aceh—where she and scores of her relatives (brothers, sisters, aunts, uncles) had attended the wedding of a distant cousin. They had all ridden up to that far northern place in a rented bus, and now she was pulling her thoughts together to tell us what the conditions of the road were like, how strongly the wind had blown, the flavor of the mango fruits from the forests they passed on the way—in short, anything that would reveal in story the intimate details of the moment and the place we had not been able to share with her physically.

Well, on that particular night, instead of using Indonesian, Ito spoke the local dialect of Batak. When she happened to notice the way I was listening (my face distorted by muscles tense with concentration), she smiled and said, "Sorry Pak Guru, I have to use Batak for this one—its just too good." My Batak friends ordinarily used Indonesian to tell stories if I was present because they knew my comprehension of Toba Batak was fragmentary at best. They said Batak was a better language for story telling because the words, especially the verbs, are more colorful and evocative. Ito turned back to the group ready to continue the tale, but hesitated. She looked back at me with her eyebrows scolding me and said: "Why can't you speak Batak yet? Why? You have already been here three months and still you are deaf! You know how to carve, you know how to eat,[1] but how can you *be* Batak if you can't *speak* Batak, eh?" I got a light slap on the knee, then she turned back to the group with an exasperated "A-uh!" before she continued on with her story.

It wasn't as if I hadn't tried to learn. From the very beginning, a week after I had arrived on the island, I had made overtures to various possible language teachers in Huta Mungkap village. Some said, "Okay, let's start tomorrow," and would then disappear. Others said things like: "Who wants to learn Batak? Who cares about the Batak language? You can talk to us in Indonesian, that's good enough. . . . English! Now there's a language to know. English is the language of business, the language of education. As for Batak? You don't need to know Batak," and that would be the end of it. I might remind them that I already know English, and that learning Toba Batak would be useful in my research, even necessary for interviews, and they would agree halfheartedly before changing the subject. (I found that these were often the same people, at some later time, who would chastise me for my lack of proficiency in the language.) As the months passed, it turned out that most of my Batak friends were either "not educated enough," did not "have enough time," or did not "speak the language well enough," so I had try some other method.

At one point, imitating the way I had learned Indonesian, I wrote out dialogues on common topics in colloquial Indonesian hoping that someone would translate them into Batak for me, thinking I could then memorize these "everyday" utterances. I carried the printed sheets to my favorite *kedai,* a low concrete building with broad open windows and doors that let the breezes flow through; a building shaded by a tree dense with small leaves and speckled with tiny sour fruits the small children crave and everyone else ignores. Since it is a rare day when the *kedai* is empty, I figured it would be easy to find a neighbor or two to help me with the translations. It so happened that three women and two young men were sitting in the shop that day, and when they heard what my project was, they leapt to the task with gusto.

All at once, they started talking and interrupting, then arguing among themselves as to the best way to say a particular sentence. Some were giving me the local dialect, others were mixing in colloquial Indonesian, and a couple of them were earnestly trying to get the first two groups to provide me with the "refined" way to speak. Sentence by sentence we worked on two dialogues. It took several hours to write out ten lines what with all the bickering, correcting, false starts, mistakes, erasures, and reinscribings. At the end, when I read the sentences out loud, all agreed that indeed the phrases contained the most proper words and forms—and that they sounded very strange and unnatural. One woman told me, "Don't use those sentences. Nobody talks like that."

So I put aside the idea of making a formal study of Toba Batak; instead, I would try "picking it up" from conversations I overheard. In a month or two I was able to comprehend basic topics, one of the first of which involved two middle-aged women complaining with bitterness and indignation about the six westerners who had moved from one of the nearby tourist hotels to an empty traditional house across the street.[2]

They were telling each other how impossible the situation was, and how embarrassed they were. I couldn't get any more of the gist of it, so I questioned them in Indonesian. Gusting, the woman who owns the *kedai,* told me that this situation was the greatest scandal the village had yet encountered in its interactions with tourists. Some young people (German they thought), four male and two *females,* were staying in the same house—without a chaperone. She told me she knew that westerners have different "ways," so it must not seem unusual to me, but for the Batak. . . .

"Look at them," she said, "they are living in a house right on the street —right in the middle of the village!" She told me it wasn't so bad for her and her friend here, for they were used to this sort of thing, but what about the old people? Must *they* have to watch this sort of thing going on right in front of their homes? Well, if this weren't bad enough, the other woman said, go see for yourself: they wear filthy clothes that are "impolite" (the other woman at this point noted that the young men sat on their haunches in rayon shorts, allowing aspects of their *kemaluan* [I: genitals; lit. "shameful parts"] to become visible), they have mean faces, AND they cooked rice in a big pot *right at the front of the house!*[3] The two Batak women had no idea what could be done about this deplorable state of affairs. Apparently, the person who owned the house had been unaware that the party was composed in part of females when he agreed to rent the house for the week, so what could be done now?

I went to see for myself, and it was all just as they said: stern faces, no chaperone, rayon shorts, genitalia, rice pot simmering. . . . It was the morning after the scandal had begun, and the owner of the house, a young man of about twenty who had inherited it from his grandmother, stopped shifting his weight from foot to foot in his side yard long enough to ask my opinion of the situation. He said: "My neighbors are so angry with me, I don't know what to do. I have the rental money and I would be happy to give it back to them if they would leave, but I don't know how they would react. They look so mean. What do you think?" I hesitated a little and he was more specific, asking me (as a westerner) if it was possible to tell them to leave. I said, "Just tell them that you made a mistake in renting the house and return the money." He seemed incredulous, saying, "Can I really ask them to move on?"

I left him to his own devices, knowing he could speak English well enough to communicate with them, and walked on my way, looking up as I passed at the two tie-dye-clad guys who, with bleary eyes, bent hair, and gaping yawns, were perched on the wooden steps to the house. They didn't actually look mean to me now, but rather fuzzy and vulnerable. I was reminded of a trio of westerners I had met some time previously on the ferry boat going to the island who had the same relaxed demeanor, and who told me how intent they were on finding the perfect place to stay (as one said) "with the primitives." With dreamy, unfocused eyes, the three told me how they had met on the road in Thailand, and how they all longed to cook their own food on a fire outdoors, not just to eat in some *restaurant* like the *tourists*. They told me they wanted to be *with* these farming folk, these Toba Bataks. It seemed to me that they stopped just short of saying they wanted to *be* Toba Bataks.

The two Germans I now saw looked so happy sitting on the steps of this ancient wooden house, the place (perhaps) they had so perfectly imagined, then found, with nothing between their skins and the morning sun and cool zephyrs but thin rayon shorts or a cotton sarong, and nothing between their hunger and a plate of morning rice but embers to cook it on. I don't know exactly how the young owner of the house (whom I last saw being joined by two pals wanting a closer look at the casually comported limbs of the Germans) managed to tell the visitors to leave, but I did hear that he sent them "up the coast, where there are a lot of nice old houses to rent." By that afternoon, the house was empty and shuttered up again.

It was not long after this that I was approached by a young Batak woman who, challenging many cultural conventions, served as a guide for westerners wanting to trek across the island.[4] She began to tell me the story of a Spaniard who paid her more than the going rate in order to take him to "a real primitive's house." They climbed to the island's 5,500-foot plateau using a defunct trail rather than the usual tourist path. At the top, with the cold mists of dusk blowing around them, she directed him to an aged traditional house standing at the end of a line of five dreary homes in a wide clearing. As they drew closer, the Spaniard saw a small wooden sign painted with the English words "Rooms Available." The guide told me he flew into a rage. She looked at me with mock astonishment saying: "What is it with him? He kept telling me he *had* to see how the primitives live. I don't know what to say to him. The man who owns this house is poor and his house is very simple—does that make him a primitive?"

The tourist pressed her to take him farther into the forests and thickets, not using the ordinary paths, but instead following the meandering trails of the *kerbau* (I: water buffalo). Dusk is a fleeting moment up on the mountain, and it is almost always accompanied by swirling wisps of fog and mist. The twilight mists blow in hard from the coastal cliffs and disorient many walkers, because familiar forms can shift from fuzziness to nothingness and then into sharp clarity within seconds. As the guide and tourist tripped on the jumbled rocks in the path, soon even the fog could not be seen, only felt, sharp on their cheeks. Finally, the guide came upon the large wooden house of a man she had once met at a cousin's wedding. She beat her fists on his small door and, shivering, begged to be taken in. Perhaps because the darkness of the night was so enveloping, or perhaps because he felt an obligation to an acquaintance, he opened the door and waved them in.

The man's wife came in from the fields, clearly exhausted from her day's work, and when she saw the unwelcome guests told the guide in no uncertain terms that she could spare enough rice to keep them from sleeping hungry but had no intention of preparing it for them. The guide fumbled with sticks and matches and a borrowed rice kettle, noticing that the Spaniard made no move to help but simply stared at the hosts, "his primitives."

I told my friends in Huta Mungkap this story I heard to see what they would say about it. They were reticent to comment on the occurrence as they had not been there to see the interaction themselves,[5] but it did allow them to ask about the meaning of the word "primitive" in English. I told them it is the same as the word in Indonesian *(primitif)*[6] but reminded them that tourists who were not native speakers of English might not know a better word. One of the group said, "So, what is the word they really want?" I had no suggestions.

Apparently they weren't swayed by my attempt at apology for the tourists and shook their heads, muttering to themselves remarks that I had heard locals make before: Why are we called primitive? What is the difference between them and us? We go to church, we wear Western clothes and shoes, so what is the difference? We serve them food in the restaurants and they are so friendly, then when our backs are turned they say, "Those Batak will cheat you because all they want is your money" and they think because we are "primitive Bataks" that we can't understand any English. Well, many of us can, and they are the ones who are wrong. Who are the primitives here? Gusting now spoke up, making reference to the six Germans, "Huh! We're primitive are we? Well at least we don't live like the *kerbau*[7]—at least we *wash* our clothes."

My carving friend Partoho took the matter much more philosophically. He told me it no longer surprises him to hear how the tourists refer to the Bataks, as he hears it fairly often when he tries to sell his carvings. He said westerners often come in to his *kios,* look at every single thing he has made, fondling them all, then select the simplest and darkest object to buy, saying something about "primitif." He said, "They look at all the fine work I do, but it doesn't fit with them. They want the simple stuff." I reminded him that he sold an awful lot of the elaborate things, and he said, "Okay, okay. Not everyone has to find the original primitive thing, but there are plenty of them. What are they doing with all this primitive stuff? Have they forgotten that *they* are the ones who brought us religion a hundred years ago?"[8]

I had been living in the village for about eight months when one night, as I sipped a beer, Partoho's brother-in-law, Nalom, announced for all in the *kedai* to hear, *"Pak Guru sudah menjadi Batak"* (I: "Mr. Teacher has already become a Batak"). I had no idea why he came to this conclusion at this particular moment and asked him how I could be a Batak if my home was in Texas, if my parents were born in America? He laughed and wagged his finger at me as though I was trying to get something past him, saying, "There you are! You have already become a Batak, that's all there is to it." I knew what he meant, that even though I was using Indonesian, I had just answered him in the kind of parallel couplet phrasing that is common in the area, but told him that I couldn't possibly be a Batak as I still couldn't speak the Batak language (What I had said was, *"Bagaimana saya bisa orang Batak, kalau rumahku di Texas, kalau orang tuaku lahir di Amerika?"* where the words *kalau* indicate the start of the paired couplets). He replied: "It doesn't matter. There are lots of Bataks living in Jakarta who can't speak the language, and they are Batak. So you see? The language is not so important." Several people listening to our exchange were nodding their heads in humorous agreement; some just looked at me glumly, as if they were not amused at the man's careless identification of me as one of them. I decided to try one more counterremark: "If I am a Batak, why don't I have a *marga* name?" Nalom didn't miss a beat, and further angered the serious-minded men in the room by saying, "Okay, so choose one!" Several possibilities were shouted out amid laughing and interruptions, those participating trying to figure out how connections with a westerner could best benefit them.[9] I waved them off, commenting that one doesn't *become* Batak, one simply *is* Batak. A few of the sullen fellows nodded quietly.

Some weeks later, I was confronted by Marbada, a portly man who owned a nearby shop. I usually avoided him because I found his personality to be thoroughly unpleasant—negative, paranoid, argumentative, snide. On this day, however, there was no possibility of passing him by. I had recently returned from doing errands in Medan and had heard that he was spreading rumors about me to the local men who gathered in his shop, saying, for example, that I was not in actuality a university researcher at all, but an exclusive tour guide. Furthermore, he said, I was in the pay of Gusting (a woman of vast wealth, he reminded everyone, though no one had any idea where her money came from) and was secretly luring westerners away from their hotels at night and forcing them to patronize her establishment. So, on this day, I felt I could not simply pass by. I had to talk to him, *terus terang* (I: straightforwardly).

I sat down in his shop and ordered a coffee from him, which he set down on the table, shaking with anger. He confronted me with all of the slights and injustices he felt I had perpetrated against him, the only one of which that had any substance was that I rarely patronized his shop. When his list of my crimes finally spluttered to an end, he fixed me with one of his eyes and asked: "How is it that the government allows you a permit to do research here when all I see you do is guide tourists to my enemies' shops? You say you come here to make a study of the Batak people, but all you do is make my business worse. If you really wanted to become a Batak—."[10]

I interrupted him in confusion, saying, "Wait a minute! I am an American and everyone knows it. I don't want to *become a Batak!*" To which he retorted, "If you don't want to become a Batak, then why did you come? It is better you go away from here if that is how it is." I asked him if he thought a person studying a culture should *change into* a person of that culture, and he answered: "Yes, I think if you want to do a study, you should be just like the Batak, and the Batak way is to spend time in everyone's shop, not just a few. But it is clear that you don't want to become a Batak because you think we are all stupid. You want to study us, but you don't want to become stupid!" I stood up from the table insulted and could think of nothing to say except that there was no point in talking to him any longer.

I walked down to Partoho and Ito's house so angry that my vision was blurred and vibrating. Partoho prodded me to tell him what had happened, assuring me that it was not considered gossip to talk about an emotional event. I finally blurted it all out, not forgetting any details or descriptions of possibly hidden slights. Partoho listened seriously, puffing on a *kretek* until my ire was fully expended, then without addressing any of my complaints said, "Marbada's view is narrow.[11] Don't be like him, okay?" There was nothing else for me to say. My story didn't arouse any interest on Partoho's part, and he clearly didn't want to hear any more details, so we agreed that I should forget it and not talk about it again. The television was on, showing some Japanese cartoon superhero in an eyeless hood flying over a smoldering cityscape. The character's voice was dubbed into Indonesian by a solemn basso, but the volume was too low to understand what he was saying. Partoho made up a crazy dialogue that transformed the show from drama to comedy, and listening to him I grew calmer.

CANNIBALS AND EX-CANNIBALS

On one of the trips I made to Medan for visa paperwork, I wandered into a dark bookstore with high nineteenth-century ceilings. The sales clerks seemed too sleepy or bored to assist me in the overly helpful way I found common in most other shops, which suited me fine. It meant I could poke around the shelves of fading manuscripts at my leisure. In the corner of the store reserved for social sciences, I picked up a book purporting to be a complete history and description of the Toba Bataks and their culture. It was written by a Toba Batak man and was a strange sort of pastiche of grainy photographs, extended treatises, and genealogical charts, some cribbed from other published works, and others original.[12] It was a thick book printed in several different fonts and type sizes, and was far too complex for me to browse through completely in the shop, so I bought it to read on the four-hour trip back to Lake Toba. As the bus passed acres of plantation palms and rubber trees, I flipped through the pages of history mingled with fables and family trees, marveling at the energy with which the author described the identity of his ethnic group. His wild juxtapositions mostly confused me, and I stared out the window pondering how difficult it is to capture a culture or a history on paper. I thought about the works on the Toba Bataks I had read by westerners, and recalled how their versions were often just as earnest and just as muddled.

Since the time of their earliest visits to Sumatra, westerners have struggled to describe the inhabitants of the interior. At first, the early explorers and traders depended on the information given to them by groups living on the coasts, information that may have had seeds of truth, but which was often misinterpreted or exaggerated. As contact with Sumatrans continued, westerners were able to create their own impressions of the inland people, but not without reference to their prior assumptions and prejudices. Western descriptions of the Toba Bataks were strongly colored by rumors of cannibalism and spirit worship, and these perceptions have remained potent right up to the present day. I often met Western travelers on Samosir Island who spoke as if they believed that the Toba Bataks only recently, and reluctantly, gave up a preference for human flesh. I knew a little about the history of interactions between westerners and Toba Bataks, yet wondered why the fascination with anthropophagy was so persistent and enduring.

In 1783, William Marsden, an employee of the East India Company, published his *History of Sumatra,* an encyclopedic work based on eight years of personal experiences in West Sumatra (1771 to 1779), and on information relayed to him by other Europeans. Because of his careful documentation of facts and his clear presentation of data, Marsden's history was well received in Europe upon publication, and remained a popular reference for decades to come.

One of the things in the book that caused an immediate sensation in Europe was Marsden's account of the Bataks' "extraordinary custom" of eating human flesh. His report of their acts of anthropophagy is written, for the most part, with calm objectivity, and only occasionally indicates his own horror at the practice. He makes it very clear that the Toba Bataks' cannibalism was not a matter of "satisfying the cravings of nature" (1783:391), but rather took place only when wounded prisoners of war were captured, or when certain legal trespasses (such as adultery) dictated such punishment.

Marsden's revelation, because it seemed to be so well founded, caused a minor uproar in certain academic circles. It seems that at this time cannibalism was believed to be an extinct human practice. While all educated men knew of historical references to man-eating, it was surely a thing of the distant past. What made Marsden's description of the subject a contentious academic debate was not that an isolated group consumed human flesh, for as late-eighteenth-century explorers came in contact with previously unknown cultures who engaged in this practice, and as the popular dissemination of missionaries' and travelers' reports increased, such information was becoming more common. What made the Toba Bataks an exceptional case for the enlightened thinkers of the 1700s was that they also possessed a well-established system of law, complex architecture, and most important, a writing system based on ancient Sanskrit. These were institutions that many post-Enlightenment westerners felt were the essential marks of "civilized" humans, not cannibals.

Marsden's disclosure showed that Toba Batak culture was not just an exotic anomaly (for here were people who could not be described as either "noble savages" or gentlemanly rustics), it was a direct and threatening refutation of one of the West's most fundamental assumptions.[13] The system of thinking about cultural diversity in the eighteenth century still had its foundations in Renaissance hierarchical thinking, which meant that human social relations were thought of as a ladder reaching from the incivility and degradation of savages to the civility and gentility of the upper classes.[14] Although the "savages" might look human, they were "unmanly," "beastly," and lacked reason (Hodgen 1964:410–413).[15]

It was precisely because the Toba Bataks possessed cultural traits that evinced "reason" that their cannibalism, whether strictly limited by legal contexts or not, was so alarming. While it is true that not all European academics perceived the Bataks' cannibalism as being unusually peculiar, the overwhelming majority felt obligated to mention it.[16] Some felt that Christianity could quell the problem, and the call for missionizing activities in the Batak area began in the early part of the nineteenth century.[17]

A report made by two British missionaries, Richard Burton and Nathaniel Ward, who surveyed the area in 1824, mentioned the Bataks' cannibalistic acts, but downplayed them.[18] It was not until 1834, however, that a serious effort to convert the Bataks living inland was made.

In that year, two American Baptist missionaries, Henry Lyman and Samuel Munson, went inland from Tapanooli (now called Sibolga), a port village on the west coast of Sumatra. Traveling with a retinue of porters and attendants, they did not heed the warnings of various Bataks they met along the way, and were promptly ambushed and killed. The fact that Munson and Lyman were killed in the midst of their evangelical efforts in the Silindung Valley caused a crescendo of horrified responses. Rumors were quick to spread that their bodies had been devoured, although there was nothing more than circumstantial evidence to corroborate this.[19]

The effects of this event were far-reaching. The martyrs' deaths of Munson and Lyman focused attention on the importance of missionary work in the East Indies, and by May 1838 new recruits for missions in Sumatra were actively being sought. Perhaps a more important effect was that the missionaries' deaths seemed to prove what westerners familiar with the East Indies already assumed—that the Bataks were cannibals.[20] What had until this time remained an arguable issue now seemed fully answered, and publications produced after the 1830s address the Bataks' anthropophagy as fact.[21]

The years passed, but Western fascination with those referred to as "lettered cannibals" did not fade.[22] Even after 1865, when the German Protestant missionary Ludwig I. Nommensen began showing remarkable success in baptizing Toba Bataks, they continued to be associated with cannibalism.[23] The Dutch colonial government finally attained control over the Toba Batak lands when they killed the last hereditary Toba Batak king, Sisingamangaraja XII, in 1907, but the myth of "civilized cannibals" is a durable one.[24] While some popular articles and books attempted to rationalize the Bataks' actions, others referred to their past acts as if they continued to occur. Melvin Hall, for example, wrote, "as to whether or not any tribes continue the practice of eating their aged and decrepit relatives, I found a divergence of opinion among the European residents of Sumatra" (1920:86).[25]

Even though the majority of the Toba Bataks are now Christian and have been for some time (indeed, many are fourth- and fifth-generation

Christians), their past anthropophagy has never left the Western imagination.[26] It is amazing to think that more than two hundred years after
it was first reported, the image of "lettered cannibals" in Sumatra still
survives in the popular imagination. Take, for example, the first few
paragraphs from the two most commonly used English-language tourist
guidebooks:

> British traveller William Marsden astonished the "civilized" world in
> 1783 when he returned to London with an account of a cannibalistic
> kingdom in the interior of Sumatra, which nevertheless had a highly
> developed culture and a system of writing. (Turner et al. 1995:520)
>
> Numerous cultural, linguistic, and physical indications of early
> Hindu contact include the Batak style of rice irrigation . . . religious
> ideas, and script. . . . The only human flesh eaters on the island, the
> Batak were the infamous "headhunters of Sumatra" in tales of yore.
> . . . Though this practice largely ceased when the Batak converted to
> Islam and Christianity, some Batak have indulged in cannibalism in
> quite recent times. (Dalton 1995:779)[27]

It is this enduring image of the Toba Bataks, constructed partly by outsiders (such as westerners and coastal Malays) and partly by the Batak
themselves, that provides one of the important subtexts for Western travelers eager to have "exotic" experiences. I don't want to give the impression that I think travelers come to Lake Toba truly expecting to see or
hear about past frenzied feasts. Still, it seems probable to me that the
Toba Bataks' connection to ancestral "cannibals" serves as a kind of cre-
dential of authenticity for travelers in a way that the more accurate designation "Protestant Christian" cannot. That is to say, reference to historical cannibalism more than perhaps anything else helps travelers to
identify Toba Bataks' culture as a legitimate "sight."

When the bus finally bumped into Parapat, I stopped my musings on
Toba Batak history and stashed the thick paperback of jumbled images
and anecdotes back into my bag. Because I knew that the very next day
I would have to go to the government administrative town to finish my
paperwork, I found an inexpensive hotel room in town. It was dusk by the
time I had put my bag up and washed the dust of the road out of my hair,
and since it is such a pleasant hour of the day, a time when wisps of foggy
cloud come tapering down the mountain forests in the east and the sun's

warmth still glows to the west, I wandered down the road that leads to the dock.

The road is slightly narrow and winding, and is crowded with shops and restaurants that cater primarily to tourists. At this hour, most of the shop owners were deftly manipulating long, forked bamboo wands to remove their merchandise from the nails and hooks that hold them out for display. I saw a young woman at a second-story window wearing the white blouse and light-blue skirt that is the uniform for middle school students. She was leaning out between two potted geraniums in order to bring in a tame and cooing pigeon. Other people were sweeping off their concrete stoops, or flinging out handfuls of fresh water to help keep down the dust from the cobble and asphalt street. It was very hard for me to imagine at that moment that some visiting westerners have come to this place looking for animist ex-cannibals, or if not this, then for "primitives."

I knew that most Toba Bataks I had talked with accepted these designations with patient or humorous resignation: in regard to the historicizing portrayals, they seemed to acknowledge the inescapability of their ancient past, raising their eyebrows to say, "Itulah!" (I: "That's how it is!"). It wasn't simply that the Toba Bataks I met accepted the mantle of outsiders' opinions, but also that they integrated certain facets of Western characterizations into their own constructions of group identity.

When the topic of cannibalism came up (which was not often, as the topic was considered inappropriate for polite company), it was usually discussed tersely as a fact of the ancient past. My friend Partoho put it like this: "Yes, yes, a long time ago there were those who ate humans, but that was *a long time ago,* you know? Lots of things have changed too, right? Christianity came and a lot changed. That was all a long time ago." A chorus of agreement from those around him greeted his words: "That's right, things are different now." The prevailing attitude during these moments was a kind of annoyed exasperation that the subject had come up *yet again.*

Still, when I asked Partoho if he was certain that *his* ancestors ate human flesh, he looked at me in surprise and told me that of course "everybody knows" the Bataks were cannibals and that there is no reason for a person, whether Batak or outsider, to lie about it. This is not to say that Bataks are proud of the fact that their ancestors might have eaten other humans, simply that most contemporary Toba Bataks assume their ancient relatives took part in this act (despite the fact that it is not clear

how common anthropophagy was),[28] addressing the issue with equanimity and succinctness.

Others, however, handled this aspect of group history with less
reproach. About twenty minutes' walk from Huta Mungkap is the popular tourist sight referred to as "The Stone Chairs of the Kings of Siallagan." This sight is an enclosed village in whose central plaza are huge
boulders carved in the shape of high-backed chairs surrounding a huge
stone table (plate 6). The tour guide (usually someone of the Siallagan
clan) informs visitors that, in the past, important negotiations and legal
transactions were discussed at this site. Next, the guide directs tourists to
an adjoining courtyard where several other carved boulders are located:
one of them is purported to be the block on which a criminal's head was
chopped off, and another is said to be the platform upon which the feast
of the victim's body took place. Sometimes a tourist is called from the
audience to create a mock reenactment of what the horrible punishment
must have been like (figure 3). One of Partoho's cousins has a stall in the
marketplace that is directly adjacent to the walls of the Stone Chairs'
enclosure, and as the tourists leave the place, they often pass right in front
of his shop. He is not at all shy in marketing his wares, and with a defi-
ant tone in his voice, calls out to the visitors to come see objects like those
once owned by "the cannibal kings."

For some Toba Bataks, cannibalism can be a humorous topic. When I
arrived at the station for my trip to the administrative town the next day,
I found that the next bus leaving was a minivan already crowded with
local people, their parcels and baggage. The one seat left free was next to
a corpulent local government official on his way to a meeting. As the
small bus wound up and down the steep mountain slopes, my seatmate
showed his talkative and chummy nature, asking innumerable questions
about my family in America. As we approached our destination, he grew
abnormally quiet. He suddenly turned to me and, with a face of calm
intent, said, "Say, did I tell you there's American blood in my family?"

I was a little confused since this guy seemed to be so clearly and solidly
Toba Batak, so I said, "No. How is that possible?" He was grinning
broadly now and shot back, "Yes, its true! My grandfather ate Munsen and
Lyman!! Ha! Ha! Ha!" The rest of the passengers, who up to this point
had been silent and dour, joined in the laughter (perhaps at his joke, perhaps at my reaction to it). On my return trip to Samosir Island I saw what
must have inspired this man to tell his joke at the moment he had. I had

FIGURE 3. *A reenactment of a beheading*

to laugh again (this time somewhat grimly), for to the side of the road outside Sibolga we passed the small stone and bronze memorial marking the place where the two missionaries were slain so long ago.

ANIMISM INCORPORATED

The more I talked with Western travelers once I was back on Samosir Island, the more I realized that cannibalism was not the only (nor perhaps the most important) aspect of Toba Batak culture that attracted them to Lake Toba. Many also seemed to want to interact with "animists" or to participate in a "primitive" lifestyle. What travelers actually see, as might be expected, is often very different from what they hope to see. In those areas of Samosir Island where the local people have begun to have more expendable income (in particular, those areas close to the tourist center), most Toba Bataks live in rectangular wooden or concrete houses, not in the traditional ornate houses mounted on stilt foundations. Furthermore, most economically solvent families have a television set (and sometimes a motorcycle), dress in clothes and fashions that are clearly in tune with Western trends, eat mass-produced candies and potato chips, and sing pop songs to the accompaniment of guitars. In short, the day-to-day lives of many Bataks on Samosir Island are not all that different from the Western traveler's life at home.

Although there are some important differences in the two lifestyles, the day-to-day life of rural Toba Bataks is hardly "exotic." This state of affairs is certainly not ideal for some travelers. A common complaint I heard was that all there is left to see on Samosir Island, in the words of one traveler, are the "vestiges of a strong culture." While the tourist guidebooks tend to foster a fossilized image of the Toba Bataks—one where descriptions of ceremonies of the historical past take precedence over present realities[29]—westerners do not seem convinced. In fact, one noted that "I found Batak people fishing, swimming, . . . cooking, going to school . . . but I think they've lost something with Christianity that I feel maybe killed their social life."

What I slowly realized is that the guidebooks' historicizing portrayals were attempting to repair the disjuncture between what visitors desire to see and what they actually see. They do this by implying that the Christian, the "modern," the "westernized," aspects of Toba Batak culture are actually just a thin veil masking their true "primitiveness" and connectedness with their pre-Christian traditions. A context in which this commonly occurs is in reference to the Toba Bataks' religion. The same two guidebooks mentioned above, for example, state:

> . . . the majority of today's Bataks are Protestant Christians. . . . Most Bataks, however, still incorporate elements of traditional animist belief and ritual. (Turner et al. 1995:520)

> The Batak are animists with a veneer of Christianity or Islam covering complex and sophisticated beliefs. . . . Eighty percent are Christian, but their religion is mixed strongly with ancestor worship. (Dalton 1995:780)[30]

The implication here is that the Christianity practiced by Toba Bataks deviates from some more pristine form that is apparently found in the West, and the phrasing of these quotes suggests that the Christianity westerners know and practice does not include ancestor worship or animist beliefs and rituals.[31] The point made is clear: the Toba Bataks (unlike westerners) have merely incorporated their animism into Christianity; while they may sing hymns at church on Sunday, they will no doubt pray to the spirits of rocks and trees later in the day.[32]

It is difficult to say to what extent Western travelers accept this scenario. Many come merely for a few days of respite from the oppressive heat of the coastal lowlands by swimming in the cool lake waters and care little or nothing for the culture that surrounds them. Numerous others, however, are like the Spaniard I was told about who came to the area looking for "the Primitives" and follow the guidebooks' advice to climb to the top of the mountain where the culture is more authentic (Turner et al. 1995:522). The hike to the villages on Samosir Island's mountaintop is a long and strenuous one, but many of those searching for "more traditional" Bataks find their exertion pays off when they meet the gregarious owner of the house-hotel the Spaniard avoided. As a man who openly refers to himself as an animist, he is popular with those travelers wishing to meet someone they believe practices the "real" Toba Batak religion.

I climbed to the top of the mountain, too. I, too, wanted to see if the people living at the top were somehow more authentic, and so climbed to the top of the mountain to stay in the house of the animist hotelier. I asked him how he dealt with westerners interested in his animist beliefs, and he answered by flipping open a thick photograph album to show me how many travelers had accompanied him to his places of worship. He said he realized that many westerners want to see how he prays because they believe he still has the "old religion," and that for them it was extremely strange and unusual. He hesitated a second and then added, with a short laugh, "I'm really Christian. I just like to pray in the old way . . . it's not really that different you know." The idea that the two belief systems are actually very similar is a point some academics have made before,[33] but it is a topic in which few travelers seem interested.

So, although it is true that tourist guidebooks do mention the Bataks' Christianity, the subtle stress of their message to tourists seems to be that Batak animism lives on.[34] Part of this is evident in descriptions of the Toba Bataks' contemporary wood carvings (which are most commonly based on pre-Christian forms), where the implication is that these objects are not just being made for sale to outsiders. While tourist guidebooks disagree about how much importance these carvings have in the religious lives of the Toba Bataks, travelers seem to have their own ideas. An unusually large proportion of the westerners I spoke with believed that the wood carvings offered for sale in the marketplaces could be used in the animist religion they believe the Toba Bataks still practice. This belief, which flies in the face of everything the travelers see being lived by the Bataks in the villages of the tourist center, is not only encouraged by vendors who say *"Majik! Majik!"* (I/TB: magic) whenever the traveler picks up an object. The belief in rampant but hidden animism is also strengthened for travelers by the two hundred years'-worth of Western writings that have depicted Toba Bataks as cannibal-animist others.

While many Toba Bataks resign themselves to westerners' exaggeration of their connection to ancestral cannibalism with equanimity or humor, they take the characterization of them as animists more seriously. This is because it is relatively easy for Christian Toba Bataks to distance themselves from the extinct practice of cannibalism, while it is often more difficult for them to express the difference between themselves and those who might still practice the old religion. Everyone I knew scoffed at the idea that there might still be animists in the vicinity, saying "We are all Christians here!" Nevertheless, I often heard whispered stories right after this comment about how this neighbor's father or that neighbor's grandmother still believed in spirits and ghosts until "a few years ago."

There is no denying that certain aspects of animism have been incorporated into the Toba Bataks' Christianity over the years, for ancestor worship, among other things, is still widely practiced.[35] Nevertheless, most Toba Bataks so fully identify with their Christian religion that any outsider's reference to their affiliation with animism implies more than mere backsliding or religious amalgamation, it implies that the Good News has been heard—and ignored.[36]

Why is this so? Well, most of the Toba Bataks I knew equated animism with "primitiveness." In their view, an animist was either a person who had "not yet" accepted "religion" (that is, Christianity), such as the naked people from Irian Jaya they regularly saw on national television news, or someone who was deliberately rebelling against "religion," such as those Toba Bataks who participate in one of the local animist-based religions such as Parmalim.[37]

This said, how does one understand those Toba Bataks who play up the image of primitive animist for the tourists? For a great number of vendors of touristic objects (perhaps to a lesser extent hotel or restaurant owners), it comes down to a very simple case of economics: as many westerners come to the area to experience the "primitive," tapping into this desire— whether by shouting *"Majik! Majik!"* or by some other similar marketing angle—is one of the most certain ways to make a sale. Although most Toba Bataks are respectful of their ancestral heritage (cannibalism and animism included), few actually identify with these aspects of their culture except to create a successful context for selling their wares. This is a situation not so different from vendors at county fairs in the United States who dress up in period costumes in order to legitimize the old-timey quality of their wares.[38]

Sometimes, outsiders' constructions are too strong for Toba Batak individuals to negotiate or contest. Toba Bataks are rarely in a position to have success in directly refuting Western constructions of their culture that have been two hundred years in the making, especially if they take part in fostering them. Often, for Toba Bataks living in the tourist center, the only way they can regain some control over their cultural identity is by encouraging Western travelers to act out their preconceived notions and possible ways of being in utopic spaces far away from them, whether it be up the coast or inland. This is part of the reason, no doubt, why the young landlord in Huta Mungkap dealt with the Germans in his *adat* house, not by asking them to change their actions or perceptions, but by suggesting that they could find a better place somewhere "up the coast."

"CHEATS" AND "SNOBS"

While sitting in a coffeehouse frequented by westerners not long after I had returned from my bus trip, I heard a tale suggesting that not all travelers view Bataks as ex-cannibals, animists, or even primitives; some create summary opinions based on their own experiences or the opinions of other travelers they have met. The coffeehouse where I sat that day was run by an expatriate Australian woman who had married a Toba Batak man and had found a niche among the competitive tourist restaurants and cafes by baking bread and cakes, and by providing a lending library and bookshop of Western-language paperbacks. I sat at a small round table on the crowded wooden balcony overlooking the lake and was soon joined by an office manager from Seattle, dressed rather formally for a traveler, who held his coffee cup and saucer as if they might soar into flight at any moment. Our conversation had a false start or two, but when I told him that I had been living on the island for several months doing research on tourism and Batak culture, he must have felt he had found an eager ear for a story about his recent experiences. This man was unlike other travelers I had met who described the Toba Bataks in positive terms, saying things such as "[they are a] very helpful, interested and smiley people," or "they are open, cheerful, hardworking, and smart."[39] Instead, this traveler told me, to his preface his story, that all Toba Batak guides were "cheats."

It seems he had contracted to have Gusting's son Sulean guide him around the island by motorcycle for a fixed price. After several hours of lurching and seesawing down the poorly maintained road that rings the island, he saw a small *kedai* at a bend in the road and suggested they stop for a beverage, to which Sulean readily agreed. He ordered a large bottle of beer, while Sulean ordered a tea and (because he is regularly famished) a bowl of noodle soup to boot. When the bill came, the American told me that Sulean made no effort to pay, which irritated him because he had not explicitly stated that the refreshments were his treat. He was angry at Sulean's insouciance, and told me he could think of little else for the rest of the day's trip.

When I returned to Huta Mungkap, I decided to talk with Sulean on my way home. I passed by his mother's *kedai,* and saw him comfortably lounging in a chair listening to Western pop music on his tape machine. I asked him about his day, about his trip with the visitor from Seattle. He responded that the American was a very strange man. As he told the story, the two of them had been having a fine time until after lunch, when the American had suddenly become very surly; Sulean blamed this on the man's physical discomfort at having to travel on the bumpy road. (In fact, he had no reason to think that the American's attitude arose from anything else, since it is common in the Batak area for a companion to suggest stopping for "something to drink" as an invitation to relax and "refuel." The suggestion ordinarily implies that an invitation to pay has been extended as well.)

Sulean continued, saying that when they returned to the man's hotel at the end of the day, he realized that something more serious than a sore backside was bothering the American, for as the bills were being counted out to pay for Sulean's services, the traveler said, "I guess that meal counts as your tip!" Sulean was saddened as he left the hotel, then perturbed as he rode his motorcycle home. He told me that this event was not all that unusual; he said that sometimes the rich tourists are the cheapest ones.

I wondered about what had happened between the two of them, how such a seemingly simple interaction could have such problematic consequences. It seemed doubtful to me that the American was truly concerned about the amount of money he had spent that day, for, as Sulean told it, the service fee was very reasonable and the price of lunch a pittance. Instead, it seemed clear that the traveler felt he was being taken advantage of by the "greedy" Toba Batak guide, Sulean; he seemed to feel he had been had by a cheat.

Such opinions are not unusual. Travelers are not very diplomatic about their views, often voicing their thoughts about the Toba Bataks, whatever they may be, to anyone within earshot. In conversations, I most often heard travelers describe the Toba Bataks as being "pushy" or as "cheats," both impressions always arising in reference to financial interactions. The Bataks' aggressiveness in the marketplace of touristic objects is almost universally commented on by travelers because, having usually come directly from Java or Thailand, places where vendors are generally thought to be more sedate and polite, they are stunned by the Bataks' direct, clear voices, their tendency to force objects into their hands, and to physically pull them into their small shops.

Descriptions of Toba Bataks as cheats usually (though, of course, not always) have to do with misunderstandings arising from language difficulties on the part of the Bataks or addition problems on the part of the travelers. Nevertheless, there are times when the epithet accurately reflected travelers' heartfelt opinion that the Bataks are greedy. It was not uncommon to hear travelers say things like, "The Bataks are just a bunch of cheats . . . everything for them is money, money, money. That's all they want is money, and they'll do anything to get it."[40] Often this kind of statement would come up when travelers were saying that they had to pay for a service they assumed had been "taken care of." Thus, in many such characterizations, as indicated in the Seattle man's interactions with Sulean, the term "cheat" seemed to include an impression of avarice.[41]

Many Western travelers (especially those on extended vacations) indicated to me that they prided themselves on an ability to deduce, or "read," the character of a particular tourate group quickly and accurately. This contradicted my own impressions: that Western travelers formed their opinions of the character of Toba Bataks based primarily on what they had heard from other travelers prior to visiting the area, only later modifying their perceptions based on their own experiences. While there is no way to understand fully how cultural characterizations are created, and verified or negated, via the traveler "grapevine," it is clear that certain "factual" descriptions (such as "cannibal," and "animist") ultimately derive from guidebooks, whereas more subjective characterizations (such as "aggressive," "primitive," or "romantic") arise from individual travelers' interactions. The existence of a complex system of information sharing (both through the exchange of guidebooks and of personal opinions) among tourists may provide a clue to why travelers like the Spaniard continue to believe that there are Toba Batak "primitives" living somewhere deep in the mists of Samosir Island's mountain villages, and why other travelers, such as the Seattle office manager, might be predisposed to blame their problematic interactions on what they come to believe are character flaws endemic in Toba Batak culture.[42]

I wondered what the Toba Bataks thought about being called aggressive, greedy cheats by the westerners, but was too shy to ask them outright. I hoped it would come up by itself in conversation someday. The topics of cannibalism and animism were much easier for me to talk about with them because I knew that most people had simple and direct ways to address them, as they had occurred so far in the past. As it turned out, I did not have to wait long for an opportunity to broach the subject, for one day as I passed down the narrow road in Siallagan (the town with the stone chairs) that is flanked on either side by crowded and dark market stalls, I met up with Ito, who sat wistfully sanding a carving. She asked me why it was that westerners so often seemed to avoid buying things in these little shops. She wanted me to be honest and direct in my answer, but I found it hard to tell her everything I had heard. I did tell her part of what I had heard many travelers say: that the vendors were too pushy (or, as the Bataks put it, *"agresif"*). She had a certain amount of frustration in her voice as she told me that westerners say they love the Batak because they are so open-hearted and *terus-terang* in ordinary social interactions, but then turn around and complain when they are too forward in selling their wares.

As it turns out, Ito and other Toba Bataks I spoke with later saw this as a Western double standard: when their forwardness occurred in a conversation at the side of the road or on the ferry, it was charming; when it was part of an interaction in the marketplace, it was obnoxious. Ito tried to overlook this seeming contradiction, saying to me: "Okay, we're too pushy, right? Well, that's just the way it is then. The tourists come into our stalls, and they look and *look* . . . and then they buy nothing! They go home without their souvenir of Lake Toba. Sometimes we are too forward, too pushy, but that may be what they *need!*"

With the topic thus broached, I found it easier to chat with Ito about tourist perceptions of the Bataks as avaricious or as cheats. She, like so many other Bataks I talked with, was confused when she found out Bataks were thought of as greedy. For her and the others this was blatant hypocrisy, because travelers have far more clothes and other possessions than a typical Toba Batak would ever have, and they continued to buy more as they traveled. Furthermore, because Toba Bataks do not perceive the accumulation of wealth in a negative light as do some other Indonesian groups,[43] their desire to maximize their financial gains was not "greedy" (or as Ito said it, *"rakus,"* implying someone who gobbles up more than their fair share) but, rather, economically shrewd.

In regard to the characterization "cheat," the Toba Bataks' attitudes were much more nuanced, partly because in Indonesian the word for "cheat" is the same as that for "trickster" *(penipu)*. Thus, when a person is caught trying to delude another person, they are shamed, not because of their intent (for that is considered part of doing business),[44] but because they did it so poorly they got caught. In essence, they were not *pandai* (I: clever).[45]

It could seem, at this point, that thinking up ways to label the other is an activity only westerners engage in, but this is not so. Toba Bataks are also prone to developing opinionated characterizations of travelers, and of westerners in general. Part of this has to do with the fact that the Toba Batak tourates' employment often puts them at a disadvantage with westerners.[46] While the tourate's assistance is perceived by visitors as some kind of culturally derived friendliness, graciousness, or hospitality, perhaps hospitality "is just another technique of selling" (Boudhiba, in Crick 1989:331). No one can deny, of course, that in certain situations (like that of the Toba Bataks who maintain control of local hotels and restaurants) tourism can provide employment opportunities for otherwise economically deprived groups. The point here is that these jobs are usually low-paying, insecure, and dead-end: when working as maids, guides, and waitpersons, Toba Bataks are put in the position of being physically subservient to visitors.

As I continued talking with Ito and other vendors, and with Partoho and other carvers, I started to hear occasional eruptions that let me know what they thought of westerners. While many of the Toba Batak tourates perceive westerners to be a mostly undifferentiated group, they are nevertheless aware of certain distinctions among them. These they base on the clothes they wear and the way they hold their bodies, their cultural "character," and their language. One Batak tour guide gave me this list: "*French:* sloppy dressers, dark hair, tan (vs. pink) skin; *Germans:* usually tidy dressers who carry backpacks on their backs (not on their shoulders); *Dutch:* very tidy dressers who are often elderly and polite; *Italians:* people who gesture with their arms a great deal." But such characterizations are not always shared. Another Batak, a carver, told me without hesitation that the sloppiest dressed westerners are Germans and Americans, and that the Dutch are the most arrogant.

Describing travelers by their cultural character is the most common way that Toba Bataks construct westerners' identities. A female Toba Batak tour guide told me if she had to rate the people she has worked with,

> "The Italians are the WORST! The English? Not much better. We call them 'The Kings of Complaint.' Nothing is ever right for them. The Americans are Okay, but they are always criticizing . . . you know, always have a better way to do something—they're know-it-alls. The Germans are pretty nice, but you know, they just come here to smoke the dope. The Dutch are the best. They are always polite and well dressed. They even speak a little Indonesian."

When I asked one vendor in Siallagan what he thought of the Western visitors who passed by, he told me, simply, that he pulls his shades down to cover the entrance whenever he hears the French coming up the path.

Partoho had his most unfortunate experiences bargaining with Germans. One day, as we were sitting around listlessly carving, he asked me to teach him some words in English. I asked what he wanted to know, and he began to give me a list of seemingly random words: "*Tersenyum*" he started; I responded, "smile."

"*Ukiran,*" "carving"; "*kereta,*" "motorcycle"; "*orang Jerman. . . .*" He hesitated a little and looked up at me. I said, "That's the same, German."

"*Kikir,*" he went on; "stingy."

"What was that one again?" he asked.

"Stin-jee," I repeated it.

"Okay, how about *kukunya?*" he asked.

"*Kukunya!?* Why do you need to know the word for fingernail?" I asked him.

He abruptly ended our session by saying, "Okay, that's enough words for now."

We sat there quietly for a moment and I was thinking what a strange man Partoho was when suddenly he began saying in a very loud voice, and with a very heavy accent, "YOU! You German! You STIN-JEE! You stinjee German! Stin-jee. German stin-jee. . . ."

I was horrified; he was very proud of himself. He asked me if he had pronounced it properly. I told him I was not going to help him speak English if he only wanted to insult tourists. He thought this was very funny and nudged me as he chuckled. As soon as Ito came home from the fields he began teaching her the words, and both of them roared happily at my strained attempts to shut them up. I told Partoho this was a terrible thing to say to someone, and he agreed that he would never say such a thing to another Batak. He tried to reassure me by saying, "Oh, don't worry, I won't say it all the time. I just want to know what to say in case they get too cheap with me the next time."

This incident introduced me to an issue for Toba Batak tourate that was repeated later again and again: the feeling that westerners did not act in accordance with their social and economic place in the world.[47] Sometimes the topic would come up when a westerner pretended penury and bargained furiously with the vendors in the marketplace, and other times it arose when a westerner entered a public place dressed too casually (or in unclean, shabby clothes). A few Toba Bataks were offended by these actions, while others were utterly confused.

Among themselves and among other Indonesians, there are clear social templates for knowing how to interact with others. With Western visitors in general (and in particular with travelers, who tend to be more interested, at least theoretically, in social equality and cultural sharing), the Toba Batak tourate find that the rules for interpersonal engagement are constantly shifting. A hotel worker meeting a guest who is friendly and chatty as they come in contact off-premises during the day may later find that the same guest is demanding and impatient when ordering food in the evening. Such a change might be second nature for the westerner who is used to distinguishing between social and work interactions, but they may seem contradictory to the Toba Batak worker. Because much of the behavior of westerners is enigmatic to Toba Bataks (primarily because their motivations to act are often so vastly different), the issue here is not necessarily that the traveler acted as an equal or a superior, but that they switched between the two roles for unclear reasons. Because of this, westerners are many times characterized as being arrogant or snobbish: they seem friendly but are also patronizing. This is no doubt what Gusting meant when she said that westerners talk in ways that imply they are more "civilized" but act in ways that betray their rudeness.

SELF-IMPRESSIONS

The stories I heard from Toba Bataks as we sat around on the brightly colored mats after dinner, or as we lounged around a table in one of the local *kedai,* did not single out Western travelers exclusively. Toba Bataks were often just as judgmental of themselves as a group as they were of others,[48] often using locally accepted character traits that are just as likely to be derogatory as they are to be complimentary. Some, like Marbada, spoke of Toba Bataks as stupid farmers,[49] but others gloried in their renown as orators and singers.[50] Traits about which Toba Bataks feel proud are often the focus of a narrative. Someone might say something like "So, about bravery. . . . You know, the Bataks are very brave, it's part of our character . . ." or they might mention their exemplary cleverness.[51]

Negative characteristics popped up in conversations all the time. A person might be telling a gossipy story about some neighbor who took advantage of another's hospitality, ending the story (for my benefit) with some line like "That's how it is! That's the character of the Batak, you know? Every single one is *greedy!*"[52] Nevertheless, an unfavorable trait usually came up in conversation in such a way that it was balanced with a favorable one: if they called themselves crude or rough, they would also note that they were candid and direct; if they mentioned their anger, they also spoke of their good hearts.

Sometimes, however, the speaker could conjure up no positive traits.

One evening, when the April winds had blown a heavy velvet cloud of rain against the hills behind Huta Mungkap, my friend Hatop came knocking at the door. He scuffed his feet all the way into the sitting room and plopped down in a chair, heaving a sigh. We chatted a little about what had happened during the day, but I heard nothing that would lead him to say: "You know, Pak Guru, most Batak deep in their hearts are pessimistic. We may do some worthwhile work, and do it well, but when it comes time to promote it, we stop. We just don't have the strength to be criticized, which is what we assume will happen." He picked up my *hasapi* (TB: two-stringed lute) and plunked on it desultorily, just staring at me. I tried to give him examples, first to refute his comments, then to cheer him up. He simply continued on with his complaint: "We are pessimists, that's all there is to it. We don't like to try new ideas because they might fail, we don't want to improve on an idea because we think it must already be adequate since no one before us has changed it. We just keep doing the same thing over and over because it can't be fixed." I was pulled down into his despondency and sat staring back at him, lacking any response. He plucked a few stray notes on the instrument in our silence. Then he smiled saying, "Yes, well! That's the way it is!" and then invited me to join him in a bowl of noodle soup at the *kedai*.

The character trait that came up most commonly, and most explosively, among Toba Bataks, was jealousy. Many times when I saw some inexplicable behavior in the village, I would ask Ito or Partoho why someone had acted that way. Almost invariably, the breezy answer would be *"cemburu"* (I: jealousy). This answer only served to confuse me more, as the behavior rarely seemed to be in sync with my knowledge of this emotional state. I stopped by Ito and Partoho's house one day and found that she was giving him the silent treatment. It seems she had just discovered that he advised his financially strapped sister and brother-in-law not to borrow money from the bank because the interest rates were too high (close to 21 percent per month).

I asked Ito why she was so angry with Partoho, and she snapped at me, "Since he is so free with his thoughts, they are jealous!" I told her I didn't see the connection between jealousy and getting advice, and she replied: "You just don't understand Bataks and jealousy at all, Pak Guru. When he told them not to borrow money, it's as if he doesn't want them to be more successful than he is. It is as if he is jealous that they might get wealthier. He is the older brother, so they will follow his advice, but everyday they will look at our house and our possessions and think how much better off we are. Their hearts will be sour and they will be eaten up with jealousy. Now do you see?"

At this point, Partoho and his eldest son, Dolok, tried to explain to me the complexities of Batak jealousy. Dolok told me, chuckling a little, "We say: 'Batak people are *HoTTEL* people,'" and proceeded to explain to me that HoTTEL is an acronym that stands for *hosum, teal, toal, elat, late.* Each of these five words expresses a subtle variation of the state of mind that, in English, is expressed by the two words "jealous" and "envious."[53] Many Toba Bataks despair that this aspect of their cultural "personality" is its greatest failing, creating trouble where none may really exist, and tearing families apart. It also may be that "jealousy," in so far inexplicable ways, is to blame for some of the marketplace problems Western travelers complain about.

Unlike the Toba Bataks, who were talkative about both their qualities and their shortcomings, I found travelers to be tight-lipped. My experiences with them led me to believe that those who truly identify with the title "traveler" pride themselves on simply "being," not constructing, themselves.[54] Still, there are some things that can be said about them as a group. What I saw on Samosir Island and the surrounding areas is that travelers quickly form social bonds with those who are traveling in a manner similar to them. While there are undoubtedly those who feel they have more right to the name "traveler" by dint of their asceticism, their adventurousness, or their ability to bond with indigenous populations, nevertheless, travelers tend to see themselves as a loose-knit group whose emblem is the backpack and whose primary foil is the "tourist." For travelers, the "tourist" represents all of those qualities of the West that they disagree with or wish to leave behind. Because of this, the "tourist" is the perfect antagonist for their narrative constructions of identity.

Travelers generally consider their lifestyles to be "alternative"[55] and so act in ways they feel to be counter to dominant Western ideologies.[56] Paradoxically, while their manner of travel may indeed be unusual to those at home, when looked at as a group, they are a highly uniform crowd: they tend to dress in a standard outfit composed of loose-fitting, unpatterned cotton garments and Teva sandals[57] or hiking boots; their hair is either cropped close or hangs drooping in a ponytail; they tend to travel the same well-worn circuit and to cluster together in hotels and restaurants built to cater to them.[58]

In spite of this feeling of universal camaraderie among travelers, there are certain contexts (such as moments of extreme loneliness or homesickness) and times (such as when holidays fall while traveling) when national loyalties are highlighted. In addition to this, certain nationalities seem to form stronger bonds with strangers from their own countries than do other nationalities.

Although travelers seemed to construct a group identity in reference to being counterideological, there were other times when they adopted the others' traditions as their own. An example of this could be seen in the sarong-draped Germans who cooked their rice in front of the *adat* house. Some travelers assumed local attitudes and behaviors that were less obvious, such as those who made an effort to change their sense of time and urgency, who tried to awaken a deeper connection to the natural environment, or who sought to form stronger bonds with a community (in this case the community of other travelers). These characteristics may represent what they understand as "primitive" life.[59]

Some travelers took on exemplary aspects of the others' life and cultural traditions superficially, that is, as a kind of prop for playacting,[60] while others integrated the ways of the other into their lives more permanently.[61] Part of the problem for most travelers who want to act out an "ethnic" experience is that it inevitably stirs up the contradictions of their existence. How can one balance a desire to commune with the other's lifestyle with the desire to relax in the evening while drinking an imported beer? How can one rationalize one's urge to stand in the muddy water of the rice field pulling weeds and the desire to wash the soil off at dusk in a hot shower in the hotel? How can one reconcile one's desire to eat what "the people" eat with an even stronger desire to shit in a Western-style toilet? The answers to these questions are far from clear to the traveler, much less to me. Fortunately for the tourism industry on Samosir Island, few travelers dwell on these issues very long. Instead, they use the very fact of the in-between-ness of cultural tourism experiences as a chance to act out a variety of their dreams.

ACTING OUT IN THE UTOPIC SPACE

What are we to make of half-naked Germans who stir their kettle at the front of an ancient house and Spaniards who stumble up mountain paths looking for animists? If, as I am suggesting here, cultural tourism can be understood as a kind of playful experiment in a utopic space that exists between reality and unrealizable fantasy and that is constructed primarily through narrative, then some of the travelers' actions become clear. On the one hand, it seems obvious that spontaneous and novel acts performed by the traveler are attempts to take advantage of the in-betweenness of the utopic space, as discussed in Chapter 1. Because cultural tourism allows a place for new and creative experiences to be enacted, and because in it travelers feel freed from the bounds and constraints of the dominant forces at home, they can act in a variety of ways that are "unpredictable," ways that on Samosir Island can at times manifest themselves as a climb to the mountain summit via thorny paths and at other times as an aggressive bout of laziness spent watching campy American television programs.

To communicate narratives of such behavior effectively to other travelers means that there must be certain common grounds, or conventions. One is a common language (English when groups are of mixed nationalities) with which the travelers' tales are told; another is a common appearance (costume, behavior, etc.) with which travelers verify the traveler identity. Thus, a narrative told around a restaurant table frames itself as a "traveler's tale" when and if the teller is identifiable by others (via clothing, demeanor, and attitude) as a "traveler." The essence of the tale's topic is always predictable (as it always involves actions that occur between mundane reality and extraordinary desire), and the form of the story is fairly formulaic (calm beginnings, unforeseen circumstances, dangerous encounters, heroic acts, nonchalant endings); these too are part of the convention. The importance of the narrative's communication is twofold: to allow the individual to revel in the freedoms found in the utopic space, and to forge (or reinforce) identity as one of the group called "traveler."

You might wonder how the Toba Batak tourate exploit the freedoms made available in the utopic space. Some of the most dramatic examples of the exploration of possible ways of being I saw occurred in the active construction of new identities. Because many of the ordinary rules and conventions of Toba Batak culture are sublimated to one extent or another in the tourist areas, some of the tourate, having been exposed to a wide variety of Western social interactions, attitudes, opinions, modes of dress, and languages, begin to incorporate, or attempt to incorporate, these into their daily lives. The most extreme examples of this kind of acculturation I saw on Samosir Island were the young male guides who sported imported blue jeans, kept their hair long and unbrushed, wore dark glasses, spoke English fairly fluently, ate hallucinogenic mushrooms and smoked marijuana, and fondled their Western girlfriends in public. Because these characteristics are often associated with tour guides from Bali, the Indonesian island most popular with Western tourists, it is said of these young men that they *"sudah menjadi kebalibalian"* (I: have already become Balinized).[62]

Although this example is not rare, it does not reflect the ways in which the majority of the Toba Batak tourate create themselves anew. The "Balinized" Toba Bataks must be understood as existing at the extreme end of a spectrum. The more ordinary response of the tourate is to be cautious in exploring their freedoms in the utopic space. It is true that some individuals adopt new styles of Western dress readily, but few speak English with any level of fluency, and fewer still imitate the ways westerners behave toward the opposite sex. Thus, while some of the Toba Batak tourate may take on some superficial characteristics of westerners, or may experiment with novel ways of being that are facilitated when they interact in the utopic space, it is rare to see them incorporating foreign morals or values while living in the homeland.

Most of the tourates' explorations in the utopic space were more subtle. For example, we have already seen how some Toba Bataks manipulate aspects of their cultural characterization by finessing the animist-cannibal characterization when and if they wish. Ordinary conventions and assumptions are in flux in the utopic space, remember, so that the tourates are able to make their own personal decisions about whether to play with the cannibal motif for the sake of visitors or not. Typical rules for polite behavior can be suspended in the utopic space, and because of this, tourate individuals like Partoho are allowed to practice calling travelers stingy right out loud.

The implication here is not that the Toba Batak tourate currently have the luxury of exploring unlimited freedom in the utopic space. It is clear that as long as they are involved in the tourism industry they have no power to construct a group identity that silences past animism and cannibalism, for they are daily encumbered by Western opinions and characterizations. Rather, the point here is to say that as active participants in cultural tourism, the Toba Batak tourate have some level of freedom, not only in embellishing notions of who they are, but also in exploring diverse manners, attitudes, and actions. In short, the Toba Batak tourate are enabled to explore possible ways of being not usually sanctioned by their own social regulations.

Ito told me that I couldn't *be* Batak unless I *spoke* Batak; Nalom said it didn't matter, that I could just take a *marga* name. The Spaniard went off on the mountain track in the mists of evening to find the "primitive" Toba Bataks because he felt they no longer lived in the tourist center. Partoho thought all Germans are stingy; and other Toba Bataks thought all westerners are arrogant. Toba Bataks are animist cannibals? Western travelers are hypocritical know-it-alls? I wondered then and continue to wonder now if any of us know who we are, much less if we know who the other might be.

From the moment westerners and Toba Bataks first came into contact more than two hundred years ago, they have been developing perceptions of each other's ethnic identity, sometimes basing their opinions on hearsay, sometimes on history and speculation, and sometimes on firsthand experience. Two centuries later, the process of constructing identities continues, modified slightly by the fact that cultural tourism has provided Toba Bataks and westerners the opportunity to develop their impressions in individual, face-to-face interactions. Assumptions and opinions about the other are sometimes so erroneous that the two parties find it difficult to interact; but so far, in the context of cultural tourism, the negotiations are still able to proceed. One of the results of direct social contact, somewhat improved communication abilities, and attitudes of greater introspection is that tourate and traveler are not just constructing identities for the other, but for themselves as well.

4

Carving a Life in Batakland

It wasn't easy to get Partoho to be my carving teacher. This seemed odd to me because for six months we had spent many hours together every day and got along well; we shared tea in the morning and cigarettes in the afternoon and never seemed to have to fumble for things to talk about. That is why it seemed so strange when he responded only with polite and smiling silence each time I asked him to teach me Toba Batak carving techniques. I was confused by his avoidance of my requests.

Partoho has a broad open face and eyes that flash with relentless and mischievous humor. He doesn't tell jokes per se, or drop witty one-liners. Rather, he sees his world's comical sides and improvises these into intricate scenarios of absurd possibilities. The ancient woman next door, he once told me, has a special stick outside her back door that is polished smooth and lustrous from slapping her sullen, thick-skinned pig, penned a short distance from her house. Each day, he told me, you can hear that pig squealing and racing around its pen in an attempt to escape the thunderous beating it will shortly receive. I could, in fact, hear the squealing and scuffling one day, and I looked past the obscuring bushes and trees in the direction of her house. Just then Partoho said, "Listen—." I flinched when I heard a smart THWACK! to which he responded, with his eyebrows raised, "—See?"

The old woman's pig slapping was supposed to be a result of some sort of marital frustration. Day by day he would fill me in on a bit more of the tale, once adding that the thwack of the wooden stick did its smacking at the same hour each day. "Just wait," he would tell me, "its almost time . . ." THWACK! "Oh, it is very sad for the pig, huh?" he would add. I asked him once *"Jam berapa, pak?"* ("What time is it?") to which he promptly answered, *"Jam pukul babi!"* ("Pig-hitting hour!").[1] A minute later, the dreaded blow was heard again. He sat down in mock sadness and suggested we take a break.

Months later I happened actually to see past the trees and hedges that sheltered the neighbor's yard from Partoho's and realized that the frail old woman was trying to feed the greedy creature and used the stick to keep its huge bulk away from her. The stick was flat on one side but clearly could do no harm to an animal that large. I told him what I had seen: that the old woman was just protecting herself while trying to feed the pig, and that it probably had nothing to do with repressed emotions. He glanced at me and said, "Yeah, maybe. . . ." He continued to call our breaks at eleven in the morning "Jam Pukul Babi."

I laughed at Partoho's crazy tales of the neighborhood; he laughed at my stupid observations and exaggerations. We had long-winded serious conversations too. He would ask me how it was possible for a strong world economic system to bypass the poor rural Bataks so completely; I would ask him why the hard-working and clever Toba Bataks couldn't seem to trust each other enough to work together toward a common goal. We would chat about these and other topics for hours, tracking down our thoughts until an issue seemed to be squeezed dry. Our temperaments seemed to mesh, so I wondered, "Why is he so coy about taking me on as his student?"

When I checked around for another way to study wood carving, the other two master carvers in the village referred me back to him. They told me that Partoho was the one who had both the talent and the disposition to teach a westerner; he was the one who knew not only the old forms but could also create new ones. "Also," they told me, "he is the one who knows all the stories, all the *ways* to carve." With equal amounts of frustration and determination, I went back to his house again the next day.

I found Partoho carving ancestor figures (TB: *debata idup*) that he was making in the antique style. A pile of sawn water buffalo horns lay on his workbench, jumbled with tools, wood shavings, cigarette packs crumpled and torn, and cast-off plastic buckets filled with drill bits and coping saw blades. The morning sun was already up and burning, so he moved a slab of tree trunk into the shade of the house eaves for me to sit on. This put me in the midst of his buffalo-horn shavings and wood scraps, and also at his feet while he worked. He carved and we talked— buzzing the same sorts of stories as usual, humorous and serious, some peppered with stray gossip heard the night before along the road or in the *kedai*. Thin tendrils of gray buffalo horn floated down on my arms as I sat there aching to create, imagining myself carving a figure or ornament.— THWACK!—I jumped a little at the crack of wood on the pig's naked

haunch, and as I heard the practiced squealing, I woke up from my reverie. Picking up a heavy shaving of wood that lay at Partoho's feet, I found
my Swiss Army knife and began whittling a human head and body out
of it.

Partoho heard the pig's slap too. After a couple of minutes, he put his
knife and hammer down, took a *kretek* out of its worn red pack, and hun-
kered down at my level to quietly watch me work. He puffed hard on his
cigarette without taking it from his lips and, squinting his eyes from the
sting of smoke, said, "Here, this is how you do it. . . ." He gently took
the wood from my hands and began fine-tuning my coarse work. The
long carving knife he had been using to shape the water-buffalo horn was
obviously too large to be doing the kind of whittling he was doing on my
figure, but he handled it as if it were a weightless scalpel. Narrow slips of
wood were pared off the figure one after another, methodically, his thumb
pressing the wood into shape. By the time his *kretek* had smoldered to a
dull black, he had transformed the figure's awkwardness into elegance.
What had started off as elephantine legs now had a dancer's lilt, and the
bulbous head was now oval with a smiling face. He reached up to his
worktable from where he was squatting and fumbled around until he
found a short-handled knife and finished the little figure, now removing
thin shavings of wood more judiciously. He knew I was following his
knife's every slice with my eyes, so he dared not make a false cut. He gave
the tiny human one last look front and back, then handed it and the knife
over to me, saying, "Here you are . . . you've got to scrape all the little
hairs off the surface."

Later on, when his wife and two oldest sons had returned from the
field, Partoho nudged me to pull the figure out of my bag. As I showed
it to them he said: "Look at this, he already knows how to carve! He has
been pretending he knows nothing, and suddenly he produces this. This
is already the work of a master carver!" Ito looked at me in frowning surprise and examined the workmanship, her sons peering over her shoulder
with looks of wonder. "Ha!" she finally erupted, slapping my shoulder
and smiling. "You didn't make this, did you? Ha! I know my husband's
work." Partoho just narrowed his eyes, smiling, and refused to look at her
as she goaded him to admit his lie.

When I returned to my stump seat near his worktable the next morning, Partoho handed me a long steel knife, brightly sharp, and said, "Use
this knife. That red one you brought from America is only good for clean-

ing your fingernails." He moved back to his vise to continue working on
his carvings. I found myself a chunk of cast-off wood to experiment with
the feel of the new knife. I awkwardly gouged my way around the wood
for a while, then I stopped to watch Partoho. He was using a broad spoon-
like adze to take the bark off a stout limb of golden-yellow wood, turning the upright column rapidly as the surface came away in jagged shards.
He marked a line halfway around the damp log with a purple felt-tip pen,
then began sketching two seated ancestor figures with elaborate headgear
at each end of the wood, base to base. He knew I was watching and said,
"If you plan a pair of figures this way, foot to foot, you know the pattern
of the wood-grain will match." He sawed the wood at the point where the
bases touched, and set them next to each other for one last scan to make
sure the schematic proportions he had drawn were the same. His discerning eye found a few minor variations that he marked with the purple pen,
and then, in a flash, he began chopping with a flat-bladed adze.[2] First one,
and then the other, he worked the figures on the ground, holding them
upright. In about a half an hour, he was done with his preliminary work.
He stood the two figures next to each other to show me that all the basic
elements were now apparent: high peaking headdress, large head and
prominent nose, tiny crouching body with hands clasped about the
knees. He seemed pensive as he looked at them, but as soon as I heard
THWACK!, I knew he was just waiting for that signal to take a break. I
gazed at the awkward face scratched into my piece of wood and decided
I would join him.

As we sat there smoking, he looked down at my feet where I had placed
my carving, saying, "Ah, a head. . . ." Instead of retrieving the thing to
work on it, he reached up to the table to find the knife I had been using.
"The problem you are having must be with the knife," he announced as
he strummed the sharp edge with his calloused thumb. As we chatted, he
sprinkled water from a dented tin can onto a light-green block of what
looked like fine sandstone. The water darkened the sloping and curved
surface momentarily; he held the blade firmly and rubbed gently and
methodically back and forth while we spoke. When I stubbed my cigarette out, Partoho handed me the knife, its mirrored blade now fright-
eningly keen. "Watch your fingers. The blade will cut skin faster than
wood!" he told me as he returned to the carving held in his vise. The wood
was easier to work with the shining knife, and in my concentration I was
oblivious to the children coming home from school and the light of the

sun casting long shadows. The head I had begun in the morning was, as far as I could tell, done. "Good enough," chirped Partoho when he saw it, continuing on, "You can try another one tomorrow."

I rose from my seat, stiff-legged, to put the knife back in his tool box, but the second son, Tanak, frowned at me and gave a little shudder, asking me softly why I was returning the knife his father had given me. He told me that I was to use this knife everyday and was responsible for keeping it sharp and free of rust. I understood then that this was the gesture I had been waiting for—this was the token that indicated I was now formally Partoho's student.

As I waited for my pot of vegetables and dumplings to boil at home that night I wondered what it was that had changed Partoho's mind about becoming my teacher. I knew that for many contemporary Toba Bataks, the relationship between the wood carver teacher and his student is fairly straightforward: an older man who is knowledgeable in the carving arts (including but not limited to experts) instructs his younger male relatives.[3] The student is ordinarily an individual who is subordinate to the teacher either through age or through social position, but given the Toba Bataks' intricate kinship system this relationship can be much more complex than simple observation implies.

Toba Bataks are bound in an extensive web of social connections in which every individual is socially inferior to a group of people (the *hulahula,* those who provide wives to the person's *marga*), equal to a group of people (the *dongan sabutuha,* or members of the same *marga*), and superior to a group of people (the *boru,* those who receive wives from the *marga*). The Toba Bataks refer to the three groups as the *dalihan na tolu* (TB: the three hearthstones) because, much as a pot in the fire pit needs the support of three stones for stability, so Toba Batak society needs the three divisions for harmonious relationships. These relationships, which are of paramount importance in terms of formal *adat* ceremonies, also affect many day-to-day interactions. A rural Batak man will act with more deference to those people who are in the *hulahula* relationship to him and must acquiesce to their requests for favors in dozens of small ways. This is why Nalom was obligated to teach Partoho how to carve, and why years later Partoho found himself in a very awkward position.

This is what happened: a member of Ito's extended clan asked if he could come over to study carving. Partoho was not impressed with this young man's seriousness, but as he was *hulahula,* Partoho had no option but to agree. The young man was given the worktable ordinarily used by Dolok and Tanak, which was fitted with the family's only other vise besides Partoho's. In addition, the young man had access to whichever carving knife and mallet he wanted. Wood for carving was also freely given. Partoho was in the difficult position of being a teacher who could criticize this student only in the most roundabout and diplomatic manner, despite the fact that the youth needed serious instruction. Both of Partoho's sons delayed their carving work for several days while the new student mangled chunks of wood and nicked the carving knives on the vise, never producing anything that could be sold. The diplomatic silence and polite demeanor Partoho had to present every day finally ceased when the young man announced that he had had a dream that directed him to stop carving and open a *kedai* on some land he owned on the tourist road. When the fellow was out of earshot, Partoho tersely reminded his sons to hurry up with their work to try to make up for lost time.

As I stood there stirring my simmering pot of stew, I thought how difficult it must have been for Partoho to decide whether he would teach me or not. During the first six months of my research, Partoho and I had unconsciously constructed a series of relationships that evolved from foreign interviewer/wary interviewee, to joking friends, to older brother/younger brother (I am three months older than he). We fluctuated between the latter two most of the time, acting as friends of comparable status until some emergency arose (usually monetary) necessitating my assistance, at which time I would become the *abang* (I: older brother) to his *adik* (I: younger sibling). Our relationship was of course much more complex, but we finally got to the point where we treated each other as *lae* (a Toba Batak term of address between men of the same *marga* that literally means brother). I could see why he would not want to teach me under these circumstances: if he accepted me as his student, he would necessarily have a dominant position, which would mean he must either awkwardly invert our *abang/adik* relationship or avoid teaching me directly, as he had the young man who was *hulahula* to him. Neither of these options seemed to suit him. His clever solution to the problem was to wait until I had started a project of my own that he could "help" me with rather than "teach" me how to do. Assistance of this sort is fully within the boundaries of the *lae* relationship.

Months later, looking back on my carving education, I realized that my student status was very different from that of Partoho's two sons. Not only was I never given specific projects or duties to fulfill, I was also rarely criticized directly unless my health or the safety of the tools was at stake. Ordinarily, when dealing with me as a student, Partoho stayed a little distant and reserved, not providing critical comments unless I asked for them directly. If I did ask, he would look my work over quietly, then utter some succinct, general observation like "In Batak carving, necks are short." The criticisms were always addressed to the object or the carving style rather than to me the carver. There were occasions, however, when he apparently thought I was being overly stubborn or inept and would blurt out some choice phrase, rolling his eyes and using my personal failure as the basis for a humorous monologue. In the midst of the joking he imbedded the true critique, and he would recarve the offending mistake while pointing out to me such things as the proper angle of the knife and its depth in the wood.

Partoho's teaching style with his two carver sons, like that of the other father–son carving interactions I saw, was quite a bit more terse and sharp-tongued than it was humorous. The way carving is taught to close family members is based on silent diligence on the student's part and concise, but sporadic, instruction on the teacher's part. If a student has been carving for some years, the teacher is not likely to actually recarve an object. Instead, he will rely on a few well-chosen words that either point out the specific problem or in some cases merely punctuate a general failing: "These carvings must be done by tomorrow—how fast is your hammer going?"

In most cases, the student accepts criticism gracefully (at the very least sullenly), but there were a few occasions when softly spoken but sharp words were returned to the teacher. The few times I witnessed this, the teacher ignored the outburst and continued working. No further communication between the two occurred until the student made some sort of obeisant comment or apology, which would open the door for the teacher to engage in a prolonged moral monologue about the value of listening to one's elders or the importance of respecting one's parents. Not long after the student quietly accepted the upbraiding, the relationship between the two would reassume the appearance of normalcy.

To rebel against the teacher is perhaps the most heinous of acts a student can commit. This occurred once during my research period. It was Partoho's oldest son, Dolok, who caused the trouble, because he wanted to create a series of figural carvings not based on Toba Batak traditional forms. His father curtly informed him that if he wanted to be inventive (which he clearly thought was impertinent, since Dolok was not yet an expert), he should do so on his own time. Nevertheless, Dolok got wood from the woodpile and proceeded to make his planned carvings. The issue lay unresolved for several days, smoldering beneath every comment or question that passed between the two of them, until one of the innovative objects sold. No apology was asked for, and none given. Partoho merely noted that Dolok's "new carvings" seemed to be popular with tourists.

I watched Partoho carve all sorts of things in the first two months I worked with him: *sahan* (TB: container for dry storage) made of glossy black water-buffalo horn and decorated with arabesques, ancestor couples whose matte surfaces were stained to show off their matching grain, tiny figural pendants of deer antler, and covered boxes whose surfaces vibrated with symmetrical vines and waves (plate 7). I tried to imitate some of the simpler things I saw him carve, but they lacked the verve and balance he was able to create. "Perhaps I should try holding my knife the way he held his," I thought, "at an angle to the wood." I tried to copy the way he tapped the back edge of the blade with the water-buffalo horn mallet (figure 4) but the knife always seemed to slip, nicking its blade or cutting my finger. I was getting frustrated because I had no direction. As Partoho gave me no assignments I had no idea of what to carve. I tried making a few more small figures from large wood chips. I showed them to him as I finished, and watched as he recarved every surface. At one point, he told me to stop making these figures. "Too small . . . not traditional," he said as he fished a wedge of water-buffalo horn out of the venomously black water that stagnated in an old oil drum lying on its side near the kitchen door. This drum was where bits and pieces of antler and horn pickled and softened for weeks, or months. "Try this," he said. "Since you make heads okay, try carving this into a head. Copy the mask I have for sale in the *kios*—look at it carefully, so you can make it Batak style." The piece of horn he thrust in my hands was sodden and slippery.

I went over to the little building and found the mask he meant. I drew its form onto the horn with the thin felt-tip pen he gave me, and got to work. Whittling on the horn chunk in the same way I had carved the wood chips, I found the horn to be dense and slick, and it took hours to produce a rough form to show Partoho. He stopped his intricate *gorga* [4] carving for a brief moment to look at the head I proffered and said: "Over-

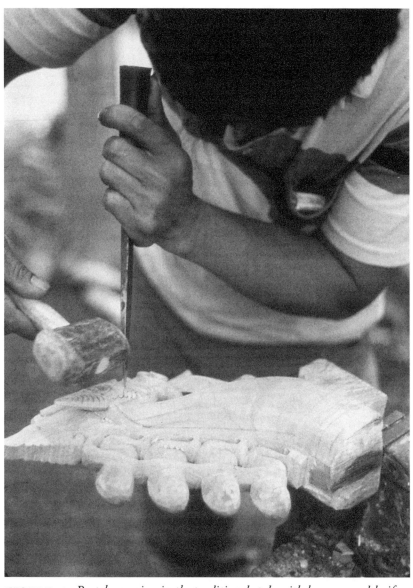

FIGURE 4. *Partoho carving in the traditional style with hammer and knife*

all. Fine. But the eyes? Wrong! The eyes are crooked. Why is that? Do you want it that way?" I took the head back from him and looked at it again, squinting. As I saw it, the eyes lacked symmetry by an infinitesimal fraction of a centimeter. "This head is wrong," he said again as he put the little thing in his vise. "You've made this face *miring* (I: crooked). If you want to carve Batak style, it has to be exactly even." He placed his heavy knife near the offending spot, and with his mallet tapped a few times gently until a sliver of horn the size of a fingernail clipping came loose. He looked it over again and, satisfied, removed it from the vise and told me to continue. "I think you should concentrate on carving heads until you get that right," he said.

I carved more than a dozen little heads while I was learning from Partoho, some from wood, some from horn, many from the hard nut of the *tuak* palm tree. Not one was free from the critique *"miring."* Each and every one had to be recut no matter how much attention I thought I had paid to their symmetry. At first he thought the problem lay in the way I was carving them: whittling rather than using the vise to hold the material while the knife was tapped along its trajectory by the hammer.[5] The use of the knife and hammer, I was told by more than one carver, is the "Batak" way to carve because it is the tradition handed down by the very first carver (the lizard-headed Tuan Rumauhir mentioned earlier). When I tried that technique, the heads still did not pass Partoho's scrutiny. Day after day, he took time away from his projects to recut the eyes of my little heads. He was growing frustrated, and so was I. *"Why? Why are the eyes always wrong? Why always so crooked?"* He rasped these words out with a sharp, breathy *"huh!"* at the end of his sentence as a verbal exclamation point.

Ito was sitting across from me one morning, splitting the rinds off the *kemiri* nuts, and looked up at me. She said, "Andru, look at me, look here," and I did. "Ha! Look Pak, look over here. That's why he makes those little heads crooked—*his* face is crooked. Look!" Partoho peered into my face and frowned. He made the windy *"huh!"* again and said in his roundabout way: "There you go! You *say* you want to carve in the Batak style, yet you allow your carvings to look like you. Let them have the face of a Batak. Look at me—look at Ito. Let the faces look like us!" His face was comically angry, and both Ito and I looked at him nervously. His face held its expression as he went on to make up some crazy story to explain why I felt I needed to carve my own face over and over. "Pak Guru has no mirror in his house in Huta Mungkap like he does in America, but still he remembers his face! To prove to us that he remembers, he carves his face over and over. He carves it once in wood, again in the *tuak* nut, then another in horn. When he is done, he begins again! Over and over!" When Partoho was done, he raised his eyebrows high and smiled, saying, "Now you know the first rule in carving Batak style: the face is always even."

THE CARVING LIFE

Partoho was born on Samosir Island in 1957 in the village of Huta Mungkap when it was still located up on top of the nearby hills. Ten generations ago his ancestor settled the land, and as the generations thrived on the hills, they terraced the *sawah* (I: wet rice fields) by stacking up the huge boulders they found in the fields to make walls. As Partoho tells it, he had a fairly happy childhood, working in the fields with his father and siblings and attending school when there was money. Though there was always enough food to eat, the family found it difficult to tap into the cash markets. Because of this, Partoho's family had only enough money to send him (the second son) as far as the fifth grade. At age fifteen, Partoho rode the ferry across the lake to seek work on the mainland. After a few years working odd jobs in the market town Parapat, he met Ito.[6]

Ito's family had lived in Parapat for more generations than anyone could count, but none of her ancestors ever seemed to find their fortune in big-time trading or in hostelry, the way some other families had done. Money was so limited at this time that Ito's mother sent her, the eldest daughter, to live with a distant cousin on the outskirts of Medan when she was thirteen. For years Ito lived a difficult life, having to cater to her cousin's spoiled children and alcoholic husband, far from her natal family. At age eighteen, she ran back home, certain that her mother would provide her with a safe haven once again. She was crushed to find that her elder brother and wife, with whom her mother now lived, felt that her return was a great imposition on them. Ito was permitted to live in their house for four months only, after which time she would be forced to move.

She had been living in her brother's house for more than two months when she met Partoho. They decided to get married. Ito's mother disapproved of Partoho from the start, first because he was two years younger than Ito, then because he had no job. Later, when these accusations did not dissuade her daughter, she complained that Partoho was too closely related to her own *marga,* making the marriage incestuous in her eyes. Partoho and Ito went to a knowledgeable elder and discovered that their relationship to each other was, in fact, distant enough to make their marriage legal in terms of Toba Batak *adat.* The marriage was sanctioned neither by Ito's mother nor by Ito's elder brother, so life in the town of Parapat was uncomfortable for the young couple. The options were few at that time, but they decided to take a risk: Partoho saw that tourism was beginning to burgeon back on Samosir Island and thought that he could make a living selling wood carvings to the increasing number of visitors coming to the area. It was the early 1970s and Lake Toba had quickly become one of *the* stops on the Western hippie-tourist trail that connects India and Thailand with Bali. Ito had two children now and was pregnant with the third when, encouraged by Partoho's sister's husband, Nalom (at that time one of the few Toba Bataks who still knew how to carve), they decided to move to Samosir Island.

With the help of his *boru* Nalom, Partoho built his family a wooden house on a sliver of inherited land near the lakeshore and set up shop making small carvings in the traditional style of the ancestors. The primary reason Partoho wanted to move is because he knew his brother-in-law's offer was the best, and perhaps only, opportunity in his life to "stand on his own—to work without a boss." He took carving lessons from Nalom and very soon mastered several of the traditional forms as well as *gorga,* the intricate relief carving (plate 8). Because he did not inherit any farmland, Partoho and Ito had to rent land to work, for the carvings were only a supplemental means of subsistence. The years passed and five more children survived infancy, making on the one hand more stomachs to fill, but on the other more potential help in farming and carving; their prayer (like that of most other Toba Bataks) to have many children to assist them in their old age had been answered.

Tourism brought a major change to the economy of many rural Toba Bataks. Until the late 1930s, occupations such as woodworking, masonry, and pottery making were thriving. By the mid-1940s, however, Nalom reported that imported metal and plastic goods had replaced most of the locally made utensils such as wooden buckets and platters, cooking crockery, and basketry. After World War II, many Bataks migrated from the old homelands in search of new jobs (Cunningham 1958; Rodenburg

1997), a social upheaval that disrupted the passing on of a number of material culture traditions. In 1952, Johannes Keuning noted that "The old Batak crafts—weaving excepted—have disappeared. Copper-, gold-, and silversmiths have vanished, and the typical sturdy, and beautifully decorated but unhygienic houses, are no longer being built" (1958:20). And in 1955, Clark E. Cunningham was led to remark that "the traditional skills of wood carving and stone work are all but lost . . . only a few remaining grandfathers and great-grandfathers can do the elaborate carving which once ornamented the fine Batak houses. Lack of the good hardwood—a result of the deforestation of the area—and the absence of desire to build in the old way are leading to the end of the adat house as a traditional architectural form" (1955:47).[7] By the 1960s, the majority of people still living on Samosir Island were subsistence farmers who augmented their produce when they could with income from fishing, husbandry, and trading (Sibeth 1991:37).

By 1969, when many Bataks on Samosir remember the first tourists coming to the island, the art of wood carving had been abandoned. Christianity supplanted the old animist religion that had inspired many carvings, there was almost nothing a Batak man or his family needed that could not be purchased from outside, and no one still living in the homeland villages could afford to build a traditional house, much less have it ornamented with *gorga*. When the westerners came buying, the last remaining antiques and heirlooms were sold off first; but they were soon depleted. In order to satisfy the needs of the tourists, anyone who knew how to carve began to create replicas of the ancestral objects. Nalom, the oldest expert carver in Huta Mungkap, was also the only one who had actually learned the art of wood carving from his father. His patriline had specialized in carving as far back as anyone could recall, so it was logical that he would be one of the first individuals to revitalize the art when the new buyers appeared, and that he would teach his family and neighbors in Huta Mungkap, including Partoho and three of his own sons.

Tourism has had its economic drawbacks, of course. Because tourism development has concentrated in limited areas only on Samosir Island's eastern coast, land values there have increased. This often means that families living in the tourist center must pay higher rent for garden plots and fields within walking distance. For this reason, among others, the importance of small-scale craft production such as wood carving to the subsistence economy for the tourate cannot be underestimated.[8]

At first, Partoho and Nalom sold their small neotraditional carvings[9] to tourists as they stepped off the ferry landing at Tuktuk, just standing there holding their things and taking in what money they could get. Later, they sold their works to an enterprising shopkeeper named Pak Sisinga in Parapat. Pak Sisinga was quickly becoming known to discerning Western collectors as someone with a wide selection of antiques as well as a good stock of contemporary carvings. The pay was not always good, but Pak Sisinga was willing to buy carvings in the off-season, which meant that Partoho and Ito could depend on some cash income year-round.

In the early 1980s, there was a resurgence of interest in traditional house carving among urban Bataks, many of whom worked for the provincial and national government. Several public works projects in the towns and cities incorporated the traditional *rumah adat*-style architecture, which necessitated the production of huge carved facades (figure 5). Through various connections, Pak Sisinga among them, Nalom and Partoho were brought from Samosir Island to the city to work on several of these projects as the master carvers.[10] Here, the pay was good; but the jobs were sporadic, and soon both men longed for the cool air of the mountains again. Partoho has stayed in Huta Mungkap ever since then, specializing in carving objects for tourists and occasionally taking on a job to carve *rumah adat*-style facades for vacation homes or hotels in the area.

When I met Partoho in 1994, he was thirty-seven years old, had been carving for over fifteen years, and was considered to be one of three master carvers in Huta Mungkap. He and Ito rented a stall in Siallagan from a distant relation of hers for a few years, but they told me the rent for the marketplace stall was eating up all their profits. Partoho said their own property's location made it ideal for a small, freestanding shop: it would be visible from the island's main paved road (in constant use by visitors traveling from their hotels to nearby towns and villages), and it was adjacent to a path leading down to a medium-sized tourist hotel and the lakeshore. There were other advantages to this move besides the financial savings: with the shop at home, Partoho could attend to customers in the mornings, and the children could assist them after they returned from school. It would also allow Ito to work in their rented fields without interruption, bringing more cash into the family coffers. So, with a little bit of borrowed money, Partoho purchased the wood planks and other materials to build the family's new small *kios* (plate 9).

FIGURE 5. *A government building in
the style of the traditional* rumah adat

From the very start, Ito had reservations about the move. She argued that a shop away from the marketplace would mean they would have no help in speaking English to the tourists, and might also lose touch with the kinds of things the visitors were buying. Later, in a quiet moment, she told me that the prospect of working in the fields alone was hardly something she looked forward to. In the marketplace, Ito was surrounded by action and conversation and friends: she was right in the middle of the excitement of the place, right at the center where interesting foreigners walked by, where deals were continuously being negotiated, and where money was being made. It was like the big city to her, she said, and she felt in control of her life. Every once in a while, she could save a little money to spend or to give to the children for snacks.

Ito, like many other Toba Batak women in the area, constructed a great part of her personal and social identity within the context of the market. Because buying and selling commodities is generally considered to be the business of women, the marketplace is the place par excellence where a woman can show her talents and abilities.[11] The move to the *kios* was unavoidable, but I knew that it carried with it a feeling of disappointment for Ito. After the little shop was built, Ito would not return from the fields until twilight, always muddy and always tired. Everyone in the family was cheered when they saw her coming down the path, but it was clear to me that a part of her (her hope? her dignity? her pride?) was bruised. After she put the firewood down by the ash pit, she would help Partoho with his carvings, either sanding or staining them, and would then start preparing the evening meal.

Partoho felt bad that he could not provide a better life for Ito and their family, but nothing could be done about the current slack market for carvings. His life was nothing if not more boring than Ito's. At least she could leave the village for a few hours, to see a new vista and to hear the sounds of the birds and the wind. Partoho was stuck at his worktable every day (except on Sunday morning, when he would go to the nearby woods to try to snare mourning doves to sell locally as pets). Although he could go into the house for a glass of tea or a rest, he could never leave the house unless there was someone to watch the *kios*. So, for the most part, he stood at his workbench carving or drawing *gorga* designs on his works for Tanak to execute once he returned from high school.

Ito and Partoho considered themselves very lucky to have so many children. The two oldest sons were already showing that they were talented wood-carvers and could help Partoho increase his output dramatically. Their home life seemed happy to me, but a slowly brewing angst erupted on occasion. The relationship between Partoho and his sons was sometimes difficult and awkward. Dolok, the eldest, had attended a computer course in the city and had done very well, but the national economy was faltering, forcing him to move back to the rural homeland, dejected and disappointed. Tensions erupted about seemingly inconsequential things, and there would be long bitter silences between the Dolok and his father. Tanak, the second son, had convinced himself that he was going on to college in Medan when he graduated from high school, a proposition that, with poverty so close at hand, everyone else in the family thought was preposterous. This conviction, however, enabled him to have a very cheery attitude about carving: why be concerned with the drudgery of stooping over a vise with a knife and hammer knowing that it was only temporary work?

One of the younger sons absolutely refused to be taught how to carve, so he and the other children were responsible for sanding and polishing the carvings, which they would do in the late afternoons or after dinner. Dinnertime itself was usually concentrated on eating, although there was always some story or gossip that found its way in. As each person finished their food, the enameled bowls were stacked and taken out to the kitchen by a daughter, and the floor swept by someone else. When the television was finally turned on, the unfinished carvings stacked on the small table, together with the plastic bag filled with sandpaper scraps, would be brought to the center of the room. The children who had finished their homework and household chores chose one of the day's carvings to finish. This was a restful time for the parents. Partoho sat smoking his *kretek*, thinking or chatting, and Ito leaned against the wall, sometimes resting with her eyes lightly shut. The dimly lit room was punctuated with softly spoken narratives of the day: stories about neighbors or school, comments about the national news, and questions to me about the incomprehensible, and usually undubbed, shows from the West that flickered on the television. The stories and conversations, often murmuring on until midnight and growing less energetic as the hours passed, were accompanied by the rhythmic sounds of sanding until, one by one, the children toppled over dreamily on the mat, or crept off to their room to sleep.

PLATE 1. *Portrait of Partoho and Ito*

PLATE 2. A rumah adat, *traditional house, carved with* gorga

PLATE 3. *Hotels in the mainland town of Parapat built in the old style*

PLATE 4. *An oil painting of Lake Toba and Samosir Island*

PLATE 5. *A view of Samosir Island rising up from the lake*

PLATE 6. *The Stone Chairs of the Kings of Siallagan*

PLATE 7.
*A lidded box covered
with* gorga *carving*

PLATE 8. *Close-up of* gorga *carving on an old home*

PLATE 9. *Partoho and Ito's new shop*

PLATE 10.
A miniature rumbi
carved by Dolok and Tanek

PLATE 11. *The souvenir marketplace in Siallagan*

PLATE 12. *The vegetable market in Parapat*

PLATE 13. *View looking down on Siallagan*

PLATE 14. *A singasinga mask on an old house*

PLATE 15. *Partoho's* singasinga *lamp*

PLATE 16. *Sulean's oil painting*

A PLOW AND A RING BOX

Partoho had finally finished the antique-style *debata idup,* items that his client Mr. Sisinga had ordered. All of them were based on the same prototype, a museum object he had seen illustrated in a Western catalog. They had been sanded smooth by the children and had been polished to a handsome glossy finish after hours of work. Mr. Sisinga, never one to compliment a carver's work too highly for fear that the price might go up, nodded his head in approval upon seeing the dozen figures. "These are fine," he said, adding, "although it will take me a while to refinish them so they don't look so new."[12] Partoho just puffed on his *kretek,* waiting for the payment to be made and hoping that another order was not forthcoming. It was good to have carvings on order, Partoho later told me, because clients are obligated to pay in full upon receipt of the items requested. The drawbacks to accepting orders are not only that the price per item is lower than it would be on the open market but also that there is a deadline for completion. To complete Mr. Sisinga's order on time, Partoho and his sons had to work on little else for more than a week; this meant that the supply of carvings in their small shop, the prices for which they themselves decided and negotiated, could not be immediately replaced when they sold.

With the set of *debata idup* gone, Partoho informed Dolok and Tanak that they must work harder each day to catch up on their backlog. Because Tanak was in his last year of high school, he was informed that he must begin working as soon as he returned home, leaving his homework for the hours after dinner when it was too dark to carve. Partoho had a long list in his mind of items to be made, instructing his sons to begin working on miniature replicas of the traditional lidded container called *rumbi* (plate 10) first, while he started on a few large horn *sahan* (figure 6). He had no sooner started roughing the shapes of the elaborate wooden stoppers for the *sahan* than a relative, a member of his *hulahula,* appeared at the door. This man, a distant cousin of his wife, had traveled most of the day from his small rural hamlet inland on the island to ask Partoho's help, a request he could not refuse.

As all his daughters were in the fields helping their mother, Partoho ordered Tanak to prepare tea for the honored guest. We moved indoors to sit on the fancy mat that Dolok had ceremoniously rolled out. As soon

FIGURE 6. *One of Partoho's* sahan

as the battered tea tray with its tinkling glasses had been lowered to the
mat and all had been served, the conversation began in earnest, and in a
tone much more formal than I had yet heard. Because they spoke in elegant and formal Batak, I could not follow the conversation closely; Dolok
translated the important parts for me. It seems that this cousin had come
to ask that Partoho make him a plow. Partoho raised his eyebrows at the
request, and even though he was speaking in delicate terms I could tell
that he was trying to avoid accepting the order. Many rural farmers in the
area use wooden plows hitched to water buffalo for their *sawah* as such
tools can withstand the rigors of use and wear for many years. Because
they last so long (a decade or longer, Dolok told me), it is uncommon for
a carver to make more than a handful in his lifetime. The cousin told
Partoho that several members of his extended family had not dried the
implement carefully after use, so the wood had split, making it unusable.
He was asking that Partoho make him a new one, with payment for it
(such as it was) to be made upon its completion. The conversation lasted
over an hour, and when the man finally left, it was clear that Partoho had
given in to his familial obligations.

The departure of the cousin was greeted by Partoho and his sons with a kind of frantic energy. The sons were instructed to get back to work as quickly as possible while Partoho checked with family and neighbors in the village to find a plow for use as a prototype. I took my seat on the wooden slab, trying to keep out of the way as Dolok and Tanak dove into their work with renewed vigor. At one point, Tanak lifted his head from his concentrated work and said to me: "My father made a plow a few years ago, but does not remember its shape well enough to make another. He needs help for this project."

It surprised me that Partoho needed to seek the help of others. Everyone in the village, even his brother-in-law teacher Nalom, credited him as one of the most knowledgeable carvers in the area. From memory, he could plan and carve replicas of many of the sacred traditional forms as well as a wide array of variations of the antique secular forms. In addition to these, Partoho was respected as a man who could create innovative forms, objects that used and manipulated aspects of the traditional forms and designs in entirely new amalgamations, objects he referred to as *cipta baru* (I: "new ideas"). I suppose it just seemed natural to me that Partoho would have a mental plan for a plow, an object whose shape appeared to be very straightforward.

When Partoho returned to the house, he had good news: one of the neighbors in the next village over had a plow stored under the house; they were carrying it over at that moment. He walked to the back of the house to survey his inventory of wood. If he was lucky, he would not have to go hunting for the right kind of wood in the right shape. After shifting several logs and limbs, he found a large heavy "Y" of a reddish wood that is easy to carve but not very dense. We dragged the huge log in front of his carving table, and as he was stripping off the bark of the huge log with the straight-edged adze, two men came down the path, staggering under the weight of their old, worn plow. Partoho looked at it carefully and nicked its surface to make certain of the species. As he feared, it was made of a slow-growing hardwood called *jior,* a wood known for its durability and weight. The men agreed to leave the plow behind for Partoho to measure and sketch.

Despite its simple-looking form, the object had complex planes and angles; most difficult of all to replicate, Partoho told me, was the long hole through its center. We marveled at the fact that the ancestors were able to create this object with tools far simpler than he had. As we tipped it over to take measurements on the bottom, I saw that smooth, rounded furrows had developed in the softer grains of the wood, etched deeply into the base by years of rolling through thick mud and weeds. After the measurements were taken, the next pressing issue was where to find the proper wood. "We can be thankful that we are just looking for *jior,* not *umbang*" he said, "At least *jior* we have a hope of finding around here!"[13]

Partoho actually knew where he could find the *jior* wood he needed, but was hesitant to pursue the arrangements necessary to obtain it. His brother-in-law Nalom (his *boru*)—his teacher and the man to whom he owed so much—had an old and dying *jior* tree on his property. His relationship as *hulahula* to Nalom meant that Partoho could ask for the wood he needed with little fear of being refused. The tree was dying, it is true, but it still provided much needed shade for the back of Nalom's house. Partoho decided to exhaust every other possibility before he approached his brother-in-law, and so scoured the nearby hills where his childhood village had been and examined every overgrown field to find a tree of the right shape and size. He found one tree at the edge of the old village boundary, but it had been pruned and chopped for so many years that the only usable branches were higher than he could safely work; he feared that one more cut would kill the otherwise healthy plant. He had no choice but to speak with Nalom about his dilemma.

Partoho and Ito invited Nalom and his wife, Gobara, to come for tea after dinner one night. I sat there with the two of them as they awaited their guests. It was no small thing to ask such a favor, and when Nalom and Gobara finally arrived, I felt an awkwardness between the family members chatting as the tea was prepared. Nalom had no doubt heard about Partoho's project, and had a solemn look on his face as if he knew what he was about to be asked. The conversation was short and formal. Partoho made his request as they drank their tea, and Nalom politely mentioned the difficulties such a favor would entail; Partoho reiterated the importance of the favor, and Nalom acquiesced. As soon as the transaction had been resolved, all four of them relaxed and the conversation turned to planning the cutting of the tree and the carving of the plow.

The huge forked branch that Partoho wanted was not far off the ground, but it took more than an hour of concentrated work to cut it loose from the tree. It took three men to drag the wet wood down the path and across the cobbled road to Partoho's workbench. After they settled the stump in a position that could be easily worked, the two others left Partoho to consider the project before him.

During the two days it took him to remove the bark and shape the dense wood into a rough shape, Dolok and Tanak had finished eight of the small covered *rumbi* pots and six assorted human figures. I did not bother Partoho as he worked on the plow, instead sitting close to the workbench that his sons shared. Dolok apparently felt he had finished enough of the backlog of carvings that his father had assigned to him, because on the third day he began carving an object of his own plan, a miniature *tunggal panaluan*.

The carving called *tunggal panaluan* is the object that many Toba Bataks consider to be most representative of their ancient culture. It is commonly known in English as "the king's staff," or "the magic staff" (figure 7). In the past, the *tunggal panaluan* was the property of a *datu,* or in some cases the communal property of a *marga* clan. It could be made from only one kind of wood and was considered to be the most powerful object with which to control supernatural forces.[14] Stories continue to be told about how an especially strong *datu* could transport huge boulders through the air to smash an enemy village simply by commanding the staff to follow his orders. These staffs were not only considered to be supernaturally powerful, but were also used as a kind of emblem around which a village would internally identify itself. People today still speak of these staffs with awe in their voices, seemingly nostalgic for the days when the village could be both socially bound together and protected by the power of such an implement.[15] During the time I lived in the area, I heard of only two *tunggal panaluan* that were still kept in their villages, and those were only rumors. All the others, I was told, had been sold off to foreign collectors over the years.

Dolok's project was based on an object he had seen in a photocopy of a Western dealer's advertisement kept by his father in a yellow folder of such images and brochures.[16] He knew the original item pictured must have been at least five or six feet tall, as they usually were, but decided to keep his carving small, so it would be attractive to Western travelers needing to store the object in the limited space of their backpacks. His creation would be no more than two feet high, and would have a detachable base. He must have told his father of his plan to carve this elaborate object, because Partoho came over several times to observe the progress of his work. This was one of the few times I saw Dolok working with some level of happiness or contentment. The vein of disappointment about not having found work in the city sank deep in his heart, and the way it most

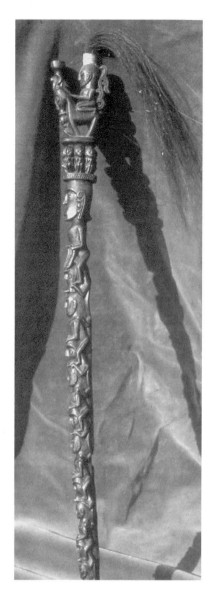

FIGURE 7.
Dolok's tunggal panaluan

often revealed itself was through his simmering anger at having to live with his parents back in the countryside. Now, however, with a plan of his own making, he chatted and joked while carving, cutting in sequence each eye, each ear, each arm and leg, as he worked his way down each of the stacked figures.

It was a high school holiday, so Tanak continued working on small items such as necklace pendants and figurines, his hands focusing on his work but his mind always slightly distracted by his daydreams of a life working as a pharmacist in the big city. His obsessive concentration on the fine and detailed work seemed to remove him from the real world; he awoke only when his father noted that someone must go in and make tea, which he did smiling and chatting. It was as if he convinced himself that if he produced beautiful, delicate work without stopping, he would then be able to realize his dream to go to college and study chemistry.

We all took a break to drink the hot tea and to look at Partoho's half-finished plow. He ran his hand over its surface, showing us where the plow bit would be attached, and where the long hole would have to be drilled to attach the handle. He had already spoken with Nalom about borrowing a bore to ream the wood out, and had also devised a plan to cut part of the long hole square with a chisel. He estimated that the drilling would take at least two days, and that cutting the square hole would take another day. "Three days more," he said, "and I will be finished with this burden."

In the afternoon, Ito came in from the fields and the other children returned from school. Ito instructed the two girls to start the dinner while she helped Dolok and Tanak sand and finish the carvings they had made in the past few days. Ito told me that everyone who knows her husband is a master carver also knows that she is a master stainer. She prided herself on knowing which dyes and waxes worked best together to provide the carvings with a finish that brought out the color and grain of the wood while still resembling the antique carvings of the ancestors. Prior to the influx of tourists, she told me, figural carvings were only occasionally finished. Usually, objects were simply left untreated after they were carved, allowing them to obtain a finish naturally through handling and the accumulation of oil and dirt. Sometimes, objects were stored in a tray above the home's fire pit and would soon be covered in a thick coating of soot and oil from the cooking food below.

These days, a "black" carving is covered with a deep purple form of Mercurochrome, which is applied with a worn-out toothbrush. Objects that are intended to be dark brown are first given an undercoat of iodine, again applied with a used toothbrush, while those that are to be tan are unstained. The final coat for all objects is ordinary shoe polish, brushed on with a toothbrush to ensure that the coating reaches all the way to the deepest corners, and then buffed with a small shoe brush with hair bristles. Black shoe polish is used on the purple undercoat, and brown on the iodine undercoat. Some carvers opt to leave the iodine's brilliant crimson as a contrast color, which is covered with a tan or clear shoe polish; Ito frowned as she told me about this innovation, saying, "That color is too bright. It's not appropriate for carvings from the ancestors."

Two days passed and Partoho (who was working on the plow primarily but not exclusively) discovered that boring the long hole down the center of the *jior* wood was taking much longer than he thought. Each of us helped him with the hand drill when his arms began to ache, but even when the bit was sharpened, only a small handful of shavings corkscrewed their way up after fifteen minutes of work. Dolok was putting the finishing touches on his *tunggal panaluan,* and Tanak had finished with the little *rumbi* and the human figures. Although Partoho was preoccupied with finishing the plow, he was able to keep a close eye on his sons' production of carvings for the tourists. He took a moment to take stock of the carvings in the shop, shifting objects on shelves and counting them. He came out of the *kios* muttering audibly about how few carvings Dolok had made since he had started on his king's staff. At his worktable once again, he found a small, stapled notebook cast off by one of the children that he had shoved in the side of a plastic bucket filled with nails, drill bits, and small pieces of wood and horn. He called Tanak over and the two of them sat on a log of *ingol* wood leaning against the house wall.

Since I was sitting on my slab of wood nearby, I could see that Partoho was drawing sketches for one of his *cipta baru,* his new ideas. He spoke in hushed tones to Tanak, no doubt fearing that one of his less creative neighbors would hear him describing the new carving and would copy the idea. On the dog-eared paper, he drew a box with *gorga* carving covering every surface, a job particularly suited to Tanak. The box had a lid, also decorated with *gorga,* which was topped with two figures back to back. Unlike other carvings, Partoho said with his voice rising slightly, these two would not be finished with shoe polish, but rather would be varnished, as he assumed carvings in the West are.

Tanak started on the new project right away. I helped Partoho with what promised to be the last few centimeters of the plow's hole. Drilling with renewed vigor, Partoho was exuberant when the drill finally chewed the last scraps of wood free; he tipped the plow to the side and peered down the shaft to see a perfectly round spot of light. He did not rest even a second in celebration of the work, but raced into the house to fetch the long rod of steel bar that would be inserted in the hole to act on top as the plow's handle and at bottom as the plow's tooth. Never have I seen a face more crumpled with exhaustion and dismay as when I watched Partoho guide the steel rod into the plow only halfway. "It's stuck," he said simply. He left the metal bar sticking out of the plow and sat down to light a fresh *kretek* and drink his tea, which had since gone cold. His sons worked diligently on their carvings and I sat next to him, very quiet. I did not stay for dinner that night.

When I arrived at the workshop the next morning, I found Partoho hammering on the steel bar. He seemed to be quite chipper, and told me that he had called Nalom and another carver over to his house in the evening to examine his workmanship. Both of them studied every inch of the plow and announced that his work was *"baik"* (I: fine) and *"bersih"* (I: clean), comments that came as close to compliments as I ever heard given between Batak carvers.[17] In particular, they scrutinized the hole Partoho had laboriously cut: Was it straight? Had the wood warped? Could it be repaired? All agreed, the hole was as perfect as it could be, which could only mean that the steel rod was slightly bent. He was encouraged by the other carvers' appraisal and woke up early to begin work straightening the metal. He was also encouraged, he told me, by Tanak's progress on the *cipta baru,* a carved lidded box with two heads (figure 8). With an almost imperceptible arch of his eyebrows he nodded toward the house, saying, "Let's go in for a minute to drink tea."

I sat down on the mat in the living room as Partoho continued on past the curtain that screened off the bedrooms. Returning with one of the boxes, he said, "I had to put this out of Nalom's sight last night. He is too eager to see my new ideas, and remembers them too well!" I turned the intricate box over in my hands, marveling at the details and variety of decorative elements. I admired its workmanship and asked if I could buy

FIGURE 8. *One of Partoho's* cipta baru: *a covered box with two heads*

it as a gift for my mother. "A gift for your mother? She would like this rather than the plow? She would like something brand new rather than something very old? How is it possible for such a thing to be true?" I reminded him that my mother did not have fields to plow, to which he countered: "No fields for a plow, but lots of gold for a box! You see how it is for a Batak carver now, Pak Guru. We must carve ancient styles and new ones, we must satisfy Bataks as well as westerners, and all the while we must make things that everyone can afford!" He agreed with me that a carved box would make an ideal gift for my mother, but insisted on designing something even more elaborate, with carved feet and heads of water buffalo horn inlaid in its sides. He stepped over to the *lemari* (I: a large cupboard) for a moment and came back in with his tattered notebook and a felt-tip pen, then proceeded to draw the plans for another *cipta baru.*

The art of wood carving almost disappeared on Samosir Island when social upheavals (such as migrations to plantations and large cities), conversion to Christianity, and superior imported goods made the production of traditional carved objects obsolete. It was only the advent of tourism, according to the Toba Bataks with whom I spoke, that kept the art form alive. While the life of a carver is not easy and the money is never really certain, it is nevertheless a profession that scores of individuals choose as their primary or secondary work because it brings hard cash to the family coffers. Of the variety of vocations an undereducated rural Toba Batak might be qualified to pursue, wood carving is one that requires only a willingness to learn and a modest financial investment in tools and materials. Because of the Toba Bataks' complex system of social obligations, those who choose this profession can usually find a qualified teacher somewhere in their extended family.

This does not mean that all who try their hands at wood carving will be successful. As the preceding stories show, a successful carver will need, not only some facility or talent for manipulating the knife in the wood, but also the assistance of a spouse and children to create and finish the carvings, and to sell them in the marketplace. Maybe more important still, a carver will prosper only if she or he can simultaneously produce a vast array of traditional forms and a continuous flow of novel ones. Partoho and Ito's situation is not particularly unusual among carving families living in the tourist center of Samosir Island. To do more than merely survive, a family must be in a position to seize all opportunities that arise, and to be inventive in creating them when they don't arise. Such inventiveness reveals itself not only in the actual creation of innovative objects such as the *cipta baru* but also in the development of ways of selling and marketing—the creation of legitimizing stories that help give the carvings value and meaning to Western buyers.

5

Creating Value and Meaning

Scattered drops of rain began falling around noon. Partoho suggested that we put our tools away early and go into the house to eat. As he and I gathered up the iron knives, the wood rasps, the saws, and the electric drill, Dolok and Tanak carried the narrow table, on which the vise was bolted, under the protection of the eaves. Someone forgot the plastic bag of sandpaper scraps (worn but still useful), and the youngest boy was sent out to retrieve it. It was only five leaping steps out the kitchen door and five back, but he returned soaked to the skin. This was the fifth day of heavy rains, and Partoho complained that it looked like another day that would have to be spent indoors sanding carvings rather than outside carving them.

We sat down on the floor mat to wait for the food being prepared in the kitchen. The rain was beating down so heavily and loudly on the corrugated iron roof that we could not carry on a conversation. One of the children brought in the large pot filled with a pile of fat, pinkish rice. Ito was close behind with a dish of *gulamo* (the spiced and fried dry sardines that are a local specialty) and a jug of boiled water and glasses. She placed these on the mat, and then began heaping the rice on enameled metal plates. Partoho pushed the *gulamo* in my direction and shouted above the din of the storm, "Eat this . . . Batak thorns," so I took a spoonful. He took some too, then passed the dish to Ito; and as she served the younger children, he smiled, picked up one of the hard and brown little fish from his plate, and pretended to pluck it out of his arm with a sharp wince, then popped it into his mouth with relish, exclaiming, "Batak thorns . . . delicious!"[1]

The rain let up a little as we finished our meal and then rinsed our hands in the communal bowl of hot water. Now we could talk. I wanted Partoho to tell me about the connection between religion and carving.

We had developed a certain rapport, so I felt comfortable asking him, "Is there a conflict for you between being a Christian and reproducing animist objects?" Partoho lit a *kretek* thoughtfully and answered: "You know I was born a Protestant, right? So when I make these carvings, it's just for the tourists, not for me. It's not like I think these things still have power. You know? I only make them to sell." I thought about this a second, then said: "I know you are Christian, but you never go to church. I've never seen you at church in all the time I've been here." He responded by saying: "I pray at home. I think about religion all the time right here on this mat. I don't have a conflict with the old ways and Christianity, none at all. Of course, I have questions, but mostly about minor issues. For instance, if Jesus was from Bethlehem, how could he be a German?"

I wondered how to understand what he meant. Because Indonesian was a second language for both of us, we sometimes misunderstood each other's sentence construction and use of words. I sat there for a second frowning and blinking at him, trying to figure out if he was teasing me, but he was looking at me with a face of pure sincerity. I said, "You know Jesus was born in Bethlehem . . . that's in Israel." "Yes," he said, "where the Jews and the Palestinians are fighting. So . . . how is it possible that he was a *German?*" His voice was now icy with accusation, and he cocked his eyes at me suspiciously. I tried to devise some answer but couldn't think where to begin: "Wait now. Why . . . ? Why do you think he was a German?"

He interrupted my stuttering, saying, "Well, he has blue eyes and long blond hair and a blond beard, just like the German tourists, so we decided he must be German." I knew what he meant now. He was talking about the Victorian-style chromolithograph that his brother-in-law, Nalom (a Catholic), had hanging in his house. I told him that Nalom's picture was not a portrait, per se, it was just an idea someone had of what Jesus *might* have looked like. He frowned at me and began asking questions in rapid succession: "If that is not a picture of Jesus, who is it a picture of? Why don't they use the real picture of Jesus instead of this imitation? Isn't it wrong to use a false picture of Jesus? If Jesus doesn't look like a German, what does he look like?"

This last question was one that interested Ito and the oldest sons too. All of them sat looking at me, waiting for an answer. What did Jesus look like? "Well," I said, "I don't know, exactly . . . nobody has a real picture of him." Everyone eyed me suspiciously for a moment while they considered the ramifications of this statement. It was obvious that they were not getting the information they wanted. Partoho took a more practical approach now, saying, "Okay, if that is so, then what do you *think* he looks like?" I hesitated a little, trying to make a safe guess, then said, "Well, let's see. He comes from a place where a lot of people seem to have dark hair, so maybe he had dark hair, not curly, not straight. . . ."

Partoho catalogued that feature aloud, saying, "Okay, dark wavy hair."

"And I suppose his skin was browner than mine. . . ."

"Okay, brown skin . . . ," he added to the list.

"Perhaps he had dark eyes, maybe brown eyes . . . and maybe he was stocky and not really tall," I said.

He continued, ". . . brown eyes . . . short . . ." He stopped abruptly, saying, "*Buh!* He sounds like a Batak to me!"

Partoho liked this idea and spent the next several minutes elaborating his theory that Jesus was, in fact, a Toba Batak man, noting among other things that Adam and Eve and the original Batak ancestors that descended from the heavens could be one and the same. As the rain finally let up and became a soft drizzle, Partoho asked me to paint him a little watercolor portrait of the Jesus I had described. I asked him what he wanted it for, and he said he just wanted something to remind him what Jesus "really" looked like.

On a Saturday afternoon several weeks later, I was sitting with Partoho near his workbench under the eaves of the house. I was telling him about my trip to the weekly market and the post office on the mainland in Parapat, and as I rummaged around in my bag looking for the cigarettes that would make our conversation more sociable, I found a letter I had forgotten to open. Partoho insisted I open it right away as it might be something important. It was a note from one of my sisters that included a thin cardstock brochure from the Metropolitan Museum of Art in New York. The brochure described a small exhibit of Batak objects currently on display, giving a brief history and general overview of the Batak culture.[2] It was illustrated with a map and photographs of five artifacts, three of which were wood carvings. When he saw the photographs, Partoho gently reached over and lifted the brochure from my hands saying, "Oh, great! I really need this!" He looked intensely at the images reproduced in the pamphlet, telling me that the head of the *sigalegale* puppet[3] on the

FIGURE 9. *Partoho carving a* sigalegale
head (note the photocopy on the table)

cover was particularly fine, that he had never seen one like it. He took
the brochure into the house, and I could hear him rummaging around in
there. He returned a minute later holding only a small log of wood, saying, "This should work. . . ."

Partoho was almost done carving his replica of the *sigalegale* head (figure 9) when I received the next envelope from home: an article photocopied from a fancy art magazine.[4] It concerned the same exhibit, but
included a dozen more photographs of objects in addition to advertisements from galleries offering to sell Batak antiques. When Partoho saw
the photocopy, it too was gently lifted from my hands and examined with
great concern. He put his tools down and went into the house (me at his
heels this time), saying, "This one is much better than the other. Lots of
things I need!"

We sat down on the mat and called to one of the children to unlock the
center drawer of the sky-blue *lemari* and bring him the folder stored there.
His daughter struggled with the small brass key until the lock finally
yielded, then shuffled through bill receipts, school report cards, and old

letters until she found what he wanted and brought it to him. He opened the yellow cardboard cover, and I saw scores of black-and-white images of antique Batak carvings photocopied from museum bulletins, auction catalogs, and gallery pamphlets from Europe, North America, and Australia. Still examining the photographs in the article, he said: "I'm very fortunate. I just got an order from Pak Sisinga for sixteen powder horns. I know how to carve the shape, but not the *gorga* designs. Look here," he said, pointing at the photocopy, "here is a beautiful example right here ..." His voice trailed off as he took one last look at the powder horn reproduced in the article in order to memorize it.

I decided that Partoho needed the photocopied article more than I did, but I did want to have a look at what had been written. Too late. The yellow folder was back in the *lemari* somewhere, safely hidden from the eyes of any competing carver who might happen to drop by. Right away, Partoho started making practice drawings of the powder horn's *gorga* design in one of the children's notebooks. He seemed absorbed in his work, so I began reading the letter that had accompanied the article. Among other things, the friend who had sent it told me that he was also sending along a photograph of an object owned by friends of his who asked if I would please tell them if, in my opinion, it was really Toba Batak. I fished around in the bottom corner of the manila envelope and found the small glossy print.

Partoho's eye lit on the photograph as soon as it emerged. "Something else? What's that? What's that?" he asked excitedly. I told him that it was something owned by my friend's friends, and Partoho moved the picture from my hand to his in a flash. "Ohhhhhh. This one is really nice. It's the stopper to a *datu*'s medicine bottle, and it's really old. See, you can tell by the way its face is carved that it comes from this part of Samosir Island. Oh yeah, I need this too. . . ." He started off to the *lemari* with the photograph. "No, no, don't take that! You can't have that one!" I was practically yelping. He looked back at me, shocked at my tone of voice, and sat down next to me, saying, "Why, Andru? What's the matter?"

"Well . . . uh, well . . ." I was stammering as I took the photo back from him. My mind was running like a rat through a maze trying to imagine all of the possible consequences of this situation. The professional quality of the photograph told me that the owners of this object were well-to-do collectors. Judging by the workmanship and age of the piece, I was guessing they had paid a fine price for it. No doubt they also valued it as a unique object. My sudden fear was that Partoho would add the form of this object to his everyday carving repertoire—that he would make dozens of little statues in this shape for years to come. Whatever value this object might have based on its unusualness or particularity would thus be undermined, especially if Partoho decided to take its reproduction one step further and make fake antiques.

Such practice was not unknown in the area, and although Western buyers (both tourists and collectors) had grown much more savvy in the past decade, there were still talented carvers like Partoho who knew how to carve so flawlessly in the antique style and, furthermore, others who knew how to mix the various herbs, oils, and solvents and how to distress, sand, and polish their carvings with such subtlety, that, with the help of a middleman like Pak Sisinga, they could still fool even the most discriminating collector. The panic I felt when I saw my carving teacher carry the photograph to his hidden folder was that the monetary value of a carving could suddenly plummet based on a decision I would have to make in this split second. I kept stammering, trying to buy more time to think: what would giving the photograph to Partoho *mean?*[5]

"I . . . well, its just that . . . well . . . ," I continued to mutter; but now Partoho interrupted me. He said: "What are you saying? You sound like a crazy person! Don't worry about the photo, they can just have another one made—its not expensive. Really." I told him it was not the photo I was worried about, but the thing itself. I said, "See, these people *own* this thing, and I don't know if they want copies made . . . maybe they want theirs to be the only one." Partoho looked at me very patiently and took a drag on his *kretek.* Then he said: "Oh, I understand now. These people want the only one; they want an original, right? Okay, fine" (he became slightly stern now), "they own the original thing and they can have it. But. This thing comes from *my* ancestors, so the shape of it belongs to the Batak. The shape they cannot own."

He gently took the photograph back out of my hand, smiling at me with a face full of wisdom, and started sketching its form into the notebook. "I will just make a couple of drawings for later," he said brightly, ". . . it will only take a minute, then you can send the photograph back to the owners." He made several drawings with a purple felt-tip pen on lined notebook paper and included notations about proportions and craftsmanship. When he was done he said: "I won't be making too many like this! It will be a very hard thing to carve—I'll only show it to the *best* tourists!" By now he was smiling again and handed the photograph back to me, then tore the drawing he had made from the notebook and headed over to the *lemari.*

COLLECTING THE OTHER'S ART

At sunset, I walked along the road pondering why I had felt so conflicted about showing Partoho my friend's photograph. In a more rational state of mind, I could see that the likelihood of Partoho's carvings having any effect on the value of their object for the Western collectors probably would be infinitesimal. Nevertheless, the situation had awoken in me, at some deep and visceral level, an indistinct worry.

When thinking about it later, it became clearer to me that this event encapsulated many aspects of my whole project in Sumatra—my attempts to understand the West's interest in collecting and valuing Toba Batak material culture, and the consequences such collecting and valuing has for the Toba Bataks. Although I had thought about it abstractly many times before, the event that had just transpired forced me to realize with new urgency that without Western interest in their material culture, the Toba Bataks might have no reason to continue reproducing objects originally made by their ancestors. It also provided me a point of reference from which to consider whether the development of Western constructions of "the Toba Batak" over the past two hundred years—as cannibals, as Christian converts, as exotic animists—consistently exploited Toba Batak wood carvings as icons of a believed tendency toward magic, animism, and spirituality.

What is it that motivates certain westerners to want to obtain, or consume, the art of the Toba Bataks? How is value created for or assigned to works already obtained and to those still desired? When is an object "authentic" and how is it separated from other works considered to be "fake"? What impact has Western collecting had on the Toba Bataks and their culture, as well as the continuance of their carving tradition? In some ways, answers to these questions are specific to the Toba Batak experience. In other ways, however, the issues raised here simply exemplify trends that are occurring in other cultures. The phenomenon of individuals collecting and valuing the art from cultures other than their own is hardly new: exchange, theft, and plundering of artworks has occurred for centuries. What is different in this situation, and others like it, is that Western colonialism seems to have opened the door for a much greater number and variety of individuals to collect the objects of their desire in larger numbers, and in many cases more easily. The individuals who have collected objects from Batakland over the centuries are a disparate group, ranging from explorers to colonial administrators to tourists, and their motivations to acquire the Toba Bataks' possessions are probably just as diverse.

Some have collected based sheerly on their curiosity. This motivation to consume is perhaps most clearly articulated by the exclamation, "Oh! Look at *that!*" and is not a measured response, nor one that is based on extended contemplation; it does not indicate taste or intellect, but rather arises from a sudden burst of unnameable longing.[6] There are times when this response increases as contact with the stimuli continues: the wondrousness of the thing perseveres and the desire to own it becomes palpable.

This must have been the state of mind of the Europeans who were trading with the Toba Bataks in order to obtain camphor, cinnamon, and pepper in the eighteenth century. For these early European traders, the objects made by these unusual, anomalous people—these "lettered cannibals"—may have struck them with some kind of wonder, for descriptions from this period, few though they are, paint a world exotic and strange:

> On festival days, . . . [the young women] ornament themselves with
> ear-rings of gold, hair-pins, of which the heads are fashioned like birds
> or dragons, a kind of three-cornered breast-plate, and hollow rings
> upon the upper arm, all, in like manner, of gold. . . . [The men] have
> machines curiously carved and formed like the beak of a large bird, for
> holding bullets, and others of peculiar construction, for a reserve of
> powder. (Marsden 1811:377)

While it is not certain why some individuals collected Batak objects, it has been said that in similar situations in the South Pacific, European explorers anticipated that their new possessions would have monetary value back home. Others, perhaps more rarely, may have seen their possession of such objects as evidence of their contact and relationship with the other (Thomas 1991:151).

The sense of curiosity and wonder that is evident in the way some of these early European traders and explorers wrote about Batak material culture was fleeting, however, and the curiosity factor soon turned into an attitude that might be called "grave concern." Objects that before might have seemed resonant with a fresh peculiarity were now sodden with an evil and vile intent, good only when separated from those who knew to what horrid use these implements could be put. Several authors writing in the early nineteenth century were missionaries, or other individuals with strong Christian principles, and were, no doubt, predisposed to consider the Batak corrupt because they believed them to be cannibals. In their descriptions of Batak possessions, varying levels of alarm are evident, as they speak of "dark arts," human scalps, and blood being drunk in association with wood carvings.[7] For these writers, the Bataks' paraphernalia gave them proof that there was much work to be done, for while it was generally understood that the Bataks believed in one supreme God, and that they did not worship idols, there were also ample reports about objects infused with terrifying ingredients such as *pupuk* (TB: magic potion).[8]

Christian missionaries began their work in the Toba Batak area in earnest in the late 1860s, perhaps gathering one or two objects out of curiosity, but more probably receiving items as gifts from reformed animists (Veldhuisen-Djajasoebrata 1988:174). These artifacts were often sent back to Europe for display in provincial mission headquarters, a practice that may have served both to educate pious individuals in the home countries and also, inadvertently, to ignite the desire of collectors interested in the strange and unusual.

The work of the missionaries in pacifying previously belligerent villages paved the way for the incursion of two other important groups of early collectors: colonial administrators and early tourists. As with the other collectors discussed here, the reasons these individuals collected examples of Toba Batak carvings, jewelry, and fabric were no doubt various and complex, but we might typify their motivation to consume as a desire for the exotic. Whatever danger or evil was thought to inhere in the sooty carvings and tarnished amulets was now inconsequential: the people who made them were constrained by colonial laws, censuses, and imported religion. The Batak artists, it was believed, were now fully assimilated.[9]

In 1915, the Dutch colonial government oversaw the building of a graded road through the mountainous terrain that had protected Batakland for so long, greatly facilitating travel in the area. While some of the early collectors were colonial administrators who were stationed in the Batak lands and obtained objects from the people living around them, others lived in Medan, the administrative and trade center on the east coast, acquiring artifacts from Batak migrants who had come to the lowlands looking for employment, or from middleman traders.[10]

Several Europeans traveled inland during this period as short-term tourists, collecting objects, as Achim Sibeth notes, to "put on the mantelpiece as souvenirs of a journey to the cannibals" (1991:225). There were others, however, whose trips were much more extensive, and whose collections were more comprehensive and better documented. One such individual was Dr. Elio Modigliani, who spent approximately seven months with the Toba Bataks in 1890, collecting scores of fabrics, ornaments, books, and wood carvings to take back to Italy with him (Giglioli 1893). Such daring excursions and extensive collections by individuals were unusual. Most tourists seem to have preferred only transient contact with the indigenous people. The wealth of the European planters made it possible for them to build pleasure houses in the cool climes of the Bataks' lands, and by the 1930s an incipient tourism industry, complete with local people selling their fabrics and carvings as souvenirs, was already established.[11]

At the same time the colonialists and tourists were building private collections of "exotica" to decorate their homes, institutions were collecting, and displaying, artifacts on a grander scale in such venues as world's fairs and trade exhibitions. These institutions were motivated in their actions by a desire to show the diversity of the dominated world—to indicate to European audiences that so-called exotic peoples were now being assimilated into the "civilized" cultures. As Nicholas Thomas says, "expositions of this type, which often included dwellings, fake streets, and live specimen natives, made an entire colonial world visible and tangible" (1991:176).[12] The fairs and exhibitions were instrumental in the development of systems of organization used to order and judge objects, and one of the results was that Western responses to the objects became less visceral or emotional, instead favoring "the more disciplinary languages concerned with authenticity, connoisseurship, provenance and patronage . . ." (Breckenridge 1989:212).

As for the Batak, one of the first major European venues for exhibition of their material culture was the 1883 international trade show in

Amsterdam, where the Dutch Protestant Missionary Society set up elaborate reconstructed villages from various East and West Indies cultures, complete with natives cooking and weaving (Valk 1988:1). This was just one of many such shows that were mounted throughout Europe, North America, and Australia, and when these exhibitions closed, the specimens of material culture exhibited were usually delivered to newly formed ethnographic museums. The museums were popular with the public and often expanded their collections, not only with donations from institutional groups and through purchases from galleries, dealers, and private collectors, but also by sponsoring their own formal collecting expeditions.

The fairs and trade exhibitions served to educate Western audiences by displaying the range of artistic diversity in the world, but they also engendered, for some, an increased urge to consume. This is because they not only showed varieties of material culture that had been virtually unknown before that time, but because they also helped to show that these items were, in fact, consumable.[13]

CREATING VALUES

While the number of collectors of non-Western artifacts was relatively small, their influence on Western attitudes about the others' material culture was often far-reaching. First, their interest helped to popularize the material culture of non-Western peoples, which often served to legitimize it as "art" and, in turn, inspired others to begin collecting. Second, the early collectors' interest in, and exhibition of, non-Western material culture often promoted the idea that these objects possessed particular potencies or "spirits."

Several previous works have discussed how the West's perception of non-Western material culture shifted from "ethnographic" to "art,"[14] and it is generally agreed that this shift coincided with the dramatic changes that were occurring in Western art between the 1900s and 1930s. Fauvists and Expressionists, following on the heels of Symbolist painters such as Gauguin, were exploring ways of portraying their world directly and boldly, often using African and pre-Columbian objects as their inspiration.[15] For many, the aesthetic appeal of these things was not in their original use but in their artistry—that is, they were valued for their form rather than their content.[16] Although masks and figural sculptures from

Africa were in the limelight of artists' attentions, focus was also drawn
to the reappraisal of other "primitive" arts as well: objects from Microne-
sia and Melanesia began to be of interest in the early 1940s, and those
from Indonesia slightly later.[17]

For collectors of non-Western art at this time, the shift in interest from
ethnographic artifact to objet d'art increased the social cachet in owning
it. In some cases, the artifact was of interest primarily because of its pure
form; but in other cases, the importance of content and context was not
lost, for part of the value of the piece was its origin in what Sally Price
refers to as "the night side of man," the place where "images of fear and
darkness, often with side journeys into unharnessed eroticism and cannibalistic feasts" are made (1989:38). Even though collectors of Toba Batak
material culture may have appreciated the prevailing interest in "form" as
an aesthetic category for non-Western art, it is doubtful that the objects
were ever completely removed from an imagined (or real) connection with
exotic rituals and cannibalism.

With its new assignment as "art"—a system within which things can
be rated as "better than" or "worse than"—non-Western material culture
gained a kind of status that was increasingly connected with price.[18] And
as prices for the "better" objects (defined as such by connoisseurs with specialized knowledge) increased, access to them decreased, creating a situation where the ability to form a collection of such objects implied elevated
status. Why? Because distinguishing between the better and the worse
depended on the cultivated taste of an aristocrat or world traveler, the talented "eye" of an aesthete, or at the very least exposure to higher education in the arts.[19]

Thus, part of the value of the non-Western material culture in the first
decades of this century came from its association with avant-garde artists,
and part of it from its new designation as "art." From the 1950s on, however, another facet of its value emerged, and that came from its increasing rarity. It could be said that rarity is a category constructed by judgments separating the few "better" works from the masses of lesser ones,
but the point is that during this period European collectors increasingly
perceived many non-Western cultures (especially those which produced
art) to be on the brink of vanishing.[20] In fact, the idea that one could
discover a "masterpiece" from a culture whose traditions were being sub-
sumed by "westernization" is what motivated many private and institutional collectors of the past four decades to consume and display "prim-

itive" arts.[21] To understand the rhetoric of this kind of thinking, consider the following excerpt taken from an exhibition catalog of Batak objects:

> When the culture changes quickly the art loses its power. In the course of the evolution of ancestral art, the same forms have been recapitulated over and over until they have acquired great authority. . . . In the case of the Batak, their culture was militarily subdued by the Dutch by 1905, and thereafter the artistic integrity could no longer be maintained and the quality of the work declined or ceased altogether. (Diamondstein and Willis 1979:4)

The response to this rarity or disappearance of non-Western objects, whether it is actual or simply perceived to exist by collectors, is addressed by collecting those objects that still remain; the act of collecting is often associated with a sense of "preserving" cultural traditions.

If there is any one motivation that twentieth-century collectors have in common, perhaps it can be considered to be "investment," for as Pommerehne and Granica show, collectors have a higher "willingness to pay" for an object if they think it is an original, or if they feel it is a replica of an original that has been irrevocably lost (1995:246). Investment is an apt term here, because it refers, not only to the fact that vast amounts of money are committed to acquiring these objects in the hope that a profit will accrue (a Toba Batak *tunggal panaluan* bought in the early 1970s for a few hundred dollars might sell for as much as three thousand dollars if sold at auction today), but also to the fact that twentieth-century collectors have invested non-Western objects with a new meaning ("Art") which carries with it implications of cachet, status, and class.

In addition to those collectors who have a sense of monetary investment in the objects they purchase, there are those individuals who collect in order to make what might be called "spiritual" connections.[22] These collectors, some of whom identify with New Age ideologies, seem to feel that so-called primitive groups produce objects that have stronger "energies" or spiritual powers than can be found in their own cultures.[23] Grant McCracken says that such objects serve to bridge the gap individuals perceive as existing in their cultures' social life—the gap between the "real" and the "ideal" (1990:105–106)—noting that one of the locations for these "displaced meanings" occurs "across the continuum of space." Collectors who travel across this continuum, among them many of the backpacking travelers who are the focus of this book, seem to find that non-

Western objects have more potential for spiritual resonance than objects from their own cultures.[24] Some of these travelers may feel that they themselves can invest the things they collect with spiritual powers—that is, they can infuse their objects with energies they direct and control[25]—while others believe that the Batak carvings they acquire possess a pre-existing, inherent power or energy (by virtue of the fact that they derive from the traditions of a "spiritual" and "primitive" group).

When I first began talking with Western travelers, I wondered if they were really serious about their beliefs in the powers objects have. One in particular, a man from Georgia on his first trip to Indonesia, convinced me that this kind of thinking was prevalent and sincere. He started off by telling me about a mask he owned while living in Bali. He said it "just attracted" him from the very first moment he saw it, so he bought it and hung it on the wall. When he came home later in the day, he found it on the floor cleanly broken in two pieces, and a more knowledgeable friend who happened to be with him clicked his tongue saying, "Oh, you got a wall-jumper there, pal." He was told that the mask had a strong energy, a powerful spirit. Because he didn't really like the idea of having such a potent object in his house, some days later he decided to burn it. Armed with his new resolve, he entered the room where it was hanging, but it was gone, and was nowhere to be found.

Right on the tail of this story, he told me another. He was still in Bali and went to visit his knowledgeable friend, a collector and an individual of mystic sensibilities. As they were sitting around chatting, he happened to feel an attraction to something leaning in the corner that he could not clearly see. He went over to the darkened corner and saw a tall staff carved of dark wood, highly polished, which was topped with black hair; it was a Toba Batak *tunggal panaluan.* His friend, seeing his intense interest, said he could borrow it to walk around with for a day, an offer he could not refuse.

He walked all over the local Balinese countryside with this tall staff and said he never felt more peaceful, centered, or energized. He said he could feel the spirit of the staff being communicated to him directly. At dusk, he realized that he had to keep his word to return the carving, but as he drew closer to his friend's house he became more and more aware that he must *possess* this staff, and so he began to calculate how much he could pay his friend for the object. As he reached the threshold of the house, the door opened and his friend said, spontaneously, "You *can't* have the stick." The Georgian lied and said he didn't want it, but his friend looked him in the eye and said again, with a quaver in his voice, "You can't have the stick." He didn't question how his friend knew his desire, but wondered if those who owned such powerful staffs also had psychic abilities. He repeated to me that he knew the staff was real because he could feel its strength. He wanted to experience those sensations again and had come to Samosir Island specifically to find a staff of his own. As we talked, it was not clear to me whether he was searching for a vehicle in which to invest his spiritual energy or an object that already pulsed with an energy he could absorb.

Another collector, I was told, found the energy-filled staff he was looking for but could not control it. Pak Sisinga told me this story that took place in the mid-1970s: a French collector came into his shop asking for an antique *tunggal panaluan,* in particular, one that was energized by the magic substance *pupuk.* He was not interested in anything but an original, beautifully crafted, ancient, and potent staff, and was willing to pay up to two thousand dollars for it. Pak Sisinga was flabbergasted at the price he was willing to offer (which was far more than he had ever received for an object) but had to tell him that he knew of no such staff for sale— they had all been sold off many years before. The collector said he would stay in the area for a few weeks, which should give Sisinga ample time to seek out such a carving.

After checking around, Pak Sisinga heard that a family living in an isolated hamlet far from Parapat still owned their venerable staff; he also heard they were financially strapped. When he first approached the head of the family, he was told that the heirloom would not be sold. He prevailed on them to reconsider, stressing that the money he would give them could solve their problems. By consensus, they finally relented. He brought the staff back to his shop and contacted the collector who, after examining the workmanship and aged patina, paid him the price they had agreed upon.

As Pak Sisinga tells it, the man came back in six months' time. His face was full of weariness and angst as he handed the staff back to Pak Sisinga, saying: "Take it! I don't want it! I've had nothing but trouble and bad luck since I brought it into my house. You don't need to give me my money back. Just take the thing away from me." Pak Sisinga made a feeble offer to return some of the money, but the man just waved him off and, with wild eyes and a haunted look, left. Later in the evening, as Pak Sisinga stored the staff in an upstairs room for safekeeping, he thought to himself, "Great! Now I can find another collector to sell it to and make twice the money!" The next morning however, the staff was gone. His house had not been broken into and nothing else was missing. The staff had simply vanished, he said, and it was not until several months later when he happened to be in the area of the isolated hamlet that he heard of the *tunggal panaluan*'s miraculous reappearance at the house of the original owners. He ended the story by saying, "Strange, eh? Sometimes these old things can find their way back home again."

This story might be apocryphal, but it highlights three important aspects concerning the perceived spiritual potency of Toba Batak objects. First, it gives some idea of the degree to which some Western collectors are motivated to possess specific non-Western objects they desire. Second, it shows that an object's "energies" are felt to be potentially uncontrollable. Third, it indicates that not only some Western collectors but also some Toba Bataks believe in the ability of a carving to have innate energy and, in extraordinary cases, agency.

Why do westerners acquire non-Western material culture? In talking to travelers in Sumatra, I found that their motivations to consume Toba Batak art were rarely consciously defined, rarely based on a single impulse. I suspect that past collectors, like present-day ones, were inclined to take possession of Toba Batak material culture for a combination of reasons, among which might be curiosity, wonder, dread, greed, or aesthetic attraction. If there can be said to be any commonality among present-day buyers, however, it is the desire for an "authentic" object.

As individuals seek to satisfy particular wants, their attitudes toward the meaning of "authentic" changes: if they are looking for the exotic in an object, then "authenticity" might be satisfied by the fact that it came from an indigenous marketplace; if they are looking for the spiritual aspect of an object, then the "authentic" object may be one whose "energy" is sensed bodily; if their interest is in investment, then they may be interested in an authenticity that is based on age, condition, rarity, or beauty. One of the reasons I have discussed the varying motivations of collectors and other buyers here is to underline the point that different desires to consume create different authenticities—just as there is no one motivation, so there is no one "authentic."

AUTHENTICITIES: INTERIORITY,
CONTINUITY, UTILITY

We now know a little about why westerners buy Toba Batak material culture, and this leads us to wonder *how* westerners (especially travelers) buy such objects. The question here does not concern the processes by which money changes hands (the topic of the next chapter), but rather the ways in which westerners determine and discern which objects they will buy. As I mentioned in an earlier chapter, when we speak of material culture that is collected while one is engaged in cultural tourism, notions of "authenticity" are closely allied with concepts of "original." This is because one of the goals of cultural tourism is to interact with original people, or "real primitives" (cf. Bruner 1991). In the early days of Western contact, of course, there was no conception of a Toba Batak who was not also a heathen cannibal; all of them were "real," and all of them were "primitive." As Western contact continued, however, there arose the notion that Toba Bataks living on the coasts, and who had traded with outsiders for generations, were somehow not as authentic or original as those living in the interior.[26]

The earliest travelers to North Sumatra who might be considered to be tourists made it clear that they were not content to visit coastal groups, or even groups who were under the jurisdiction of a colonial administrator, for the true and original Toba Bataks were those who lived in the interior, beyond the borders of European settlement.[27] Consider, for example, the words of world traveler and adventurer Madame Ida Pfeiffer:

> My intention was to stay only a short time at Padang itself, as I wished to visit the highlands . . . and to go among the wild cannibal Battakers [*sic*]. People tried to dissuade me from this plan . . . [telling] me that, in 1835, two missionaries . . . had been killed and eaten by the Battakers, and that no European could possibly venture among them without a military escort. They advised me to content myself with the Dutch settlements (on the coast), and not to expose myself to the danger of terminating my life in so horrible a manner. It was, however, precisely for the sake of becoming acquainted with these Battakers—a people so little known to Europeans—that I had chiefly desired to come to Sumatra. . . ." (1856:135)

Or, consider that the collections of Toba Batak material culture that Modigliani was able to make were considered to be particularly important because they came from "the heart of the *independent* Battak country" (Giglioli 1893:111 [italics added]), that is, those places beyond the reach of colonial administration.[28]

The idea that there are interior areas where Toba Batak culture is somehow more pristine and more original continues to the present:

> If [the Western tourists] were interested in the people and if Lake Toba represented for them more than a name on a travel itinerary, they would hire a small boat . . . and go off along the shores of Samosir Island. That way they could escape the well-worn tracks which always end up (at the towns in the tourist center). (Barbier 1983:28)

> Most foreigners stay in Tuktuk (in the tourist center). . . . Those with a serious interest in Toba Batak culture will gain more satisfaction from scrambling over the mountain ridge to the villages on the other side of the island. (Turner et al. 1995:522)

What all of these quotations imply is that the "original" (the "authentic") is to be found in those cultural places farthest away from the centers of cultural contact: if one is on the coast, the original will be found in the interior; if one is in the interior, the original will be found in the margins of colonial control; if one is on Samosir Island (the very center of Toba Batak traditional life), the original will be found down the shore, or over the mountain and beyond.[29] Recall that the Toba Bataks themselves have a similar concept when it refers to the more original culture.

That "originals" are more likely to come from places farthest away from centers of cultural contact is a concept held by collectors of Toba Batak material culture as well. One of the important aspects that defines the authentic object is its (to use the French term of art collectors and art historians) *provenance,* that is, its origin of manufacture or purchase.[30] For modern-day travelers who collect Toba Batak material culture, the value of their touristic object is appreciably higher if its provenance is an antique store in Medan rather than a department store in Jakarta, higher yet if it is from a shop in Parapat, and even higher if its provenance is the tourist marketplace on Samosir Island. The reason for this might be obvious: the closer one is to the center of traditional manufacture of an object, the less likely the object is to be machine- or mass-made or created by outsiders, and the more likely it is to be handmade, culturally authentic, and original.[31]

Oddly enough, this pattern is not necessarily followed through to the most extreme interiority. That is, not all traveler-collectors consider objects offered for sale in an artisan's studio (or, more central still, from the workbench of a carver or the loom of a weaver) more valuable than a similar object found in the marketplace.[32] There may be many reasons for this: the marketplace has more selection; there is the promise of better prices through competition; and it is more likely that a vendor, or someone nearby, will speak English or some other European language. Another reason, expressed to me by more than a few travelers, is that buying directly from an artisan feels too intimate: the collector feels *too* close to the center, making the interaction seem like a social relationship rather than a financial transaction.[33]

In such cases, travelers say that when they see a close-up view of the artisan's home life they are hesitant to bargain as vigorously as they might wish and are hesitant to walk away empty-handed, even though they are not attracted by what they see. It has been said that tourists are forever trying to get into the farthest back regions of a tourist site in order to discover the authenticity they are seeking (MacCannell 1976:100–101), but here is evidence to the contrary. Here we find support for the notion that travelers prefer touristic encounters to occur in the utopic space that exists between cultural reality and unrealizable fantasy: for the traveler, interactions at an artist's studio may feel too close to the reality and too far from the fantasy.[34] The marketplace, on the other hand, is already perceived as a space where social interactions have limited liabilities, and so naturally seems more neutral to the traveler. Not only is evidence of the lived reality of the seller completely absent (allowing the buyer to avoid feeling obliged to buy), but the objects are usually sold by brokers (making a refusal less personal). Thus, the conception of place, or *provenance,* that travelers in North Sumatra use to evaluate an object's authenticity concerns closeness to a center of cultural tradition, but not necessarily closeness to an individual artisan—the value of provenance tends to derive from place, not person.[35]

Akin to the travelers' concern with provenance as an indication of an "authentic" or "original" object's value is their desire that the item reflect some aspect of cultural use. Two aspects of cultural use are of interest here: actual physical use and what might be called "imagined" use. The first, for many collectors, is the indication par excellence of an object's authenticity, because for many there is no more real and original thing than that which has actually touched the other's hands and participated in the other's life; the visual evidence of an object's actual physical use is referred to as its "patina," as was noted in Chapter 1.[36] As discussed earlier, the Toba Batak sold off most of their antiques and heirlooms long ago and, in the case of objects of daily rather than ritual use, replaced them with similar objects of metal or plastic. While evidence of use, such as patina, may be foremost in travelers' minds when looking for the "best" object in the marketplace, it is a rarely used determinant, as most of the traditional-looking objects offered for sale there are new.

If I am correct in saying that collectors are concerned with an object's use as validation of its cultural continuity, then what we might call "imagined" use is the most pertinent to present-day travelers. By imagined use I am referring to those objects based on antique forms that Western buyers believe are used by local people. This group of items constitutes the vast majority of carvings made by contemporary Toba Batak carvers. An example would be the traveler who purchases a replica of the *tunggal panaluan* because she or he knows there are *datu* "up on the mountain" who are still using such objects. This is not to say that the buyers actually think the thing they have bought has the power they admire (although some do believe this), but rather that the object they are considering buying *could* be used, under the proper circumstances, by such an individual.

Closely allied with travelers' concern with *provenance,* and their valuing of an object's cultural uses, is their desire for cultural continuity. Here, they are looking for a piece that is "traditional," just like the original one used by the *datu:* it is a kind of synecdoche, where the replica is a part representing the whole "bundle of emotional conditions and social circumstances" (McCracken 1990:114) that the buyer values. This desire for an object with a clear cultural heritage is often closely related to the motivation to own a Toba Batak carving that has "spirit" or "energy." If travelers can see that an object descends from an ancient and illustrious form, then they can better imagine its potential for being charged with energy.

ANTIQUE, "ANTIQUE," AND *ANTIK*

The longer I stayed in Huta Mungkap, the more I became convinced that travelers are looking for a vast range of authenticities. Some wanted a thing that came from an authentic place, while others wanted something that had cultural continuity—that was "real," not made for tourists. There were still others, like me when I first went to Samosir Island looking for an ancient and polished object, who valued age and patina.

Now carvers know about buyers like me, people who place a high value on antique objects and are willing to pay a high price for them, and to satisfy us they will often attempt to make objects that copy the form, design, and finish of the things we desire. When these newly made objects are advertised as copies, of course, they are called reproductions or replicas. When they are offered for sale as actually being old, then they are fakes, and those who make or sell them are spoken of with scorn as frauds, cheats, and swindlers. Here, the difference in artist intent is of crucial importance.

What is at stake for Western collectors of non-Western art who accidentally buy fakes? For some, monetary value is lost: a fake is a bad investment, money thrown away. This is because fakes, for the majority of collectors, have no intrinsic monetary worth because they cannot be resold for the amount originally paid. For others, pride is lost: purchase of a fake indicates gullibility or lack of knowledge. A collector who owns and displays fakes is seen as someone who has more money than expertise, someone who has access to the rare, the old, the original, but does not yet have the discernment necessary to select and acquire the real things. For yet others, a belief in "truth" is lost: a fake is an intentional lie, a deceit. For these individuals, the fake represents a moral (and perhaps an intellectual) forgery. Whatever the case, collectors ordinarily remove fakes from view and sequester them, sometimes for centuries, as they rarely lose their stained reputation.

As I mentioned in the Introduction, some will argue that the difference between "imitation" and "real" is a slight one, if it even exists. But for many Western collectors there *is* an authentic (no quotation marks needed here), there *is* an original, and there *are* antiques, because for them the meanings of these terms are not culturally constructed but rather are among the most primary categories that create sense in the world. My interactions with the Toba Bataks showed me how limited and culturally exclusive this kind of thinking can be.

After I had lived in Huta Mungkap for a few months I began to realize that there was a serious gap between the way I talked about old things and the way my Toba Batak friends talked about them. One of the first lengthy conversations I remember having had with Partoho, in fact, was on this very topic. When Ito first introduced us, she said: "This is Andru, an American. He is interested in Batak carvings. He wants to know about the antique things, right?[37] So, maybe you can talk with him."

I chimed in, saying, "Yes, sir, I'm interested in Batak carvings, but not just antiques. I'd like to know about the new things, too, especially those made like the old ones, like those from the ancestors. If you have the time—."

Partoho was a little suspicious, and responded by saying, "You want to know about antique things? And you also want to know about the things I make now?" He laughed. "What's the difference? I'm the one who makes the antique things. All those things there?" he gestured to objects hanging on the walls, "I made all those. Those are the ancestors' things, but I made those antiques there, see? Ok, let's talk."

As the conversation continued and we got to know one another, I asked him if he would mind talking about how, exactly, he made "antiques." He was very willing to talk all about it, which surprised me since I didn't see any fakes in the stock he had on display. He called me over to his workbench, picked up his carving knife and hammer, and tapped away on a piece of wood that was already fastened in the vise. He created an arabesque or two and then puffed on his *kretek* a little, saying, "That's pretty much all there is to it."

I thought perhaps I hadn't asked the question properly, so I said, "And so, the finish, what do you use for the finish?" He looked a little sheepish and I thought I would now hear the list of things used to achieve an "antique" patina. He said, "Well, we just use this (showing me a can of Kiwi brand brown shoe polish). We put it on with an old toothbrush. . . ." I was still confused, so I suggested, ". . . and then dirt (I: *kotoran*) or something?" Partoho looked at me with a very stunned look, clearly thinking I was making some sort of American joke. He looked over at Ito with wide-open eyes and shrugged his shoulders up around his ears, laughing, and said, "*Kotoran!?*[38] Huh? Do you mean *soil?* Yeah, after I put the shoe polish on, I put soil on it, then I eat it. Bataks love to eat dirt, you know? De-licious!" I could tell I was on the wrong track with him, but I didn't know yet if he was suddenly being protective of his secrets or really didn't know what I was talking about, so I dropped the subject.

Later, when I got to know Partoho better, I brought the subject up again. This time, we both understood what the other meant when the word "antique/*antik*" was used: he understood that when I used it, I meant "*barang tua*" (I: old things), and I understood that when he used it (if he didn't clarify the meaning further), he usually meant "things in the old style." This was the basis of our first conversation's confusion: what he was telling me was that all the things he made were in the antique style, that they were all inspired by the ancestors' things. I asked him once if he had ever made "*barang antik palsu*" (I: fake antiques). He looked at me very seriously and said he knew how, and that at one time he had made such things, but that was a long time ago, adding that he did not do it anymore. He told me that he and many other carvers had made scores of fakes and sold them indiscriminately in the late 1970s and early 1980s to whoever would pay the money. After a few years, tourists stopped buying these things because word got out that they were being cheated. The carving business took a nosedive and, as he tells it, has never fully recuperated.[39]

Over a period of several months, I heard more of Partoho's stories about the revival of carving on Samosir Island and realized that my questions about the carving of antiques were heavily weighted with my own assumptions about what the term encompassed. The meanings of the terms "fake" and "replica" are too specific to Western twentieth-century culture to make much sense when applied cross-culturally (Jones 1990). The story I heard from him, which was echoed by his brother-in-law, Nalom, was that in those early years they were simply making *barang antik* of two sorts: one with brown stain and dirt, and the other without.[40] I am not so naive as to suggest that they did not know the brown stain and dirt made their carvings look much older, and that because of that appearance of age the pieces could be sold for more money. However, I want to make the point that one can intend to make an accurate replica of an aged object without intending to deceive a buyer. In the 1970s and 1980s the same dialogue no doubt took place as it does now: a tourist speaking English addresses a carver or vendor saying, "Is this antique?" to which the Batak individual, speaking Indonesian, replies, "*Ya, . . . antik!*"

It is still not clear to me how, or if, all of my carving friends on Samosir Island draw the distinction between reproducing antique forms and antiquing reproduced forms, but it is true that some carvers are still trying to sell fakes, and clearly understand the meaning of "antique" in the Western sense of the word. I found this to be the rare exception, rather than (as its seems to have been ten years earlier) the rule. Most of the carvers I talked to simply have the habit of eliding the meanings of antique, "antique," and *antik*.

This is not to say that Toba Bataks are unaware of, or lack appreciation for, "original" things.[41] Partoho's dissatisfaction with the authenticity of the chromolithograph of Jesus shows how strong opinions can run, for as soon as he found out that the picture was not an original (or even a copy of an original) but rather an invention (albeit a well-intended one), its value to him, as a material object and as a symbol of religion or of spirituality, was lost. The valuing of originals is perhaps most strongly connected to family heirlooms. While I heard on numerous occasions that it was proper for certain old animist carvings such as the *tunggal panaluan* to be stored in foreign museums because they might still be magically powerful, other old things, such as a necklace owned by a beloved parent or a favorite bowl used by a grandparent, were wistfully missed. For most of the people I spoke with, these latter things were considered to be unique and, unlike such objects as the king's staff or the *datu*'s medicine horns, were more readily referred to as *"pusaka"* (I: heirlooms).

Western travelers' and collectors' avid interest in, and aggressive collecting of, Toba Batak material culture in the late 1970s, coupled with a general and persistent poverty in the area, caused the wholesale liquidation of the material culture of entire villages. In 1994, when I questioned the inhabitants of Huta Mungkap about their family heirlooms, not a single family reported having such things for over a decade. Aside from the feelings of loss and sentimentality for certain objects such as those already mentioned briefly, the wholesale depletion of traditional material culture in the Toba Batak area has had other effects as well.

MISSING HEIRLOOMS

I asked Partoho about this mass sale of material culture, and he told me that many families saw this time as their golden opportunity to convert old and useless wooden objects into cash: capital that could be invested in small business ventures, long-postponed house repairs, or the education of their children. Other families were not so happy to sell their heirlooms, but crushing poverty forced them to take advantage of any chance to get ahead. He said that not all the sales of heirlooms were voluntary, stating that this was also a time when family treasures, which are owned not by a single person but by the entire lineage, were actually stolen. Sometimes the theft was perpetrated by a rogue member of the lineage who removed a sacred carving or ancient porcelain from their attic storage places in the family *adat* houses. Other times it was a neighbor, who waited until villagers had left their homes to work in the fields, stealing whatever seemed salable.[42]

These days, such acts are considered to be old history. There is no way to get the objects back, Partoho told me, so there is no reason to think about them any longer. In fact, the prevailing attitude of Toba Bataks I spoke with was one of strong practicality: whoever sold the heirlooms must have needed the money. On occasion in the marketplace of Ambarita I would see a lone antique being offered for sale. These were not the large and potentially valuable wood carvings, but rather small, worn things like bamboo storage containers or trinket baskets. I asked my friend Inang what she thought about the sale of old things. Inang is a matronly woman of great respect in her town, and has been selling in the marketplace as long as tourists have been coming. This is how our conversation went:

> Andrew: How do you feel about people selling the old things?
> Inang: Well, you know, I don't think it's good. What if all the old things from our parents are carried away to some other place? There is nothing left here. No, it's not good. But all the old things, the ancestor carvings and the *tunggal panaluan,* those were all sold off a long time ago. . . . We sold those off when we were really poor. I think those things were already gone in the sixties. People came here to buy the old carvings and we just sold them. We were poor. At that time, I heard of people selling the ancestor carvings for 500 thousand *rupiah* (about $250). One guy sold a *tunggal panaluan* for one million (about $500)! That was a long time ago. But you know what happened? People told him not to sell the old things from the ancestors, but he did anyway. From

that time on, his family was sick. It's the same with the ancestor carvings. That family became sick too. . . . Those families are still up in the mountains. They still pray to the old things, give them food, and pray to them.

Andrew: Are those people up on the mountain Christian too?

Inang: Oh yes, but there are still some who believe in the old things, and pray to the *tunggal panaluan*. You know, when it is the dry season, they take them up to the top of the mountain, and pray, and ask for the stick to bring rain. The very next day, there is rain. It's like that. They are Christian, but they still believe the old things have power.

Andrew: I still see old things for sale in the market here, like old baskets, and *sirih* (I: the betel nut blend that some people chew), containers, and the big wooden bed-chests for storing valuables.
. . .

Inang: Yes, those things are still for sale, that's no problem because the baskets and bed-chests, they are not really the same (as the other things). We get those from the people up on the mountain. They don't mind selling that kind of thing because they probably say, "Oh what's this old thing? A basket? What do I want that for? I have a nice new container from the market, so what use is this old thing?" They bring it down here to sell. The baskets— there is no problem selling those, because they can be replaced. They are already old and have no use anymore. But the other things, the carvings and all, those cannot be replaced. When they are sold, they are gone.

Inang, like many other Toba Bataks I came in contact with, values the antiques and heirlooms from the ancestors but does not feel financially able to keep them. Although she is not much more affluent now, she has managed to put several children through college (one of the few avenues for rural Toba Batak families to improve their financial and social standing) with the money made from her sales in the marketplace over the years, first from the sales of family antiques, then from sales of carvings and leather handbags.

The antiques that appear in the marketplace nowadays are from financially strapped people living in isolated rural areas, who are no doubt selling them for the same reasons Inang and her family sold their heirlooms twenty-five years ago. They bring them to Samosir Island because they know Western buyers of touristic objects can be found in the market-places.

With all the antique prototypes of carved forms sold and gone, it is almost a wonder that it was possible for the wood-carving tradition to be revitalized in the 1970s. The way Partoho and his wood-carving brother-in-law, Nalom, tell it, when the demand for neotraditional carvings started, they had nothing left to copy. Nalom was the only man in Huta Mungkap who could remember any of the old forms and designs. He told me that when he first started carving, he could do nothing but make the same few objects over and over. Now, almost twenty years later, both carvers have memorized the complex forms of over twenty-five tradi-tional objects, as well as the numerous innovative forms that each of them makes.

How can we explain this increase in forms made knowing that there is a lack of tangible antique prototypes? There are several ways a carver might examine ancestral carvings. One is to visit the small private museum in the village of Simanindo, where a modest collection of old carvings is displayed. This is not the best explanation, because only two carvers I spoke with had ever been there; I was told the bus fare and entrance fees were beyond their means.[43] Other carvers have access to one of the glossy books on Batak art published in the West.[44] Ordinarily, though, such books are owned only by middlemen, such as Pak Sisinga, who maintain small private libraries.[45] Carvers who work with middle-men are allowed or encouraged to look at the photographs in these albums as inspiration for their work, or, as in the case of Partoho's *debata idup,* are shown particular objects to copy.[46]

The greatest exposure to traditional forms Toba Batak carvers have is through photocopies of museum catalogs and books given to them by westerners. In many cases, tourate carvers request such copies to be sent them by travelers who have stayed on Samosir Island long enough to develop a relationship. Occasionally, the copies are brought along by westerners to supplement the guidebooks' information. Clearly, not all carvers have access to this kind of imagery—those who must depend on middlemen to sell their wares, or who live far from the center of tourism, are unlikely to come in contact with westerners, and so are unlikely to be able to request or acquire photocopies of publications.

As the story at the beginning of the chapter illustrates, photocopies of antique forms are highly valued and are literally kept under lock and key. This is because competition among carvers is fierce. Currently, there is a glut of carvings on the market, most of which are reproductions of the same five or six forms. Travelers regularly commented to me about what they saw as endless repetition in the marketplace, saying, as did one German tourist, "the carvings are very nice, but everything is the same." A carver who has the means to create a traditional form that is unusual (that is, an antique form no one else is making) will thus have a slight edge over his competitors for as long as he is able to maintain exclusivity of the form; once an unusual form is offered for sale in the public marketplace, of course, it is seen by competing carvers, who can add it to their own repertoire.[47]

Now it becomes clear why Partoho was eager to get hold of the museum pamphlet, and even more anxious to get the photograph. The former, he could easily see by the date of exhibition printed on the cover, was "hot off the press" and contained images, such as the powder horns, that he could use right away.[48] Still, there could be other carvers with American friends who might also receive this publication, meaning he did not have exclusive access to the images. The photograph, on the other hand, being a representation of an original object owned privately, was an image only he would see. As long as he could hope to acquire more images of privately owned objects, he could continue making unique replicas, and the more careful he was in selling reproductions of these forms to a select group of consumers—"the *best* tourists"—the more likely he was to maintain exclusive rights to them. For a carver like Partoho, the hard thing is successfully to walk the tightrope between offering novel forms for sale and keeping them out of the view of other carvers. If he can do this, his position is potentially secure.

For a hundred and fifty years or more, the purchase and sale of carved wood objects has provided westerners and Toba Bataks with a venue for interaction. The carvings, used as tangible evidence of Toba Batak traditions, have provided westerners with a foundation on which to construct conceptions of the character of Toba Batak culture. At some times westerners celebrated the wondrousness of the Bataks' creative output; at others they were stunned with horrific fascination at their past uses. For contemporary travelers who see Toba Batak wood carvings as financial or spiritual investments, the prime concern is whether these things are "authentic"—whether they are "original"—which has been, especially recently, of serious concern.

Westerners' drive to locate and collect "original" carvings has impacted the local culture in two ways. First, the demand for ethnographic objects pushed Toba Bataks to sell their carvings, in the beginning heirlooms and then replicas, as a way to access capital they could use both to relieve some of the weight of daily crushing poverty and to invest in future endeavors. Selling old family possessions brought families cash but also hastened the loss of their cultural patrimony. Further, they lost something more: with the original treasures from their ancestors gone, carvers had nothing left to copy when tourist interest in their art grew. This predicament led to the second impact on their culture: a revitalization of the once-dying carving tradition. In trying to satisfy the increasing numbers of visitors wanting to buy some physical reminder or evidence of their trip to Sumatra, Christian Toba Bataks have found a way to keep their animist ancestors' traditions alive. For some carvers, continuing the carving tradition means re-creating the same historical forms over and over, but others realize that westerners' uninformed interest in their work offers them an opportunity to innovate forms in the antique style, or to create imitation antiques.

Contemporary Toba Bataks must be adept to survive in the business of manufacturing neotraditional carvings. Not only must they maintain strong connections to their cultural traditions in order to continue selling to westerners who are interested in authenticity, but they also must find ways to keep their art vibrant for buyers who are looking for uniqueness or originality. Because of this, surviving in the marketplace means that the Toba Batak tourate must guess what westerners want; at the same time they must be creative in interacting with them to develop the values and meanings the carvings will have.

6

Locating Spaces of Interaction

It is hard to say really when the heavy rains started to pour down out of the skies, because it happened so gradually: first, gray shadows blocked the sun not just in the afternoons but in the mornings as well; then low-slung and dark blankets of cloud dripped all day long. Finally, it rained. There was a steady rain for a day, and mist for a day; later it was just rain. The gutter trench that surrounded my house, and supposedly drained the water that fell on the small hill in my backyard, puddled up white with mud water, then flowed translucent gray, then surged with water so quick and clear that it looked black. The gutter trench could not drain the water from the hill quickly enough, however, and soon the path that connected me with the island's paved road, and with the rest of the village, was part of a wide, shallow pond. Now, my shoes were always either wet or damp because rain and pools of water were unavoidable.

The songbirds all seemed to have left the area. If they were still around, they were huddling soggy under the leaves of forest shrubs instead of darting in and out of the hedges and fields as they usually did. The trills and arpeggios of yellow weaver birds and indigo mynahs were gone. Now, the thick, damp air was filled with the wheeze and croak of frogs in the newly formed pond or in the black trench water. Some nights, when the rain let up and became a sprinkle, their high-pitched croaking would drown out all other nighttime sounds so effectively that I could not tell if what I was hearing was a seamless amphibian chord surrounded by the vibrating sprinkle, or just ringing in my ears. If the drench of rain started up again, it only served to muffle their roar, not to obliterate it. Almost everyone in the village went to bed early on these drizzling nights because the sound of the TV could not be heard over the constant trilling of the frogs in the wet fields and ponds in the village.

When the rains became persistent and regular, the smells on Samosir Island dissipated like the birds' songs. Now, I only smelled an occasional damp mildew, and even then the scent was very light—a whiff of some slight trace of something that was hard to recall. During these long wet days, I would think about my home in springtime, when the air was succulent with the scents of iris, honeysuckle, and wisteria that hung layered in the atmosphere like thick, warm waxes. In my memory of home, every breeze had a smell. One moment the air might cling with the odor of flowers and asphalt; the next minute it would be mown grass and pecan leaves. And when a summer rain came by at home, the streets smelled acrid and the gravel walks fresh; the sluggish rivers smelled like suntan oil and bubbling algae.

My house on Samosir Island was surrounded by a gardener's dream of hibiscus bushes, yellow gladioli, and strange tropical plants with glossy variegated leaves, and the soil in the fields next door was constantly being plowed up with weeds turned upside-down and left to rot, but there was never a smell from any of this. When I planted a small garden at the base of the small hill in the backyard thinking that the rains would make corn and radish seeds luxuriantly burst up from the ground, I picked up a handful of the sticky gray soil I had dug, ready to enjoy a deep noseful of humus. But there was nothing. Then I sniffed harder. There, far below the sensation of inhaling humidity, I caught a whiff of a very faint stink, something like a summer day's discovery that clothes had been left too long in the washer. Even the water-buffalo shit didn't stink, and I know because I put my nose very close to it to see. The rain just washed everything away. During this time of constant rain, the days were sullen, people kept their umbrellas close to the door, and families spent more time in the house together.

Whenever I thought my coat could deflect the rain, I would head over to Partoho and Ito's house. Though the smells of nature might have dissipated outside, their kitchen was redolent with the scent of hot oils, wet children, and wood smoke. Many times I would walk the half-mile to their house holding my umbrella against a steady but soft shower, only to find myself holed up with them for hours as we waited out a cold tropical downpour. They always implored me to eat dinner with them when this happened, Ito calling out to us to sit down on the mat as she fried up some *gulamo,* or boiled some long green beans in coconut milk to go with the rice. The delicate scents of these would mingle with clove fumes as Partoho invited me to join him in a *kretek*. After the enameled plates and aluminum bowls were cleared away and the floor swept of whatever crumbs the dogs did not find, amber glasses of sweet tea were brought in and offered as dessert. It was then that Partoho, Ito, and I would sit around chatting and weaving stories, watching the children fall asleep arrayed around us on the mat, and holding in our thoughts and words when the sound of cloudbursts on the metal roof overwhelmed our small voices.

On one such night, the storm raged and the wind whipped the *kemiri* tree sharply against the roof, knocking the electricity out temporarily. Ito went to the kitchen and got a piece of sap-filled pine wood (since there were no candles), lit it, and put it in the mouth of an empty bottle so we could have some comforting light. The young children were scared and restless, so Partoho sang a few songs from the old days, one of which recalled a family happily sitting by the light of the fire as they talked. This got him to talking and telling stories as we all stared into the flame.

The time seemed right to ask him if he would tell some old Batak folktales. He said he didn't know any. I couldn't believe that there weren't stories that parents used to tell their children, or that the grandmothers and grandfathers used to tell each other. No, he said, there are no such Batak stories.[1] I must have looked very disappointed, for he said, "Honest, Andru. You know I want to help you with your research, but there are no Batak folktales! What about something else?" I agreed that some other story would do just as well. He said, "Okay, here is a story about why cats bury their shit—" Ito interrupted him suddenly with wide eyes, saying, "Don't tell him that one! Oh! How impolite!" Partoho just looked askance at her, laughing, and said, cryptically, "Okay, this is a good one for your research: the situation is almost the same as it is here in Huta Mungkap with the tourists. . . ."

And he began the story:

This is a story about the tiger. There was once a tiger and a cat. Tiger was very clever at *silat* (I: a kind of martial art), right? [He mimed a cat stretching its front legs.] But, Cat at didn't know anything at all about *silat*. Tiger lived in the jungle and Cat lived in a house . . . it was the house of his grandmother, see?

Well-ll, the one met the other in the jungle one day. So, they met up with each other, and Cat said to Tiger, "Won't you teach me how to do *silat?* And then, when I know how to do *silat,* then I will teach you how to climb to the tops of trees," like that he said it, right? Well, here's the tiger: "Oh, yes, I want to climb to the tops of trees!"[2] says the tiger, right?

Well-ll, he went ahead and taught the cat how to do *silat,* right? And, uh, he taught him all the time. So because the cat was very clever, he soon knew how to do it. Okay, so, uh, Cat is practicing his *silat* and here comes Tiger who says, "Now I want to say to you," he says, "I want to be taught how to climb to the top of the trees."

So, when the tiger said that, Cat ran straight up to the top of the wood—to the top of that tree—that showed him! So, here comes Tiger, right? "Okay, me next!" But the cat said, "I ran away because I don't want to teach tigers. I don't really like you . . . because some-day you'll eat me!" he said, something like that, right?

Well-ll, the tiger was really mad then, and said, "Later you will have to come down out of the trees. And when you come down, I'll eat you!" So, here's the cat talking now: "I won't come down! I can stay up in the trees here *forever!"* he said. The tiger said, "Fine, but later you will have to shit . . ." he said, right? [Partoho used the polite term now, and turned aside to me saying, "Its like defecating, you know?"] So, the cat says, "I don't shit when I'm up in the trees. I can wait and shit at my grandmother's house," he said, ". . . at the house of my granny," he said it like that, you know?

So, the tiger says, "You! I will track you down forever." But that tiger, because he sat waiting down there so long, he dropped off to sleep! Well-ll, after he was sound asleep, Cat jumped all the way down to the ground! And he went home, straightaway, to the house of his grandmother.

At his grandmother's house [Partoho gave me another aside: "Her house was just like the houses in some village or like the ones on Samosir Island here."] there was what people call the "waste-place," you know? It's the kitchen's fire pit. Well, the cat went ahead and shat, he dug a hole in the soil there and buried it back up so . . . so that no other animal could see it again.

So, that's the way it is with respect to Cat . . . he didn't want to be defeated. Now then, you know that's how it is, up to this day, there is no one who has seen cat shit, right? So, there you have it, the story of Tiger and Cat. The cat is smarter and the tiger is dumber . . . yes, dumber, but stronger. He can eat—can prey on—whatever he wants

. . . whether it is a bird, or some other thing, he can eat it. There you go.

The children loved the story and stared intently at him as he told it. Ito laughed naughtily at the parts involving excrement and nudged Partoho several times when he got to these parts, playfully scolding him. Ito started to tell a similar story, this time about Kancil (I: Mouse-Deer), a favorite Indonesian trickster, and his friend the monkey. Her story, however strayed from its course so many times (one time she said monkey, another time she said humans), and was interrupted so often by the children (first trying to help her and then trying to confuse her), that she finally gave up, throwing her hands up and laughing. The rain became a sprinkle and the wind stopped; I decided to take advantage of this short window of opportunity to race home before the next cloudburst.

I thought about Partoho's story for several days and was slightly uneasy and confused by it. What did he mean the situation was "almost the same" as in Huta Mungkap? I asked him just that a week later when I thought he was in a pensive mood, but all he said in response was, "Who knows? I don't know why it's the same exactly. That's just how it is." I probed a little bit more, wondering if he was just being coy or enigmatic, but he really had nothing more to say on the topic.

Not far from Partoho and Ito's house is the tourist hotel where I lived for several months before I found a house to rent. One clammy day, I stopped by the restaurant at the front of the hotel for a cup of coffee. The place was almost deserted. Partly on account of the cold rains, the great hordes of Western travelers had stopped coming; now it was only lone stragglers. When I walked in, there was just one traveler, a very secretive older man wearing shorts, sandals, and an anorak over his T-shirt. He was writing industriously in a banged-up journal, sitting far off in one corner of the tiled room, apparently preoccupied with his introspections. The seven other tables, heavy mahogany pieces with cabriole legs and topped with thick stone slabs the color of honey, were spotlessly clean and were set with salt and pepper shakers, glass bowls of sugar packets, bottles of soy sauce, and water glasses poked full of paper napkins in light pinks and greens. The room looked as though a boatload of weary travelers was expected at any moment. The tall-backed chairs were pushed up to the tables, and the large windows were wide open, lighting up the room with a hazy gray light, which wavered through the drizzle.

The five young women who worked at the hotel as cooks were loung-ing at the far table, flipping through German beauty guides and Aus-tralian news magazines (all of which were several years old and bloated through handling) as if they might see an image they had not seen before. One of them kindly got me a glass of coffee, and the eldest of the group told me they were having a "staff meeting." She told me they had just agreed that, from now on, no tourists would be allowed into the kitchen that adjoined the restaurant. I asked her what had brought this on, and all five began answering in a spate of words. "They are too close to us!" I heard. "They stand in the doorway!" Another said, "First they follow us to the door telling us how they want it cooked, then they put their heads in watching us! Finally, they buy food at the market and say, 'Cook this, fry that!' and suddenly *they* are the cooks!" The eldest said: "It's not safe. It's not their job. They should stay out in front and drink beer, not come back here and tell us what to do! It's too close to our room, and for the men, you know, that is very improper."

The voice of the eldest worker, the cashier, drowned out the others as she began to tell how this all had come about. As she told it, a few months before, at the end of the tourist season, several travelers staying in the hotel started to become very good friends with each other. They spent all their evenings in the restaurant, drinking beer, singing songs, and inviting the Batak guys who worked around the hotel to join them. Soon the young women workers were also invited to join in, and they all sat together at the tables while one person strummed a guitar and another rapped on a bottle to accompany the increasingly louder singing and laughing.

It was like a big, loud family, she said. But soon, like a family, the trav-elers were wandering into the kitchen, nibbling on sliced carrots while they chatted about their day to the cooks. Then, on a Saturday, one of the Western men brought in a plastic bag, which he insisted must be stored in the refrigerator, telling them that it was bacon he had purchased on a special trip to Medan. He said he would cook some that very night as a treat. In fact, he would cook dinner for everyone. The cashier said: "Well, after that, they were in the kitchen every night. First to show us how to cook things from their countries, then to tell us how to cook things on our menu, then to cook for us. I finally had to tell them they must not come in the kitchen because the stoves are too dangerous."[3] She told me the travelers agreed to leave the cooking to the cooks, but continued to chat while leaning up against the doorjambs. This meant that none of the five workers could take a nap, because their communal room was partitioned from the kitchen only by a thin curtain, and it was inconceivable that a young woman would fall asleep in such close proximity to an unrelated, unmarried male. The cashier could think of no polite way to discourage the travelers' behavior, and all the young women were secretly relieved to see them go after two weeks.

Sometime later, I told this story to Ito. She said: "That's how it is! With visitors, you must attend to their needs. You have to respect them." She told me that in the time between giving up the stall in the marketplace and building their *kios* at the front of their own property, she and Partoho had tried to sell things out of their house. "Those were very difficult times," she told me, "because we don't have a real *ruang tamu*. The visitors just had to come and sit down here in our big room;[4] they had to sit down next to the *lemari* and the bed to look at the carvings hung on the walls. I would have to stop and make tea,[5] no matter what else I was doing, and often they would leave without buying anything, *and* without drinking the tea. We were losing lots of money on that tea!" When the *kios* was finished being built, Ito felt much more at ease. Not only were the carvings no longer cluttering up the small house, but she no longer felt obligated to entertain Western "guests" there. She said, "It was hard . . . having guests so close to the inside of the house, you know?"[6]

I felt suddenly insecure and asked her if it was difficult to have me "so close to the inside of the house," too. She patted me on the leg and told me I was no longer a "guest," then added an odd tag line, saying, "Never mind, Andru. With you, we still have an inside to the house . . . there," and pointed to the doorway to the two bedrooms screened by a length of checkered fabric. It felt nice sitting there knowing that I was no longer a "guest," and that I was welcome to be sitting with them in social part of the house; it also felt nice to know that I was not an intruder into their privacy—that they still had another "inside."

On another occasion during the rainy season, Partoho told me his cat shit story again. One night at my house, as we sat around drinking the last few drops of the Benedictine liqueur I had brought back from Jakarta months before, he told me to get out my tape recorder, saying, "I'll tell you the stories you want to hear now." He told the cat shit story again; again prefacing it with the unexplained comment that it was good for my research. When he got to the end of it, I begged him to tell more. The talk roved around for a while, but the stories grew more disjointed and hazy. He stopped because Ito broadly hinted, "You've already taught Andru a lot of stories now . . . ," and I wondered how the three of us sitting there were reflected in the story of the cat in the tree.

UTOPIC SPACE

The majority of Western tourists come to Samosir Island when the hard rains of January, February, and March have stopped, but there is always a trickle of visitors coming to the island. Most of the Toba Batak tourate engage with the other (the travelers) both because they have to and because they want to, with feelings ranging from trepidation to curiosity and desire. Because of the regularity and intensity of their interactions with westerners, the tourate must be vigilant in their attempts to locate and define spaces for themselves that are beyond the "tourist gaze."[7] This does not mean the tourate are trying to avoid all interactions, just that they are hoping to mark boundaries between public and private spaces. Because there are bound to be differences of opinion about what divides these spaces when two cultures come into contact, one wonders how is it that the two parties are able to maintain some kind of equilibrium wherein the tourate continue to welcome travelers, and travelers continue to frequent the Lake Toba area. For both these parties, the commonality that keeps their interactions mutually beneficial is, at its most elemental level, desire: the desire for financial gain, or for sensual experience, respectively.

At another level, however, interactions between tourate and travelers indicate a common interest in exploring ways of being and acting in a space where their respective cultural rules and mores are suspended. That is, both groups seem to be interested in investigating possible behaviors that are in some sense "ideal." For example, the tourate are interested in increasing their finances while remaining in the homeland, and are interested in exposure to Western culture while maintaining ties to their own traditions; the Western travelers are interested in experiencing an "exotic" culture without leaving behind the comforts they have become accustomed to, and are interested in possessing the material culture of a "primitive" group that conforms to their aesthetic tastes. At this other level, the common interest is desire for the utopic space.

As I noted in the Introduction, one way to understand the interactions of cultural tourism is to think of them happening within a stage-like "place" where participants—tourist and tourate, and occasionally researcher—explore possible ways of being that are often counter to the dominant ideologies of home. This "place," referred to here as "utopic" because it playfully engages with extremes found in between reality and unrealizable desire, is not *necessarily* a bounded geographical point, but rather a series of unfolding and dynamic events. It is a space where touristic actions are extemporaneously narrativized by tourists and tourates in such a way that does not (and cannot) engage with one single script of action. In addition, the spaces where the interactions take place are neutral: they are places where all assumptions are contested and negotiated by both parties in myriad ways. The marketplace of touristic objects is one of the sites where the utopic interactions are most clearly enacted, for it is here that roles are continuously developed, and continuously constructed through narratives.

My observations of tourate/traveler interactions led me to believe that these roles are neither mantles assumed with full conscious awareness, nor the acting out of an unexamined self, but rather something subtle and fluid in between. What I often saw were individuals using aspects of their selves (composed with respect to the rules and mores of their culture) as a theme around which they would spin variations: explorations of possible ways of being not ordinarily sanctioned outside the utopic space. What I also saw were individuals constructing roles for the other that were founded on dreamy expectations and flimsy assumptions. All of these roles were communicated spontaneously and extemporaneously, using only minimal access to a mutually intelligible language. The acted roles writhed and bumbled, confused and charmed, and each step forward elicited a counterstep to the side as both parties either reconfigured their role or retrenched.

THE LANGUAGE SHUFFLE

The language used between tourate and travelers in the marketplaces was almost always English. Despite the fact that several local tour guides can speak some French, and others can communicate effectively in German, they rarely use these languages. If they meet travelers from France or Germany, they will open with a few awkward words to start a conversation but quickly switch (by mutual consent it seems) to English in order to chat. In the marketplace, vendors who are able to use the most basic words in ten languages[8] often revert to English when speaking with travelers since it is the foreign language with which they have most practice.

By contrast, incredibly few westerners make any attempt to use Indonesian, even though it is said to be a language that is easy to acquire, and even though all guidebooks provide elementary phrases that can be memorized and put to use very quickly. The use of English in touristic encounters sometimes puts the Toba Bataks at a disadvantage, because they are not able express themselves clearly. But this is not always the case. While it is often true that Europeans who are taught English as a second language have many advantages in the process of learning (similar language family, cognate words, regular exposure to the language, everyday applications for practice), it is also true that many of them have just as much difficulty with English as the tourate do.

If they have no common spoken language, how do tourate and travelers communicate in their touristic interactions? Sometimes the participants happily converse as if the other spoke their language, prattling away until some sort of understanding forces its way to the forefront. This is very rare. More often, the interacting parties try to use exaggerated gestures and movements to make themselves understood. Most gestures I saw used (especially when in conjunction with commonly understood or cognate words)[9] were immediately understood by the one being communicated with, usually because they involved common human functions (miming the drinking of a glass of water to mean "thirsty," or brushing the hand from backside to ground to indicate the need for a toilet). In a more inventive instance, I once stood in the Siallagan marketplace watching a particularly demonstrative woman vendor who met her match in a French package tourist. Without a word, he indicated to her that her price for a carved figure with dangling legs was too high. He mugged, winked, frowned, and then began mock weeping. She responded to his miming, just as quietly, with poses of shock, disgust, incomprehension, and scorn. He acted the part of a small, overindulged child; she acted the part of one who is betrayed. Shopkeepers and tourists alike began to gather to watch what seemed, for all the world, to be a vaudevillian show or passion play, and the two of them increased the intricacy of their histrionics. He pulled his pockets inside out, tipping back on his heels, and she took hold of a snot-nosed waif, tousling his dirty hair with sadness; he gestured the number ten (thousand *rupiah* [I: Indonesian currency]) and she gestured twenty. Just as he was about to walk off shaking his head in dismay, she grabbed him by the arm. He said, in English, "Fifteen, Okay? Fifteen," as he pulled his wallet out, smiling. She responded with a hearty, "Okay-*lah!*"[10]

Unfortunately, charades and gestures are not always clear. The most confused display I witnessed was one time when Ito saw a Western woman traveling with a young child in a backpack carrier. Ito was smitten with the towheaded child as soon as she saw it and gestured with a finger circling her own face, starting off in English, then reverting to Indonesian, saying, "Baby, *mukanya cantik! Mukanya cantik*" (I: "The baby has a beautiful face. A beautiful face.") The tourist smiled weakly and tried to ignore her, but Ito was persistent because she wanted a closer look, so she acted it out again, saying the same thing. I was sitting down on the concrete floor of the *kios* chatting with one of Ito's children and happened to catch the tourist's eye. She looked slightly miffed, and said to me, "I don't need this woman telling me I should cover my baby's head from the sun! He's *fine!*" I told her what Ito had said and she softened her attitude a little, but made no move to let Ito any nearer.

If they are unnecessary, the charades are dispensed with. In a bargaining situation, communication can be effective by using only smiles ("yes") and frowns ("no"), and fingers held up to indicate price. A great deal can be communicated through silence. One very old woman (Inang's aunt) spoke nothing but the Toba Batak language; in addition, she always had a huge red wad of betel chaw in her lip, which made her mumble terribly. In the marketplace, she was usually silent around tourists, instead creeping up quietly behind them and then just standing there, smiling adorably. When startled tourists noticed her at their elbow, she would then very softly put her hand on their upper arm and with great calm and ease slowly lead them to her stall, all the while explaining to them about her fabrics, using nothing but a hushed stream of Batak words. She had a steady business.

ROLES OF INTERACTION

Both Toba Bataks and travelers interact with each other on the basis of assumptions and expectations they have gathered from a number of sources, including personal experience and representations found in books or other media. Depending on the context, individuals may accept and

enact aspects of the identity constructed by the other, may attempt to
refine it, or may reject it altogether. There are few constraints in the way
these identities are negotiated. A person can accept the other's impression
or can invent a new identity at will; there is little or no corroboration of
factual data, so the spectrum of possibilities is great.

Western travelers tend to perceive Toba Bataks in general as being
"traditional," "animist," or "primitive," as discussed previously. Because
of these broad glosses, travelers often expect all locals they meet to be able
to answer their questions about cultural rituals, pre-Christian religion, or
something arcane, such as the names of flowers and their medicinal uses.
Most of the time, given this situation, the Toba Batak tourate will try to
answer the traveler's questions simply out of politeness; often enough,
however, I have seen hotel maids telling wild ghost stories with straight
faces but glints in their eyes, or hotel guides pontificating on the supposed names of trees and their ancient uses. When I first arrived on Samosir Island, I happened to be talking to Sulean as we sat in his mother's
kedai. He seemed very bright and well informed, so I asked him about
land inheritance rules: was it possible in this patriarchal society for a
woman to inherit land from her father? He leaned back in his chair with
a look of weary insouciance, tapped some stray ashes from his cigarette,
and told me that it was, in fact, impossible for such a thing to happen.
He was just about to give me details when his mother, Gusting, happened to walk in from the kitchen, having overheard some of this conversation. She listened for a second more as her son described how land
tenure worked, made a wide-eyed frown and said: "*No!!* What did you
just say? That's a *lie!* Those are empty words!" Sulean looked chagrined
and slumped down in his chair as she proceeded to ask him, slapping him
on the shoulder with each question: "Where in the world did you think
the property we farm every day came from? Huh? Who do you think gave
that land to me? Was it directly from God? *No!*" she answered herself.
"It's all from my father! And you'd be smart to remember that!" She finished by saying to me, "You'd better be careful with your questions, Pak
Guru, there are a lot of know-it-alls around here!"

It's not that travelers are being "lied to" by Toba Bataks. Rather, in
touristic circumstances, where the utopic space allows explorations of
ways of being, individuals may get carried away in playing up to travelers' expectations of them. When they are among their sage elders, young
people like Sulean might be considered witless and culturally unin-

formed, but in the touristic environment they are able to express their thoughts and knowledge to listeners who are often willing to accept their words as truth. Perhaps Cat was in a similar situation with Tiger: having an intense desire to interact and learn, the cat would agree in principle to practically anything, even teaching a tiger to climb.

Toba Bataks are not the only ones playing in the utopic space of cultural tourism—Western travelers are avidly engaged as well. Freed from their past histories, often with no one to contradict them, they are well positioned to make the best of the assumptions local people have about them. In the utopic space, a traveler can possess several higher-education degrees, can have worked as a doctor in Africa, or can have made dozens of sexual conquests. Toba Bataks generally consider westerners to be well-read and knowledgeable about technology, world economics, and politics, and often ask them difficult questions: "How does a computer make letters out of electricity?" "Why does the exchange rate make westerners richer?" "Why can't Indonesia have democracy like the West does?" Rarely have I heard a Western traveler hesitate for more than a moment before answering these sorts of questions. Like an immature Toba Batak trying to explain rules of *adat,* these westerners quite often provide misinformation, but it is important to focus not on the content but the style. Travelers' responses in such situations are narrative explorations of possible selves with possible knowledges.

The culture-specific assumptions and expectations of the other are not always accepted, or refined; occasionally these constructions are flatly refuted. For example, Toba Bataks who persist in believing that all westerners are enormously wealthy are certain to be challenged; Western tourists who refer to Toba Bataks as "primitive" may be set straight just as quickly as they use the term. Individuals who cannot communicate their rebuttals through language are, of course, frustrated, for charades and hand gestures are unable to dispute those facets of an identity construction that are often the most inaccurate.

In talking about touristic interactions as occurring in a conceptual place referred to as a utopic space I do not mean to imply that the participants are on an equal social footing. There is no arguing that Western travelers come to Lake Toba with many unexamined feelings of superiority, whether these are based on better education, more secure financial situations, or perceived higher social class. That their touristic interactions are in some ways comparable to relationships between westerners and Bataks that existed in the colonial past does not elude all travelers, but most perceive their travels, because they are done on a "shoestring" budget, to be in some way egalitarian. This, of course, is one of the fantasies that gets played out by travelers in the utopic space: the ability to live in luxury while imagining oneself to be one of the folk, all for a relative pittance.

One of the most common attitudes assumed by Western travelers is that *because* they can pay for their travels, they *deserve* them. That is to say, travelers seem to feel that their finances free them from certain social constraints, obligations, and responsibilities. Similarly, in the minds of some, because the Toba Batak tourate have "chosen" to be in the tourism business (which the West defines as part of the "service" industry), they have *accepted* their work (that is, to serve). Two brief examples will illustrate this attitude. A British traveler kept turning up the volume on the television set at his small hotel as he watched a loud rock-video program late at night. The owners were trying to sleep in their rooms nearby. When they complained, he shouted, "I'll bloody watch what I want! I paid good money for this trip!" In another instance, a Dutch woman sent back an omelet at a small restaurant because it contained tomatoes (which she had not ordered), even though she could see that absorbing the cost of the mistake would create a hardship for the owners, saying, "If they want to stay in the tourist business, they *have* to learn to do it right!"

I do not mean to vilify those travelers who act in such ways. The fact is that some westerners do not understand or fully appreciate two things that, when written down, seem to be perfectly obvious: (1) that they are in someone else's land where particular traditions and morals are in force, and (2) that the area constituting the tourist center may include individuals who do not wish to be part of the tourism industry but are compelled to be so because of the location of their homes. It is because of this blind spot, I think, that travelers have expectations of the Toba Batak tourate that are unrealistic, for if they are under the impression that everyone with whom they engage has actively chosen to dedicate themselves to tourist service careers in a place that was unoccupied beforehand, then of course they will feel dissatisfied when their needs and desires are not met. This is one of the reasons that the notion of utopic spaces in the context of cultural tourism is an important discursive tool, for it helps to clarify why certain dysfunctions occur. If travelers consider the entire tourist center to be a place where they may express themselves freely (a utopic space) rather than a place that is riddled both with territories they may explore and others that are more private, they will no doubt experience interactions that are below their expectations, and will also find themselves in situations where local people will be critical of their behaviors.

Not all interactions are as challenging as the ones I have described, of course, and there are many opportunities for Toba Bataks to engage with westerners in somewhat equitable encounters. In the story above, the young women in the hotel restaurant found themselves in a position where food was being prepared for them, where they could sit back, join the party, and sing. Here, the familiarity of the interactions spun out of control in the minds of the Toba Bataks, but this was an extreme case. It is not uncommon to see westerners treating Toba Bataks with honest respect and helping them in ways they are able—giving them surplus clothing, paying for their children's school fees, or bringing them bags of expensive fruits. It could be said that all of these small acts are, in fact, patronizing, yet they are always accepted by the Toba Bataks without reservation. For, if the westerners tend to treat locals with underlying suspicion, the Toba Bataks tend to treat travelers with unrestrained avarice. Social inequality works both ways in the context of cultural tourism on Samosir Island: travelers may want to act out their part as "folk," but the Toba Bataks fully expect them to act out their part as "patrons."

Some travelers implied that their patronage of a place should allow them to choose to what extent they would engage with the local people. The majority of Western travelers who responded to my questionnaire said that their primary reasons for coming to Samosir Island were to "relax" and to "see the view"; a smaller proportion said that they came to "see the culture." One of the common complaints I heard during chats with travelers was that they felt pestered by local people who wanted either to practice English or to ask innumerable questions about the West. For those people who come to the area to relax or enjoy the landscape, interactions with the local populace may be considered an infringement on their time and thus a drain on their financial investment. For these visitors, local culture is a part of the ambience of travel, and local people a part of the background. Such travelers are often just as kind and open as those who came to the lake primarily to experience the local culture, but they prefer to interact with Toba Batak waiters, maids, guides, and vendors only as service employees, ignoring them and their culture when they are in non-service contexts. In effect, this group of travelers treats the Toba Batak tourate as though they were "incidental" to the environs. Many of the tourate told me that these were some of their most difficult customers because they refused to engage interpersonally. For the gregarious Toba Bataks, not participating in the creation of some kind of relationship was almost worse than participating through anger or suspicion. These travelers were called *"sombong"* (I: arrogant) by the tourate, who characterized other travelers as *"baik hati"* (I: good-hearted) or *"ramah-tamah"* (I: friendly).[11] The tourate's reaction was to deal with them in a reserved but civil way, in effect, to mirror their own treatment. It becomes clearer now, perhaps, why Ito so disliked showing westerners the carvings in her home. She assumed they understood that a social bond was being initiated when they accepted her invitation to enter the main room; when they refused to drink tea, she could not imagine that they might have felt ensnared by someone whose relationship to them was primarily and simply that of salesperson.

SITES OF INTERACTION

Western travelers and the Toba Batak tourate meet in a variety of public spaces, some of which allow the traveler more control of the situation, some of which favor the Toba Bataks, and some that favor neither. In the tourist hotels and restaurants, where westerners often substantially outnumber locals, interactions may encourage the former to engage in self-indulgent behaviors, such as wearing inappropriate comfortable clothing or voicing opinions aloud rather than waiting for the locals to get out of earshot. Likewise, in the *kedai,* on roads and paths, or in private homes, interactions may allow Toba Bataks to play out their own self-indulgent acts. I often saw pairs of adventurous westerners who were waiting out a storm in an isolated *kedai* being joked about behind their backs as they sat patiently and somewhat sheepishly, sensing the awkwardness of the situation. In both these contexts, however, each of the participants (Western travelers in the first, Toba Bataks in the second) are constrained from exploring the full extent of possible behaviors by the dominant ideologies of home: their respective rules of politeness, decorum, or avoidance will not allow them free rein to act out in ways that they might wish to. As was shown at the beginning of this chapter, these public venues are sometimes uncomfortably close to private spaces for the Toba Bataks, forcing them especially either to change their customary behaviors or to articulate their boundaries more clearly.

Even those among the tourate who are the most fervent about the benefits of tourism want to have a place that is beyond the boundaries of the touristic utopic space. The desire to be off the stage is not unique to them of course, but as the ones who are the object of the tourist gaze, it may be more difficult for them to find, or actively create, the "inside" place. Western tourists have paid for spaces that are primarily theirs (or nearly so): hotel rooms, lobbies, restaurants. On the other hand, because there are few, if any, boundaries that exclude tourists, the Toba Batak tourate may feel constantly on display. Ignorant of what constitutes a private and what a public space on Samosir Island, westerners must have them indicated and articulated by the tourate, who often feel such things should be merely assumed and understood.

The public spaces that truly permit the spectrum of possible behaviors to be explored by both parties are those areas which are most neutral. Such spaces include the ferryboats, the restaurants and *kedai* that do not specifically cater to either visitor or local, the tourist sights, and the marketplaces. These neutral spaces do not inherently favor one party over the other, whether because the number of participants from each group is fairly equal (such as on the ferryboats), or whether because some other factor tends to balance what might otherwise be a disparity (in the marketplaces, westerners are usually outnumbered by locals, but because their money is so desperately desired, they are dominant in financial transactions). Here, behaviors are not only less constrained by cultural customs but they are more actively negotiated with the other party. In the hotel restaurant or the isolated *kedai* one party might feel free to take advantage of the other, but in these more neutral contexts, both parties are equally free to spar and play.

The marketplaces of touristic objects are ideal examples of these most neutral spaces of interaction between travelers and tourate. In the large marketplaces in Siallagan and Tomok, the contexts of interaction are spaces through which individuals can freely move because scores of separate stalls line the paths and streets. There are no dead ends, no places in which to get honestly trapped, and there is always the possibility for both parties to move on, or away. This physical freedom helps to create a conceptual freedom for interpersonal engagement. Travelers may decide to respond to the calls of the vendors, and vendors can vacate or close their stalls if they feel they want to avoid travelers. For those who wish to participate in an interaction, whether it actually involves bargaining or not, the marketplaces are spaces where individuals voluntarily choose to engage with each other.

This statement risks oversimplifying a complex situation, and for this reason I want to reiterate that travelers, because they are economically dominant, have more freedom to engage or disengage as they please than do the Toba Batak vendors. This does not mean, however, that the vendors are without agency in the interactions. No vendor I knew in any of the marketplaces was so financially strapped that she or he was forced to sell below cost or forced to deal with rude or otherwise difficult buyers. It did not happen frequently, but I did see vendors (whom I knew to be struggling to make ends meet) turn away from parsimonious domestic tourists,[12] and others who would pull down their blinds when they saw (or heard) particular nationalities coming their way. Because most vendors in the marketplaces have alternative means of obtaining their family incomes (through a spouse who farms, fishes, or works as a government servant), they are not slaves to the market or the tourists who buy from them. The situation is only slightly different for vendors who sell from their homes or from small shops outside the marketplaces.

A DAY IN THE MARKETPLACE

There are actually two kinds of marketplaces in the tourist center: one (such as is found in Tomok and Siallagan) specializes in wood carvings and fabrics of interest to the tourist trade (plate 11); the other (such as the Saturday market in Parapat) specializes in vegetables, fruits, and other food, as well as clothes and utensils of interest to the local inhabitants (plate 12). While the vegetable market is almost completely composed of women (both as buyers and sellers), sellers in the marketplace of touristic objects are almost evenly divided between the sexes. Sometimes a carver sells his own work; other times his wife, sister, or child is in charge of the selling; and sometimes a couple will take turns selling, expecting that their children will take their place if they must attend to other work.

Western tourists rarely go to the food markets as a tourist "sight." While they may take photographs from outside its boundaries, if they do shop in the Saturday market, it is because they are trying to save money, or because they want to try the variety of tropical fruits that are plentiful in Sumatra.[13] Tourists do buy a lot of fruit, and for prices that astound the locals; but in general they simply pass the chaotic market by, preferring to spend their money in the shops and stalls on the island.

The souvenir marketplace in Siallagan, like that in Tomok, is composed of a hundred or more boxlike stalls, one right next to the other. A typical stall is about eight feet wide, ten feet deep, and seven feet high. It has no doors or windows, but rather opens up at the front by the removal of planks set in slotted runners at ground and ceiling levels. Sometimes, the planks are removed and then used as makeshift shelves. Other times, they are stacked and used as a long low bench on which vendors and visitors can sit and visit. Most stalls have shelves or tables inside used to display carvings and other small objects, behind which is a mat and pillow or fabrics for napping. At the front of the stalls are boards prickling with dozens of half-submerged nails aimed in all different directions. It is on these nails that the vendor suspends leather purses, hangers of sarongs and *ulos* (TB: traditional fabric shawl), string loops of inexpensive metal key chains, and T-shirts. These objects are ordinarily crammed so tightly around the edges of the opening that entry is sometimes difficult for tall westerners. Protruding onto the street are more benches or tables displaying other carvings, brass work imported from Java, and postcards (figure 10). In the areas of the marketplace where the paths are narrow, bags and clothes completely clutter the top of the passage.

Tourists pass down the narrow roads to casually "window shop" among the stalls. This act of browsing, or "just looking," is one that Toba Bataks find very strange. A rural Batak wanting or needing to buy a certain thing would save money until the very day the thing was needed. The idea that a person would wander around looking at things they might or might not wish to purchase was considered, first, to indicate an excess of free time, and second, proof that the person had so much money that decisions to buy were based, not on necessity, but rather on whim.

This is one of the reasons that vendors in the souvenir marketplace are so outspoken: they want to do what they can to stop visitors from "shoppingshopping" as they say it, and encourage them to *buy*. They do this in a variety of ways, some of which are successful, others of which serve only to scare potential buyers away.[14] One of the subtle ways in which vendors try to attract a buyer's eye is by pretending to rearrange stock at the front of the stall, the movement of which may cause a passerby to turn briefly. This glance is just enough of a pretense for the vendor to initiate some small conversation. Sometimes, a vendor will simply push the backs

FIGURE 10. *A typical table in Siallagan*
with carvings and other souvenirs for sale

of some hanging purses to jangle them, hoping for the same automatic response from a tourist.

Sellers may also call out to a person passing by, using words from any number of languages, but usually those he or she thinks might be the mother tongue of the tourist (judging by the way they are dressed or some other overt indication). They might say in a loud voice, "Helloooo, Sirrrrr," or "Bonjourrrrr Madammmmmm," or they might say something else to attract the visitor's attention: "Sirrrr, Sirrrr, this for sale. Cheap!" Of course, those who speak a language more fluently are often more likely to catch the notice of a tourist, who can understand them because they have more words at their disposal with which to converse. This does not mean, however, that they always have more success in selling.

Sometimes, merely one word in a foreign language can make a sale, if I am at all a representative Western buyer. One day I was standing in the marketplace watching tourists pass, when I was approached by a kindly gentleman. I had been doing research in Siallagan for many months but did not recognize him, nor did he seem to know me. I spoke to him in Indonesian and asked how long he had been selling in the area. He answered that he was watching his daughter's stall for just a few days.

He hadn't had a sale all day, he said, so perhaps I would be interested in buying something? I asked him if he had anything "traditional," and he scooped up a handful of fabric strings dangling with the most preposterous wooden dolls I had yet seen. Crudely turned on a lathe and painted in bright greens and yellows, these creatures had holes drilled in their torsos to which cords were glued to imply arms and legs. The old man held them up to my nose, peeking around them. He smiled with sparkling eyes and shook them till they trembled, then said, "Pinocchio!" which I thought was pretty funny. I asked him if he meant they were *sigalegale* (the life-sized marionette puppet that is only found among the Toba Batak), but he said, "No, no. This . . . Toba Batak Pinocchio!" There was something so enjoyable about the encounter that I bought one, particularly since I would never have the chance again to buy a real "traditional" Toba Batak Pinocchio.

Sometimes business is very slow in the souvenir marketplace of Siallagan: no westerners are riding rented bicycles on the road, and no Malaysians or Taiwanese package tourists are wandering up from the dock. At these times, the vendors are worried sick, because they have invested so much money in leather purses imported from Java, T-shirts and shorts printed with the words "Lake Toba, Sumatra," and racks of glossy photographic postcards, things that now hang limply in the breeze or sit fading on a makeshift table. Wood carvings done in the traditional style are crowded in the stalls too, often far in the back, in the darkest corners. Inang tells me that the profits made on the small carvings are ordinarily much less than those made from the sale of bags and clothes, so there is no point in having them take up all the prime space out front. She goes on to tell me that some people think differently. These people put their carvings on a shelf by the entrance to their stall because they know that many westerners do not like to enter the dark stall because it makes them feel trapped. "They like to know they can run off if they want to," she says.

DESIRES AND NEGOTIATIONS

It took a long time for me to make any sense out of the Siallagan marketplace, but after months of hovering around the stalls and paths, some patterns of behavior and interaction began to emerge. Although many questions remained unanswered, I did begin to understand some of the processes of buying and selling in a context where more than material desires were satisfied and much more than price was negotiated. In short, I began to see the marketplace as a space where people got much more than they were bargaining for.

One of the questions that interested me from the beginning was how travelers knew what they wanted to buy. I pursued this question, partly in an effort to assist my Toba Batak carver and vendor friends, but also to begin to understand how individuals manage to identify the specific object they want from the hundreds of choices they are offered. It is an amazing thing to witness when a tourist wanders into a stall to buy a small souvenir carving for a roommate back home, does not find the "right" thing, so leaves, going in and out of most if not all of the spaces in the marketplace, and finally decides to return to the seventeenth stall. By what criteria is the object in that particular stall selected?[15]

I am not the only visitor who caved in to an impulse to buy something like the Pinocchio, but I may be one of the few who talked about it. Generally, I found that travelers keep their buying interests and, later, purchase selections, to themselves. Why? Well, it seems that they want to keep their purchase options open. If they express a vague interest in, say, a T-shirt, they will find that vendors will not leave them alone until they buy a T-shirt. By feigning disinterest in all the objects in a stall, they hope the seller will not pressure them to buy any one thing. Furthermore, vendors assume that prior purchases indicate what future purchases will be. When a traveler who purchased a carving one day happens to return to the market and is recognized, it is assumed that she or he has come back to buy more carvings; word will travel fast among vendors, and the buying travelers will be proffered carvings almost exclusively.

If a traveler is interested in something, I found, he or she will ask about several other objects in the stall rather than the object in mind. By asking the price of postcards, T-shirts, leather bags, and carvings, the traveler can get a feeling for the vendor's prices while seeming to show interest in a variety of things. One cagey traveler told me that he always pulls down three or four objects, only one of which he wants to buy, and puts them on a table in close proximity. He will ask the prices of these things, never starting with the thing that is of prime interest. His thinking is that initially vendors always give high prices, lowering them if a visitor seems to show a lack of interest in the objects (as evidenced by asking for the price of the next object).

It is at this point, when they are weighing the desirability of an object, that travelers most often begin to feel taken advantage of. As noted previously, vendors will sometimes exaggerate about (if not actually misrepresent) their wares. Because the marketplace is one of the most neutral spaces for acting in a way that is outside the constraints of ordinarily accepted behavior, these embellishments are not censured by the vendor's neighbors, no more than a traveler trying to convince a vendor that she or he is actually poor is censured by fellow travelers. In the marketplace, if either party believes it to be a place of earnestness and honesty rather than a neutral space of playful behavior, they may become annoyed or distrustful. This is probably why some Western travelers become so incensed when tourate vendors push the margins of truth while selling: they feel there is an assumed social contract concerning what is referred to in the West as "truth in advertising." It is also probably why some of the tourate become displeased when they find out that poor-mouthing travelers actually have ample expendable funds.

Feelings of unease or suspicion usually increase during the bargaining process. Many westerners refuse to bargain, I found out, because they find this method of purchasing goods too stressful; some will return home empty-handed rather than attempt to engage in bargaining with the vendors. The Toba Bataks, who bargain for everything they buy in the rural areas, are much more adept at the system (knowing, for example, how to counter an offer and when to stop bargaining) and so might seem to be less uncertain than the westerners, but this is not necessarily the case. Because they must often bargain in English and, worse yet, in terms of foreign currency, they lose their comfortable footing.

In an ordinary bargaining situation, whether it involves Toba Bataks exclusively or Toba Bataks and westerners, the buyer shows interest in an object either by asking some question about it or by actually asking the price. What some travelers do not realize is that asking the price of a commodity is often considered a sign of serious interest in buying it. Thus, when they ask the price of a carving, then move on to the next carving and ask its price, and so on, they may end up either confusing the vendors (if they are not experienced selling to westerners) or annoying them. On the other hand, if the vendor offers a price without being asked, there is no obligation on the part of the buyer.

After the price is uttered, the buyer is usually expected to offer a little more than half the opening price. This is another detail travelers do not really understand, for they will often counteroffer a price that is so ridiculously low that the vendor will steer them to something else. Extremely low counteroffers are sometimes made by Toba Bataks to each other in order to politely curtail a bargaining session, for it communicates the limits of the buyer's finances in such a way that does not embarrass either party. What irritates the tourate sellers is when a westerner offers an outrageously low price and then continues bargaining for the item. For the Batak vendor, such a move indicates that they are dealing with an uninformed buyer, or someone who is "stingy." Either way, vendors often avoid this situation for fear that they will have to bargain too long and even then may not get the price they want.

Sometimes, the vendor tests the buyer, starting with an exorbitant price to see how much she or he is willing to spend. Savvy travelers will counteroffer with a price much too low, then move on to the next item of interest, hoping the seller will quote them a more reasonable price, or at least one they are willing to pursue. (It is for this reason exactly that the traveler described above never asks about his primary interest first.) The process of offering and counteroffering sums of money continues until both parties can agree on some median price, but as the negotiation unfolds each side may offer little asides or comments, acted out or spoken, explaining why the latest price offered is a good one: the vendor will point out the quality of the merchandise, and the buyer will point out its flaws. The price is finalized when one or the other party stops bargaining, usually ending the session by saying "Okay!" or "Good" in English. Payment is always made at that point unless some other agreement was reached prior to the start of bargaining.

That bargaining is a time of great stress for both vendor and buyer was made clear to me by observations and conversations with both groups. Interestingly, when asked in written questionnaires if they had problems in tourism encounters, very few individuals of either group mentioned bargaining or money misunderstandings. In fact, contrary to what they said in conversations about bargaining sessions, a great majority of the westerners told me that they enjoyed the experience. It is not clear, but it may be that the "stress" they speak of is actually a kind of exhilaration, and that it is somehow an exciting part of an otherwise relaxing visit. This much seems clear: for many travelers, the bargaining process seems to accentuate the exoticism of their buying experiences on Samosir Island. For some, the fact that they manage to bargain in the marketplace might be one aspect of their trip that makes it truly "authentic."

SITTING AT THE TOP OF THE MARKET

Inang has sold carvings and fabrics to tourists for twenty years or more. Her stall has a prime location at the top of the market, facing down the path to the dock while being visible from the main road. I sit with Inang on many slow days, talking about her business, about Western visitors, and about the other vendors. One day she was particularly talkative, and we had the following conversation about her portrayals of tourists, the marketplace and its history, and the practicalities of working in a difficult business. I asked her, "How long have you been in this spot selling?" and she responded: "Oh, about twenty years I guess. I wasn't the first one here. There already were some places selling down there (down the path to the dock), but in those days it wasn't fancy. We just put up whatever we had, wood, plastic, whatever, and sold from there. We sold carvings and fabric then. Now you can see things are much fancier, and there are a lot more people selling. Before the tourists began coming here, this all was just a pasture for the pigs."

"Have things changed much since then?" I asked.

"Oh sure," she said. "Business was really good in the seventies and eighties. We would sell all day long. Now, I guess it has started to fall. It's been like this since around 1990. Things have been very slow since then."

"Have tourists stopped coming here?"

She replied: "No it's not that. Every year it seems more and more come here. But nowadays they just pass by and don't buy. You know, there are so many other places to go now. You can go to Bukittinggi, to Brastaggi, to Medan, to Padang and other places,[16] and they all have the same things. Tourists have told me that they have seen the same bags as I have selling in Bukittinggi for a much lower price. But I already have so much in the price of the thing, how can I come down to their price? I'll go *bankrupt*.[17] It used to be that we were the only ones selling *souvenirs,* but now you can find the same thing everywhere."

I asked her, "Before, if someone wanted to buy Batak carvings or fabrics, they had to come here to get them?"

"That's right. But now, people from those other places come here and buy carvings and fabrics. The carvings are all made on Samosir Island, but they sell them everywhere, and I hear at a lower price!"

"When did the tourists first start coming here?"

"I guess that was in the seventies. We were really poor then. They came to see the stone chairs and the old houses here . . . they came to see the way we lived. And they started to buy things the day they got here. We didn't have too much to sell then, but now, look at all the shirts, the bags, the *statues!*"

I asked her if the westerners liked to barter and she said: "Oh yes! All the tourists like to barter. They like to get a lower price. Even if they don't speak Indonesian and we don't speak English, that's no problem. If they can't speak, we just write a price down on paper, and then they change it until we get a price we both have a happy heart about. Like the Italians, the Spanish, the . . . who else . . . oh, the French. They can't speak Indonesian at all, but they do like to barter! We just write numbers down until the price is right."

My observations of travelers made me wonder if all westerners liked to barter, and Inang replied: "Sure! It's like I said, they all want a better price. If they want a purse and I start at 50,000rp (that is, about $25), they want to come back with a price of twenty-five (thousand). Oooo, that's too low! But I can go to forty. *"No, no, no,"* they say, *"thirty, thirty."* Oh. I can't do it. But we will both be happy with thirty-five, so I say, *"thirty-five."* I sell it for thirty-five.

I have no idea how much Inang paid for the purse she is using as an example, so I ask, "Are you making a profit if you sell it for thirty-five?" And she says, cagey as ever, "Sure. I'm making enough profit to eat."

"Are there ever people who sell their things for the price they paid, or for less?" I ask.

She jumps a little and stares at me, saying, "Huh? How is it possible? If they don't sell for more than they pay, how could they stay selling? That's no business. No, I have never heard of a person selling things for the price they paid or less. Never. Maybe they will sell something for only 500rp (that is, twenty-five cents) over what they paid. But, well, that's still a profit of five hundred. You can still eat on that. . . ." She goes on to give me a concrete example.

"If we have a child that is going to university and she or he needs money, we will bring out anything to sell—'*Okay, how much, how much you take this for?*' Whatever we can get, we'll take to send our kids to school. You see it wasn't a problem before, because no one sent their kids to school. But now, every Batak goes to school. You need money for that. So if you have to sell something, you sell it. It's better to see your kids advance than to have some old thing, some old basket. It's much better to see all your children going to school, going to find work in Medan or Jakarta. That's how the Bataks will progress."

I asked her, "So that's the only way for Bataks to make their lives better, through education?" To which she replied: "That's right. What other way is there? All of our children have to get advancement through education. That's why we work so hard to send our kids to school. How else can they advance? How else can they find a job? If they go to school, they can read—like if a letter comes from some office. The man calls on the phone: Brrring! *'Halloo?'* (she says, making her voice sound hesitant and frightened). 'Yes, madam' (her voice is now an imitation of a European male), 'did you get the letter I sent?' If I can't read, I'll think, 'what letter?' He'll say, 'Oh, you can't read? *Okay, no job for you!'* And if our children don't go to school, how will they find their way around the big city? 'Oh yes, the address is on Sudirman Street . . .' And the kids go up and down the street asking, 'Do you know where Sudirman Street is?' How can they get a job? Oh yes. Education is the way to advance for the Batak. It makes us proud to say that all our kids have finished at least high school and have jobs in Jakarta, Medan, Kalimantan, and like that. But also, what kind of life do they have here? They will just end up working in the fields like their grandmothers. What kind of life is that? It's better to get an education and find a job, so you don't have to stand in the sun all day!"

Inang then changed the subject, saying, "I thought we were going to talk about tourists. Why don't you ask me about the tourists?" I agree, asking, "So, what about tourists here? Are there any problems?" And she answers: "Problems? What problems? The tourists give us no problems. We like the tourists here. They bring money to buy *souvenirs,* stay at the hotels, and sometimes they want to make long-lasting connections. Sometimes they want to send our kids to school. Of course we like that! There are no problems with tourists!"

I decided to prompt her a little more: "Well, what I mean is . . . Okay, here is an example. Before tourists came, you could buy land for only a little bit a square meter. Now . . ."

"Right!" she continued, "Now, it is one million *(rupiah)!* It's very expensive now. But that's no problem. What did we use the land for, before? Now we use it to build hotels or stalls. The tourists bring in money and we can afford more for the property, see? Yes, it's a small problem, but you see, with the tourist money we get, we can send our kids to school. We couldn't do that very often before. I'm a good example. My parents had no money to send me to school. I had to work in the fields. But now, look! I can sit in the shade all day long. I sell now; I don't work much in the fields anymore. Life is better since the tourists came, better for us, and for our children."

Inang's words, so positive about the benefits of tourism, echoed what I had heard from many of the Toba Batak tourate. Nevertheless, there are many Toba Bataks outside the tourist area who do not want to see an increase in tourism. These are primarily people whose lands are not in the tourist center and, more rarely, people who see their culture being diluted by outside influences. It is not certain why these individuals want to see tourism decline, or completely disappear, but it may be that some feel if tourism were to increase, it would remain centered on the east coast area, continuing to leave the majority of island inhabitants out of the profits. In the case of others, it may be that their jealousy blinds them from seeing the benefits of which their neighbors assure them. Perhaps it is because they want to protect the most sacred and essential place in the Batak homeland. Whether or not Toba Bataks are in favor of tourism in the area, and despite the recent decline in numbers of tourists visiting the island, it appears that tourism on Samosir Island is unlikely to disappear.

By its very nature, cultural tourism brings individuals from unlike groups into interaction with each other. On Samosir Island, most people who participate in cultural tourism (both tourate and traveler) do so willingly, but this does not mean that boundaries are simply erased. On the contrary, the places and behaviors of interaction must be defined, developed, perhaps guarded, by those involved. Tourate and traveler work together, oftentimes spontaneously, in an ongoing effort to define where the divisions between public and private spaces will be drawn, and to negotiate the parameters of the roles they will enact in the process of meeting their needs and desires. One place the unfolding of such interactions occurs is in the marketplace of touristic objects, a place that possesses a neutral quality, as neither tourate nor traveler has the upper hand there. I have suggested that the marketplace is a utopic space, a stagelike area where individuals can explore who they are (or who they want to be) by testing the separation between what they know (reality) and what they want (desire). The utopic marketplace is a space where tourate and traveler narratives extemporaneously vacillate between explaining and defining their actions: there is no prior script for these interactions; rather, they are being constantly and tentatively improvised by the parties involved.

It is hopeless for me to try to guess what connection Partoho saw between the story of the cat and his shit and Western tourism in Huta Mungkap. Still, there might be some general conclusions to be drawn from it. Like the cat in the story, the Toba Batak tourate are often in the presence of a daunting persona, the Western traveler, who wants something from them ("authentic" culture, perhaps) and is in many ways more powerful than they. And, like the cat, the tourate must learn what they can from the powerful persona, whether it be new languages, new technologies, or new customs, in order to prosper. To survive, however, they must realize the limitations inherent in their interactions with this other and must actively set boundaries, always ensuring that they will have a place where they can disengage—an "inside" place where the authentic ("the real shit," so to speak) is distant and safe from encounters about which they are still wary. Because engagements with the other are not culturally "scripted" in cultural tourism, but rather are emergent and are spontaneously acted out by both parties in playful spaces that are neutral and utopic, the Toba Bataks (perhaps more than Western travelers, who are actively seeking a place to enact aspects of their desires) are both cautious and exuberant, exploring a variety of behaviors made possible by the neutrality of the utopic space, but also keeping an attentive eye, like the cat in the tree, on the potentially dominant other.

7
Innovating Traditions

There is one particular place on the road from Huta Mung-
kap to Siallagan where I often stopped just to look at the view (plate 13).
From this vantage point, where the road begins to dip down and around,
following the contours of the hill, I could almost see the place where
Inang sits, waiting for visitors to pass her stall on their way to the stone
chairs. As the road enters the town, it is bordered on one side by open-air
shops and on the other by the huge stone walls of the ancient compound.
At the corner of the compound the road forks—to the left, passing a
gigantic ficus tree and a creek, then on to the towns on the north end of
the island, and, to the right, down to the wobbly wooden dock where the
ferry stops. All along the meandering, cobblestone dock road are scores of
shops. Unlike the shops on the road, whose owners have erected all kinds
of sunscreens made from bamboo slats and plastic tarps that have little
success in keeping out the glaring sun and heat, the shops lining the path
to the dock are cool and dark. The path is only nine or ten feet wide in
some places, which makes it much easier for the stall owners and renters
to overlap their homemade umbrellas and wood-framed shades to keep all
but the thinnest streaks of sun from penetrating (figure 11).

In the middle of a sunny day, this crazy quilt of faded old fabrics and
raveling mats, bamboo lattices, strings, wires, and sticks blocks out the
direct light, dappling the stony path here and there with deep blues and
umbers, and making it seem like a place far under water. And like a place
far below water's surface, things move slowly and almost soundlessly. In
the midst of a hot day in this dark crevice, one can occasionally hear the
muffled sound of a woman scraping her rubber sandal as she shifts her
leg to a more comfortable position while picking wilted leaves off the
stems of a dark leafy vegetable. There is silence, and then the faint sound
of another woman softly snoring at the back of her shop while her baby

FIGURE II. *Marketplace scene Siallagan*

toddles around the tables, watched by the unfocused eye of a neighbor. Sometimes a snack seller ambles by, carrying a large fabric-draped metal tub that wobbles on her head at each step as if it were part of her body. She does not hawk what she is selling, because everyone along the path already knows what she has. An almost imperceptible wave of the hand and a smile is her signal to stop, kneel, and set the tub down to serve the greens stewed in chilies and coconut milk.

There have been lots of hot, slow days recently, and no one really knows why. The vendors wonder: is it because tourists don't like the carvings and fabrics being offered for sale, or is it because there is too much competition between vendors all selling the same bunch of things? I myself have heard tourists talking as they walk down the middle of the road (seemingly afraid of some contagion they think festers at the margins but really just trying to avoid what they think are pushy sellers in the roadside stalls). What they say is that there is so much of the same stuff in every shop, crowding the tables and overflowing into the street, that it *all* looks cheap and tawdry. "Touristy," they say, and they walk right on past.

There are good days too, though. Days when the marketplace in Siallagan pulses with the energy of hundreds of individuals: tourists from dozens of countries, vendors and wood-carvers, and mobs of others, all mingling in a spontaneous dance that murmurs with voices that cajole, entreat, exaggerate, refuse, offer, counteroffer, and very often burst into laughter. On the good days, when the boats from the mainland arrive so loaded with visitors that the benches in the hold, the white metal settees on the roof, and even the railings are bent with their weight, it seems as if *anything* (not just the replicas of traditional wood carvings, but also the tin coins, the plastic key chains, the fabric hats), *anything* will sell.

Such days were common ten years ago but are exceptional now. Although tourists still seem to flock to the area,[1] sales of carvings, fabrics, and trinkets have faltered, pressuring Toba Batak crafts- and salespeople to find ways to be more competitive. Some have tried to increase their sales by offering a wider selection of goods, adding clothes and leather bags to their stock, while others handle only the cheapest of wood carvings, lowering their prices in the hope that they can sell in quantity. For several months, as Partoho and Ito saw the profits from their rented stall in Siallagan dropping steadily, they thought that the lack of sales was due to the fact that there were too many sellers in the same place who were so desperate to sell their carvings they would accept any price, even a price that brought little profit. It was then that they decided to give up their stall, hoping that a more spacious shop on their own land in Huta Mungkap would have less direct competition and they could begin asking fair prices again.

Partoho designed his shop so that the two walls nearest the path to the lake and the tourist hotel could be dismantled completely, allowing the westerners who passed by to see everything clearly without feeling "trapped." He and Ito had big plans for their new *kios* and filled it up with fine carvings as quickly as possible. Partoho and his two oldest sons carved from early in the morning till late at night, making replicas of the traditional forms that travelers seemed to favor (such as the *tunggal panaluan,* and the *sahan*) as well as some more unusual forms (such as the *sigalegale* head and the bottle stopper). Partoho even decided to begin making an almost forgotten form called *pukkor unte,* the citrus fruit reamer used in the old days by *datu* for curing patients or making prognostications (figure 12). Most of the carvings in the shop are replicas of antique things, but other forms he simply makes up.

Partoho once told me that, as he sits quietly resting in the afternoon, he stares up into the dim recesses of the open ceiling, looking at the roof

FIGURE 12. *Partoho's replica of the* pukkor unte *with miniature version nearby*

beams, trying to make out the grain of the wood. It is then that he sees the images he will create the next day, objects that are part tradition and part innovation. These are forms only he sees: they are his "new ideas," his *cipta baru*. Because of his vast carving knowledge, he has no difficulty inventing new ideas, and he figures that selling them should be just as easy: since tourists can get these things only from him, there will be no rivals to contend with.

Yet there is a problem. His new shop is so open and exposed that it invites the scrutiny not only of passing tourists but of competing carvers. One day he told me in a resigned voice: "They come over to say hello when I'm sitting in the shop. They are on their way down to the lake to bathe—since I built my shop here, this part of the lake has become a *very* popular bathing spot for the carvers in town! They stop by to ask how my children are, but they are not looking at me—they are staring as hard as they can at my new ideas up on the shelves behind me . . . so they can steal them! One day, I am the only man making a thing, but give it a week and you'll find bad imitations in every shop in the village."

His words were true, if not prophetic, for within a week of the first appearance of the unusual *pukkor unte* form in his new shop, I saw imitations in the shops of Nalom and another neighbor. When I told Partoho what I had seen, he seemed to take it pretty well, shaking his head and emitting a long, soft sigh. He said, "They are so quick! How can I keep ahead of them?" I left him sanding carvings in the house, and as I passed his new shop on my way home, I happened to overhear a tourist saying with a sneer as he browsed with his friends, "Ugh, it's the same old stuff in every single shop! I don't think its real—it's all made for tourists." As the days passed, the high hopes for the new shop waned and Partoho and Ito grew worried.

One evening after dinner, when the floor had been swept and the hot sweet tea had been brought in, the words began to flow: Partoho and Ito began talking not about their imitative neighbors but about westerners. They grilled me, badgering me with questions they thought it natural that I (as a representative of the West) should have answers for: "What is it that westerners *really* want? Why do they look at each and every one of our carvings, then leave saying they will come back tomorrow? Why don't they ever come back? What are they *looking* for?"

How could I answer them? Even though I was talking with westerners practically every day, all I had found out was that there was no consensus among them. The more I talked with travelers, the more I realized how little I understood. Still, I tried to answer their questions. I ventured what I thought was a safe, even harmless, response. I told them that because tourists seem to come to Lake Toba to see a different culture, they should continue to make traditional things; but, because tourists often have limited money (a suggestion they scoffed at) and limited room in their bags, they might think about carving smaller things and making them useful. Partoho listened to my suggestion as the smoke of his *kretek* slightly veiled his face from me, saying he would give the topic more thought the next afternoon.

A day later I found Partoho and Ito in the yard behind the shop, their children arrayed around them, all hard at work either making, sanding, or polishing carvings. Partoho called me over to look at his latest *cipta baru*. "See," he said, showing me what the children were polishing, "necklaces for the tourists—just like you said: small, useful, and traditional!" He held out fifteen or twenty oblong figures, in a variety of sizes, carved of black water-buffalo horn and white antler. He called them a "new" form, but they looked very familiar to me, and in fact, it did not take long to realize that they were miniature *pukkor unte,* the shaman's citrus implement (figure 13).

FIGURE 13.
A miniature version of the pukkor unte

As it turned out, the neighboring carvers quickly caught on to Partoho's idea for pendants, making them smaller and more quickly, which undercut his price tremendously. His own brother-in-law was the most prolific, as his attention to craftsmanship was relaxed and he had three sons helping him churn the objects out. The neighbor across the street started making the pendants out of wood, a material much easier to carve and less expensive than horn or antler, and even sold some to a cousin up the street. Thus, within three days there were four shops in the village with ample supplies of the same new form, of which Partoho's were the most elaborate and expensive. And so it was; despite his vast knowledge of traditional forms, his knack for invention, his talent for elaborate craftsmanship, and now the spacious new shop, the sales of Partoho's carvings were sluggish at best.

Ito blamed herself for all this, saying that their lack of success was her fault because she could not speak English well. She told me about a vendor in Siallagan who was also the high school English teacher. Each day after school let out, he would stand in the path sanding or polishing carvings, striking up conversations with the Western tourists who happened to pass by. Jealous of his ability to sell so easily, she asked him what his secret was, perhaps hoping it was something besides his language abilities. He told her that when he meets a buyer who acts hesitant even after a friendly greeting, he will start telling the story of one of the objects on display near them—for example, how in the old days a king used his carved staff to hide entire villages from the Dutch invaders, or how a powerful sorcerer used it to make boulders fly hurtling across the island just to impress a rival. After this, he told her, the success of the sale is often certain.

Ito is not completely unfamiliar with foreign languages, for like most sellers in the markets and shops, she knows the words for numbers in several languages as well as some other phrases in English such as "You buy—magic," and "Good! Old Batak—*antik.*"[2] Nevertheless, she knew her few paltry words sounded very abrupt and got little response from westerners. She asked me to help her with longer sentences, saying, "They always come in here asking questions. I give them a price and there are still more questions! What can I say to them?"

Some evenings as we sat around on the mat, I practiced English with Ito and Partoho, saying (almost shouting), "THIS IS A MEDICINE HORN .... THIS IS A POWDER HORN .... THIS IS A KING'S STAFF...," but they would quickly forget how to make the cumbersome sounds, look-ing at each other, earnestly frowning and mumbling some kind of lop-sided gibberish until all of us gave up laughing. After several evenings' attempts, Partoho said, "Andru, as a teacher of English you are NO GOOD, NO GOOD! If you want to help us, how about just working in the shop for us?" I accepted the designation of failed teacher but declined the offer to work in the shop.

For a few weeks, business at the new shop was slow. Then things started to pick up a little. I came for my carving lesson around noon one day, and as I walked up to Partoho's workbench, all I could see was his back as he leaned closely over his vise. I peered over to see what he was carving and he said, "Another new idea! I finished one yesterday, and right away some Danish girls bought it!" He called his new carving *cankir mewah,* which means fancy cup (figure 14). It was easily the most intricate Batak carving I had seen made in the area, and I asked him about this. He said: "I wanted to make something no one could copy. These cups are too hard for anyone else to make." He told me it took him half a day just to carve the object's roundness since he had no lathe, and another half a day (or more) for his most talented son to execute the elaborate surface dec-orations. "It's a completely new idea—no one has seen anything like it," he told me.

He was mostly right, I guess, for it *was* new. But like many of the *cipta baru* I saw Partoho make, his fancy cup was, essentially, completely tra-ditional: it was based on the old-style footed plate and lidded container forms, was topped with the double-figure motif that is sometimes found on knife handles, and decorated overall with *gorga* variations.[3] To Partoho and Ito's great pleasure, the *cankir mewah* (no doubt because of its com-plexity) was not copied. It sold regularly and for a fair price.

This success seemed to heighten Partoho's energy for new ideas. After a few weeks, he told me he had yet another new idea, but this one was not a carving. He took me into the house and told me that he and Ito had come to the conclusion that their weak sales were due to the fact that they could not communicate well enough with tourists—they were asking my help to prepare handouts on my computer that would describe each of the traditional carvings. "Each carving will have a tag telling everything. That way we don't need to tell stories, we can just bargain!" I agreed to help them, and with a flourish Partoho instructed one of the children to bring me some paper and a pen, then dictated while I translated in my

FIGURE 14.
The cipta baru
called "cankir
mewah"

head and wrote the explanations and stories down in English. After narrating the information about the king's staff, the shaman's magic medicine horn, and the citrus implement, among others, he hesitated, realizing he had forgotten his *cankir mewah,* and prompted me to add this to the corpus. I protested a little, saying: "Wait a minute, is that one traditional? I thought you made that up yourself. What story could *that* have?" to which he replied, "Just write this down. Say: 'In the olden days, this was the cup from which the Batak kings drank their water . . .'" and he continued on, making up a story that he thought fit his *cipta baru.*

I used my computer to print the information sheet, four descriptions to a page, and gave them to Partoho. He locked the originals in his sky-blue *lemari* for safekeeping, telling me that he would photocopy them sometime in the future in the big town to the east, so none of the neighbors would know his business. In the meantime, however, I found that I was not off the hook, for Ito roped me into translating for her whenever possible.[4] I wandered by the shop one day and she waved me in frantically, whispering, "Andru! Andru! These two have been here for half an hour and they keep asking me things! Find out what they want! I think they want to buy something." The shoppers, a young couple from Holland, told me that they were very interested in the carvings in this shop but had no idea what these things *were.*

"So far," the young woman said, "she's told us everything in the store is 'magic,' but that's all we know." I showed them Partoho's most elegant *sahan*—a form that the Batak themselves consider to be exemplary of the elegance of their traditional art—and told them the story I had been told, that these elaborately carved horns once held potent herbs and leaves used to cure virulent illnesses. The young man scowled, pointing out the intricate *gorga* carving, and said, "That's exactly the stuff I *don't* like." Instead, he picked up a figure they were both particularly attracted to, a small, crouching human with its face buried in its hands carved in light-colored wood (figure 15).

I knew that Partoho had just invented this figure a week or two before, inspired by a popular Balinese carving of a balled-up Buddha. It was certainly not a "traditional" Batak form, so I turned to Ito and asked her what I was to tell them about it. "Uh . . . tell them it is called '*Orang Malu*' (I: Shy Man). Tell them that he is ashamed because he has no clothes on," she said. I translated this to them and I could see their interest increase. Ito was now chuckling with a bold look in her eye and (seem-

FIGURE 15.

The "Orang Malu"

ing to make an oblique reference to the overly casual dress of most westerners) added, "Tell them that the Batak people would have to hide their faces if they were like this man—naked."[5] I added this part to the story, and the young man said, "Okay, tell her we'd like it, but that we'd rather have a more primitive-looking one . . . you know, black."

I told Ito what they wanted and she responded with a frustrated frown, saying, "Ach! Wrong again. If we make them black, people want them pale—so we make them pale and now they need black. Which is it?!" I told her these two liked the "primitif" look. She waved me off, clearly annoyed, and shouted down to her husband, Partoho, to see if he could make one especially for them by tomorrow. He mumbled "okay" back, the price was agreed upon, and they promised to return. That evening, Ito told the family the story of the Orang Malu: how she had invented the story of the figure, and how the tourists believed her, promising to return and pay a good price.

The next morning, Ito waited hours for the couple to return, but they never did. She walked to their hotel, and the cook there said they had departed on the first boat, leaving behind the message for Ito that her prices were too high. When she got home, Partoho was almost done rubbing black shoe polish on the couple's carving. He listened to her story, then shrugged, saying as he began to shine the waxy finish: "It doesn't matter. It's one small carving . . . if they don't buy it, someone else will."

Business steadily improved for Partoho and Ito. As the days grew more balmy in the lowlands, the numbers of travelers coming up to cool air around Lake Toba increased. The hard work that Partoho and his sons had put into making carvings showed, for the shelves in the shop were now lined with a wonderful assortment of things: huge *sahans* with meticulous *gorga* designs swirling all over their surfaces, and small *pukkor unte* necklaces, tan *orang malu* as well as black ones. There were now as many faithful replicas of ancestral forms as there were *cipta baru*. Perhaps because of his ample stock, Partoho seemed to become slightly less frenetic in his work. After a few days spent out of town, I arrived late in the morning for my carving lesson and found that he had just started work, hammering his knife deftly into a large square plank of wood held tight by the vise. I wandered over and stood watching him for a moment and asked what he was making. He stayed quiet and kept working; I pretended not to snoop. Whatever it was he was making was at least twice as large as his largest medicine horn and had the shape of a trident—or maybe it was the shape of a *singasinga*.

Singasinga[6] is a purely Batak form made up of a humanoid face with a three-part upper head (plate 14) and is found in a number of contexts, both antique and modern. In the old days, I was once told, a masklike *singasinga* was placed directly above the entrance to a king's house in order to "make one respectful before entering." It is almost safe to say that the *singasinga* is a "ubiquitous" symbol for the Toba Bataks, for it is found on dozens of other objects, from powder horns to *sahans* to *hasapis* and king's staffs, as a kind of "good luck" image. I had never seen Partoho carve a *singasinga* house mask before, so while I sharpened the tip of my knife on the large gray-green whetstone at his feet I said, ". . . perhaps you are making a house mask?" He seemed ready to rest for a minute and made a triumphant face as he took the carving out of the vise.

Indeed, the carving had the outline of a *singasinga* house mask, but that was the end of the similarity. On the top of each lobe he had carved seated king figures with bowls on their heads. In the center of the main lobe he had roughed in a place for a another, but much smaller, *singa-singa* head. He told me he had been working on this new thing for two days. He was now ready to begin the intricate and time-consuming *gorga* designs. I looked the thing over, noticing that each lobe had a hole drilled down its center, and asked again, "So, is this a house mask?" He shot me a look both hurt and annoyed and took the carving back to look it over for imperfections. He responded to me as if I must be blind: "No, it's not a house mask! It's a brand *new* idea of mine. I'm making a table lamp to sell to the tourists! See," he said, indicating the holes drilled in the top, "this is where the bulbs will go. Its something people can *use*" (plate 15). My heart sank as I realized how literally he had taken what I said about the tourists' wants and needs.

For the whole day he carved the decorative *gorga* in focused oblivion, but stopped at one point to tell me that he wanted this piece, his proto-type that would garner him possibly fame and almost certainly ample money, to be as elegant as possible. This was now the third day he was devoting to the *singasinga* lamp. His shop already had plenty of carvings to sell, it's true, but this new lamp idea still represented a major invest-ment of time, energy, and materials. As a poor man, he was taking a dar-ing risk by devoting so much time to one unproved carving. Ito was standing by him as he worked and asked me what I thought of the lamp so far—would it sell? Then she answered her own question: "Well, it's really different—it's beautiful, and no one else has anything like it, that is *certain*. I don't know how to sell it, though. Who can buy it?" She twisted her lips in a funny smile and tweaked her husband's upper arm: "Who will we sell this to, eh? What tourist needs a Batak lamp?"

When I asked Partoho where he had gotten the idea for the lamp, he told me with very little explanation that he had "seen" such a shape on a westerner's table. He is not a man who gets out much, or visits the hotels that cater to Western tourists, so I suspected that he must have gotten the idea from one of his favorite imported television serials depicting wealthy westerners, *Santa Barbara*. I guessed that he felt this lamp was a faithful interpretation of a candelabra but had no conscious intention to evoke the form of the *singasinga* mask. At a later date, I again suggested to him that the mask and the lamp shared an uncanny formal similarity, but he just shook his head in denial.

After Ito had stained it red and covered it with brown shoe polish (which was shined to a high gloss), the lamp graced the top of their TV set for a month, so the family could admire it. After that, it went out to the shop. Months passed, and it was moved from the top shelf at the front of the shop to the middle shelf by the back door. Once in a while a tourist would look at it, wincing with what seemed to be utter incomprehension: "A wooden candelabra with small red and blue bulbs on top. How . . . *weird!*" The lamp was finally stored down on the floor, out of the way, and stayed there for over a year until I finally bought it and shipped it home.

DECIDING WHAT TO BUY

I stood at the edge of the marketplace marveling as a traveler scrutinized a vendor's collection of carvings. She seemed to be looking for something, but it was not clear what. Several minutes passed as she stood silently, seemingly oblivious to the vendor's patter and entreaties to buy. Suddenly she picked out a carving that appeared to be identical to the rest, asked and negotiated the price, then placed the newspaper-wrapped object in her knapsack. I shook my head, wondering, "Why that one?"

In conversations about the marketplace, Western tourists often stated that they were most afraid of being cheated—not simply bilked of their hard-earned money, but also duped into believing that the object they were holding in their hands was in fact traditional. The issue is not simply the fear of *losing* money, but also of *wasting* it—for the only thing worse than spending too much on something, according to those with whom I spoke, is spending too much for something that is "made for tourists." Because many travelers are passing through Sumatra, coming either from mainland South or Southeast Asia (India, Nepal, Malaysia, or Thailand, for instance), or from one of the other Indonesian islands (such as Java, Bali, or Sulawesi), and because Toba Batak vendors occasionally purchase various carvings offered by itinerant traders, if travelers have nothing in mind but a generalized notion of "Asian primitive art," they might buy a Balinese or Javanese carving in the marketplaces of Samosir Island thinking it is an example of local art. It is not surprising, then, that travelers commonly mention the souvenir marketplace as the place on their trip where they feel the greatest discomfort, for not only does it embody the stress of negotiations around money and object, but it also threatens to be a site where cultural authenticity is disjointed or corrupted.[7]

This is not to say that tourists avoid the souvenir marketplace. On the contrary, more than half the tourists I spoke with purchased some form of locally made handicraft from Samosir Island, although many had had no prior intent to buy. While some tourists are able simply to pass by the numerous souvenir stalls that line the streets leading to the tourist sights, most eventually succumb to a seller's friendly face or engaging patter, or are seduced by the profusion of objects hanging from rafters and crowding the tables.

In many parts of the world where westerners engage in cultural tourism, they have a clear (albeit possibly inaccurate) conception of what kind of art they *think* they will find to buy. That is, they have some idea of the "style" of the area they are visiting. "Style" here is defined as the amalgamation of a set of particular distinguishing features, and is like a touchstone for tourists when they are trying to discern to what extent an object is authentic or original: the object is mentally compared to a template of specific characteristics (that is, the culture's "style") to see how closely (or if) it corresponds. In North Sumatra, travelers are often stymied because their own conception of Toba Batak art "style" is not clear. Because of this, they must create their own conceptions of Toba Batak art style while in the field.[8] With no preconceived "master list" of form and design characteristics in mind, they are forced to guess which objects are most representative of local traditions, basing their decisions on preconceived notions of what a pretechnological, or "primitive," culture might produce. This is why magic staffs, shaman's medicine horns, and masks fit their notion of "traditional" works, while bongs, key chains, and salad forks do not.

What seems to happen in the souvenir marketplaces is this: a traveler selects an item, compares it to mental images of the most general category (in this case, what might be called Asian "primitive" or rural art), discerns if it is "authentic," "traditional," and "unique,"[9] and only then decides whether it meets other criteria such as size, color, and price. During their excursions, travelers continually refine this base "ideal type" construction into regional substyles by discerning what constitute the "typicalities" of the new examples they experience.[10]

But how is it that travelers refine the typicalities they know in order specifically to evaluate and select Toba Batak carvings? There are no locally produced books or pamphlets for tourists explaining the cultural significance (or in some cases nonsignificance) of Toba Batak wood carvings, and government tourist bureaus have not yet familiarized tourists with the forms available in the Lake Toba area.[11] For this reason, visitors unfamiliar with Batak art who wish to purchase "good" (that is, regionally representative) carvings depend on information expressed in one of three ways: published in tourist guidebooks, recounted by other tourists, or provided by the Batak salespeople.

Tourist guidebooks are often limited in scope when it comes to describing Toba Batak material culture, sometimes focusing only on the most dramatic artifacts (such as the shaman's bark books or the king's staff) and their connections to spirit worship and magic, regardless of the fact of the Toba Bataks' entrenched Christian affiliations.[12] Some westerners are more attentive to the advice given to them by their fellow travelers than to the information printed in the tourist guides. Often, while sitting around having refreshments at the end of the day in one of the numerous lakeside restaurants that cater to them, tourists will swap information about the meanings and prices of carvings. Some travelers are authoritative in presenting their views, but individuals looking for factual data about Toba Batak art forms in these encounters will probably be disappointed. Often, those sharing their thoughts may themselves be recent arrivals to the island, having acquired their knowledge in exactly the same restaurant only days before.

For some travelers, the company of other westerners seemingly more knowledgeable than themselves creates insecurity about their own ability to choose an exemplary object. I often saw such travelers walking hastily away from the marketplace, trying to hide what were quite obviously large carvings wrapped in newspaper. Once, while sitting with a group of travelers in a restaurant, we watched as a young man with a packet in hand walked quickly by. One of the travelers who knew him called him over. When asked to show his new purchase, he simply made a bald-faced denial of the purchase. Many such travelers seem to be shy to show their purchases because they are not sure their selections are "good," or "traditional." They appear to be fearful that someone in the group will criticize them or their taste, and thus will occasionally preempt the other's derision with a defensive move, saying the reason they bought an object was because "It's special and I like it."

Thus, because the guidebooks are limited in scope, and fellow tourists' "expertise" is often suspect, many Western tourists depend to a great extent on the tourate salespeople to help them understand something about the carvings' cultural contexts. Although there is usually a severe language barrier in these interactions, the vendors' contextualizing narratives are nevertheless regularly communicated. As was shown in the introductory stories above, the narratives can range from a few descriptive words illustrated by a great deal of gesturing to complex written translations that make use of the skills of passing anthropologists, and can vary wildly in their faithfulness to historical truth. As the stories also show, travelers often (though not always), depend on these narratives in order to verify the authenticity and value of the objects they purchase.

Western travelers may gain some idea of the meanings or cultural contexts of the carvings offered for sale but still hesitate in making a purchase. Most of the travelers I observed who were reluctant to buy carvings seemed to be unable to find exactly what they had in mind. Occasionally, this was because they had confused the Toba Bataks with some other Indonesian culture. For instance, an American woman learned what I was doing on the island and asked me if I could help her find "those fancy wooden puppets"; since she was not interested in seeing the life-sized *sigalegale* puppet on display in Tomok, I guessed (correctly, it turns out) that she was searching for the carved and elaborately painted *wayang golek* puppets from West Java. More commonly, travelers have some appreciation for the local style of wood carving but want something slightly different than what is offered to them in the marketplaces and *kios*.

For those expecting to see "primitive" Asian art, Toba Batak carvings may seem to be too formal, stylized, or refined. Many westerners who have never previously seen Toba Batak pre-Christian carvings usually assume that the florid *gorga* designs and symmetricality of the contemporary carvings displayed in Samosir Island's marketplaces have been "cleaned up" or "westernized" in order to satisfy their tastes—the preference of the Dutch couple for the black, or "primitive," *orang malu* in the incident related above is not at all unusual. For this reason, many travelers select those carvings that are the least ornamented, and sometimes those which, in the eyes of a carver such as Partoho, are of the crudest manufacture.

Nevertheless, it is also important to note that not all travelers share the precise "ideal-type" notion of what Toba Batak art should look like—if all westerners shared a taste for black, undecorated, and "primitive-looking" carvings, the job of Toba Batak carvers would be much simpler. Rather, there is a variety of traveler tastes that must be considered if a carver is to be economically successful. As noted, some travelers are aware of what antique Toba Batak carvings look like and so expect to find this tradition reproduced exactly. Others may be appreciative of the more elaborately carved objects but will avoid buying them because they are too large, too awkward, too heavy, or too expensive.

Still others (a minority) tend to select the most elaborated examples of a particular form. These individuals examine the spectrum of carvings offered in the marketplace and finally choose those which are the most extreme in their decorative elements, presumably because they represent the "fanciest" of the local forms. Travelers who select these carvings encourage Toba Batak carvers to make such things as *hasapi* lutes that are twice as large and wide as an ordinary one—and that are completely unplayable—and spirit dance masks that (counter to pre-Christian tradition) are decorated with *gorga* filagrees and two-tone coloring.

A great number of travelers will examine the entire stock of a stall or *kios* in their search for the appropriate object. Not finding it, they will leave silently. Apparently wishing to avoid the possibility of a high-pressure sale, they would rather vacate the shop rather than ask the vendor for the variation (smaller, lighter, etc.) for which they are searching. (Perhaps these are the shoppers whose habits so mystified Partoho and Ito.) There are some travelers, however, who indicate to the sellers, through words or charades, that they will purchase an object if it can be modified to suit their needs. While travelers are rarely on the island long enough for a special order to be completed, commissioned work does occur, sometimes inspiring a carver to incorporate the new form into his standard repertoire.

Travelers who seem to know what they want are an important link in the transformation of Toba Batak carvings, for they communicate a hint of an answer to the question that is on the minds of most carvers: What do westerners want? Through their queries, and even more through their purchases, travelers who request modified carvings indicate to carvers what they should continue making, what they should discontinue making, and what they should possibly make. This does not mean that transformations in Toba Batak carvings are completely consumer-driven.

Rather, it shows how consumer desires are revealed to the carvers. It is the carvers themselves who then must decide whether they choose to, or are able to, cater to the travelers' tastes. Some of the important transformations in Toba Batak carvings that can be directly identified with Western traveler preferences or requests are such things as miniaturized forms (such as Partoho's *pukkor unte* necklaces), and *tunggal panaluan* whose three socketed sections are measured to precisely fit in a backpack.

In these ways, Western travelers' preferences and purchase selections serve to change the character and form of Toba Batak so-called traditional carvings. Some of the changes might be inadvertent influences of the travelers (such as the partiality for black or unornamented forms), while others are made more intentionally (such as the preference for miniature or specially commissioned forms). Whatever the case might be, the effects of the travelers' tastes and desires are long-term, for the changes, whether minor adjustments to a form or design or novel proposals, soon become the foundation on which future innovations will be based.

CONFLATIONS: BRINGING THINGS TOGETHER

I watched with great curiosity as carvers re-created and invented forms.[13] Why did some things sell, and others not? Did they conceive of tradition and change in ways similar to Western travelers? I tried to put myself back in mind of how things are at home, where for many people the strength of "tradition" comes from the conviction that a set of beliefs is bounded and unchanging, and that it is transmitted from past individuals to present individuals directly and forever. Intellectually, however, I knew that the beliefs that make up "tradition," in actuality, are changed as they are transmitted, usually maintaining some connection with the past, but being modified to suit the needs of individuals in the present. Looking at the carvers making replicas of antiques and antique-like innovations, I finally concluded that if they share nothing else, Toba Batak and Western notions of tradition share similar disjunctions and complexities.

But what is really going on when traditions transform? One thing to consider in the context of cultural tourism is that changes can originate from inside the culture or from outside of it. And while it may seem natural to attribute outside influences to the pressures of a dominant on a subordinate group, this does not adequately explain the complexity of the interaction. Contemporary carvers are both freed from many of the cultural restrictions that constrained their ancestors at the same time as they are patronized by foreign buyers with differing desires and tastes. This means that changes can occur as a result either of the carvers' own artistic explorations or of their customers' preferences.[14]

The stories about innovations (the *cankir mewah,* the *orang malu,* the *pukkor unte* necklaces, and the *singasinga* lamp) concern just a few examples made by one man, yet they give a good indication of how interactions between Toba Batak carvers and Western travelers can change what is commonly referred to as traditional art.[15] It is difficult to discuss such a process of change theoretically, because the terminology used often betrays a condemning stance: a changing art style is sometimes described as somehow less pure, even inferior, to the traditional one.

Even talking about transforming art is difficult, because the words used to frame it are often inadequate.[16] Some have used the term "hybrid" to characterize transformations, but in regard to material culture, this term is insufficient: because it originates in the biological sciences, it carries with it metaphorical implications that can subtly, perhaps unconsciously, conjure up associations that may not be intended.[17] I think it is more fruitful to consider transforming arts such as the Toba Bataks' carvings as "conflations." *Conflation* comes from the Latin meaning "to blow together" and thus conjures up images like a street corner piled with dry leaves, paper cups, newspapers, string, and dust, all mixed together by the wind. For me, this image is an accurate metaphor for transforming art, more clearly evoking the haphazard and spontaneous joining of styles that portrays the character of creative synthesis that I observed. I prefer the term "conflation" for another reason: it specifies the agent of innovative creation as the artist—in this case the carver, the one blowing the elements together.

Tourate artists who create conflative carvings (such as Partoho making *cipta baru*)—objects that combine and reconstruct traditional forms in novel ways, sometimes with novel uses—are motivated, not only by the urge to edge out less inventive competitors in a tight souvenir market, but also by a desire to relieve the boredom of reproducing the same forms day after day. Most of the carvers I knew tried to balance their carving work with farming or fishing so they would not be stuck at home all day.

Partoho and Nalom were two of the most diligent carvers and rarely left their workshops for any but the most essential agricultural work. Partoho told me that when he became bored making the same limited number of items popular with tourists, he would try to think up *cipta baru*. Often, he would set himself a task that was deliberately difficult just to make it more interesting. That is one of the reasons why he made the *cankir mewah* so tall and cylindrical (to see if he could do it without a lathe), and why he invented the *singasinga* lamp (to see if he could figure out how to hollow out the arms of the object to connect the electrical wires inside).

We can look at the *singasinga* table lamp as an interesting case of the way in which traditional forms are conflated. Partoho, you will remember, protested when I suggested that his lamp looked like a *singasinga* house mask. Why would he do this? My guess is that he was committed to the idea that he was making something entirely new, something that departed dramatically from his ordinary work. When he himself saw the connection between the shape of his lamp and the mask, he seemed frustrated, as though he had suddenly realized that his vision of novelty was really still well within the canon of Toba Batak art style. Even so, I think it is important to see this unique piece as an example of how influences from outside as well as inside a culture can become "blown together," or conflated. The *singasinga* lamp is not just a conflation of traditional Toba Batak and Western art styles (that is, of Batak *gorga* decoration on a Western table lamp), but also a conflation of Batak tradition and Batak innovation (that is, *singasinga* mask as candelabrum). The *singasinga* lamp shows how a carver's creative urges interact with westerners' presumed purchase preferences to create change: if a westerner had bought the lamp as soon as he displayed it, Partoho might have been encouraged to make more. While it appears that Partoho might never again replicate the dramatic changes he incorporated in this piece, it seems probable that one or another of the incremental innovations he devised will appear in later conflated carvings.

Innovations can be risky. As Partoho quickly realized, he must display his *cipta baru* publicly in order to sell them. Because of this, he constantly fears losing his competitive edge to the less inventive carvers who see, then copy, his works. In Partoho's case, all the carvers who live in his end of the village (that is, those who use the path to the lake that crosses in front of his *kios*) have access to his new ideas. This means he will rarely have a monopoly on any of his own inventions. The one tactic a carver can use in order to safeguard his ideas is to keep them hidden. This is the strategy Partoho planned to use with regard to the bottle stopper he copied from the photograph sent to me by the Western collector.

Another risk that innovative carvers must address concerns their buyers, the Western travelers. Because a carver is usually uncertain what it is exactly that travelers need or desire, he may put his time, energy, and materials into a form that turns out to be unpopular. Toba Batak carvers themselves may see their innovations as minor fluctuations in the continuum of an ever-changing and improving (but still tradition-based) carving style; and in fact a few travelers might accept the *cipta baru* as being *both* "authentic" *and* "unique" since they seem to be inspired by antique objects and are made individually. The paradox of the situation, however, is that a far larger number of Western tourists seem to interpret the conflations (when they recognize them) as flawed imitations, or worse, cultural degradations. So, in order to prosper, the carver of innovations must be able either to create carvings that are attractive to the tastes of Western travelers, or they must compose contexts and narratives that validate the "authenticity" of their *cipta baru.* Despite what seems like an impossible situation for carvers, innovations continue to be produced *and* continue to be purchased. How is this possible?

Well, like the interactions between travelers and tourate described in Chapter 6, the production of contemporary Toba Batak carvings is greatly affected by the context of cultural tourism, for changes are sanctioned, if not encouraged, by the explorations of possible behaviors that are the hallmark of the utopic space. Thus, it seems that Toba Batak carvers internalize outside influences to the extent that objects being produced are perceived (both by Toba Bataks and Western travelers) as being culturally "possible."[18] The innovations I am referring to as conflations are primarily made possible because the negotiations occur in the touristic spaces where both parties (but in particular the Toba Batak carvers as producers of the objects) can explore what the boundaries and possibilities of that art style might be. Despite the fact that Western travelers and Toba Batak carvers rarely share a language in which they are both fluent, the process of buying and selling constitutes a negotiation that goes well beyond mere price: it is a process in which that thing called "Toba Batak art" is itself being dynamically restructured. What this means is that the

seemingly static categories "tradition" and "authenticity" are actually flex-
ible, and that daydreams, consumer desires, conflations, and creative narratives are what determine their definitions.

BUYING AND SELLING IN THE UTOPIC SPACE

Toba Batak vendors and carvers are keenly aware that they must do
more than sell their carvings cheaply; they know they must also find ways
to actively engage with Western tourists' desire for cultural authenticity
and "specialness" if they are to sell to them. It is no secret to the Toba
Batak tourate that about half the number of Western visitors who come
to Samosir Island do so simply to sit around relaxing, and nothing else.
This means that only half of those arriving in the area are potential buyers. Furthermore, although Batak sellers try to maximize their profits,
they are also fully aware that competition for the tourists' money is not
limited to Samosir Island's marketplaces, but includes all of the other
sales arenas in Indonesia and Southeast Asia that are frequented by Western tourists during their travels.

I do not mean to imply that rural Toba Batak wood-carvers and sellers
are such consummate marketers that they are aware of all the variables
and vagaries that determine how Western tourists select and purchase
touristic objects. What I do want to highlight here is that, after more
than two decades of selling to visitors, the Toba Batak vendors know that
the travelers' interest in (and eventual purchase of) carvings hinges at
least as much on their perception that the carvings have strong ties to
Batak culture as on their price. It is for this reason, then, that all sellers,
even those with limited English, seem to know and regularly use the English words that indicate culture (such as "tradition," "magic," "old," and
"antique"), as well as words that indicate cost (such as "cheap" or "good
price").

Considering that the travelers I am discussing here are usually on shoestring budgets, it might seem counterintuitive for me to state that their
need to hear a cultural or historical context is at least as important as price
(if not more so) when they are considering the purchase of a Batak carving. Yet my observations show that this is in fact the case. Why? I suggest that the answer is threefold. First, travelers are rarely so strapped for
cash that they must bargain for carvings in earnest: if the starting price

for an object they are interested in is not outrageous, they will bargain furiously and at length—yet in the end they hardly ever save themselves more than a dollar or so.

Second, my conversations with Western travelers indicate that they often purchase an object because they feel they have developed some brief but personal bond with a particular salesperson. In a context such as the marketplace of touristic objects, where hundreds of stalls offer essentially the same stock at the same price, it is understandable why a tourist's decision might be influenced by the interaction with the seller. The brief bond that is formed appears to arise from a combination of factors such as personal compatibility and friendly gestures, but it also includes efforts by the seller to convey descriptive information about the object. In the above stories, Ito and Partoho's narratives, in conjunction with pleasant and friendly demeanors, particularize the event of the purchase, distinguishing them as individuals and contributing to an exchange that seems heartfelt rather than impersonal.[19]

Third, a carving's story legitimates the object's existence in the specific social setting for the tourist.[20] As has been noted, Western travelers are usually traveling from spot to spot, country to country, ordinarily not knowing much about the cultural group they are visiting prior to arrival. By the time they set foot on Samosir Island, most have, no doubt, seen thousands of Southeast Asian touristic objects, many of which may seem identical to those displayed in overwhelming numbers in the marketplace at Siallagan. If a touristic object is to serve as an effective icon of place, as a proof of travels made, it is only when it is believed by a buyer to have local *meaning* that it can rise above the rest and achieve some level of cultural specificity. That local meaning, of course, is provided in part by the salesperson's contextualizing story.[21]

So, now one might ask if the brief narratives told by tourate vendors in order to situate their carvings historically or culturally are simply a marketing ploy. Despite the fact that Toba Bataks converted to Christianity in the early part of the century, and despite the fact that they are currently modernizing as quickly as any other group in Indonesia, they maintain passionate bonds to the ways of their ancestors. Though it is true that carvers continue to produce carvings based on traditional forms and designs specifically for sale to tourists, one should not assume that their personal connection to this material culture is somehow lacking. Many carvers told me that tourism single-handedly revived the dying art of wood carving in the area, and simply shook their heads to think what their culture might have been like if such a thing had not happened.

The Toba Bataks, both rural and urban, are extremely proud of their carving traditions. Every child knows the names of and the meanings behind the basic traditional forms, even though they no longer come in contact with them in their daily activities, and most adults can point out and name the parts of the elaborate traditional houses, indicating with equal ease those sections that represent the areas of finest craftsmanship.

This active engagement with the traditions of wood carving by the Toba Bataks on Samosir Island leads me to believe that the narratives told, or attempted to be told, about carvings in the marketplace are not *simply* meant to manipulate westerners to buy. They are also a way for Toba Bataks to reaffirm their own connectedness to their culture at a time in their history when the pressures of "national" identity are stressing their cultural identity, and when influences from the West seem to be supplanting customs and mores passed down from the ancestors. Narratives such as Partoho's about the ancient Toba Batak kings' elaborate drinking vessels may serve to bolster cultural pride, and those similar to Ito's extemporaneous tale about the "shy man" may serve to underline local moral values. In both cases, the stories are at least as important in conveying information to outsiders as they are in reinforcing a Toba Batak individual's bonds to cultural traditions.[22] That there is a great deal of latitude in how the stories are formed and the facts upon which they are based is, I think, more a factor of their being told in the context of a utopic space, where explorations of creative refashioning are made possible, than of their being manipulations conjured up in order to deceive Western buyers.

This section would be incomplete if I were to ignore or trivialize my own place in the interactions between Western travelers and Toba Batak carvers and vendors. I was only occasionally a direct participant in the encounters between the two parties, and so hesitate to refer to the part I played in influencing either of them as "mediator." Instead, my place in the utopic space was usually characterized by actions that tottered somewhere between confused reticence and high-minded altruism. Never, in the fifteen months I spent on Samosir Island, did I feel that I had a stable position in the diverse playful actings-out of which I was continually finding myself a part. Sometimes I was a spy-like informer to the Toba Batak carvers, trying to translate the behaviors of travelers (whose thinking was so varied and unfathomable that I could find only filaments of a thread to bind them together) into a language and a culture with conceptual categories that did not seem to fit them. At other times, I found myself trying to give to westerners what little fragmented information I possessed about an alien culture in such a way that simultaneously attempted to inform them, to intrigue them, and to break the news to them ever so gently that the object they just bought referred, not to a culture whose value and importance was welded to a "primitiveness" they imagined existed, but to one that was emerging and transforming, due, in part, to their own appearance on the island.

As I have tried to indicate, I was rarely able to observe interactions from the margins, for I was regularly being drawn into the explorative acts either by the language-frustrated Toba Bataks, by the underinformed travelers, or by my own curiosity. The part I played in the interactions may have long-term ramifications or may be inconsequential, I do not know. Nevertheless, I was involved in the encounters I describe between Toba Bataks and Western travelers—watching, interrupting, translating, guessing, suggesting, and explaining—and in general being a part of the changes, incremental and dramatic, that transpired in that particular place in time. The interactions I was part of were rarely straightforward and understandable, and the parts people played—the possible selves they enacted in the utopic space—were rarely fully planned, much less completely understood. Rather, these events spontaneously unfolded and to a certain extent were improvisational and playful, characteristics that are exemplified in the following story.

THE *TUNGGAL PANALUAN* FROM THE *"NENEK MOYANG"*

Partoho was crouching next to me in his new *kios*. He said, "O-oo, you better get up off the floor or you'll get rheumatism." He pointed down to where his bare feet had just been and I saw damp oblongs. "The concrete has finished drying," he said, "but the water seeps up where it's warm . . . where there is skin." I got up and felt my hips creak, stiff and jagged. He made a joke about how large the damp spot was, to which I jabbed right back, "It's because I am so hot from all the work you make me do. . . . Work with no pay!" Partoho heaved a sigh and Ito pinched me hard on the tender upper inner side of my arm, laughing and saying, "Ach! Partoho can never win can he? You *always* have to win! *Always* have to win!"

She meant that I had had the last word again. Partoho and Ito and I often sat in a threesome, each thinking up new ways to weave a verbal trap for the other two—something that could not be ignored, something randy, or lunatic, or on that edge of teasing which is furthest away from insulting—to which the others would have to respond to save face. We were never mean, and the feelings of the other were almost always spared: if one of us could not think up something fast enough and the moment was about to be lost, it was practically essential that the instigator think up something self-deprecating to rescue the other's fragile ego from a black hit.

I was helping Partoho with the sign for his new *kios*. He had finished the little building a week ago, and the day before we had had the "Grand Opening," which consisted of the three of us and the kids sitting inside, making damp spots and eating toasted peanuts-in-the-shell. Partoho was not at all confident about his lettering abilities and insisted that I be responsible for the lettering of the *kios* sign. I tried to get out of it by saying how busy I was with my research, but he sniped right back: "Oh, you always *say* you are so busy with doing research—what is it, this research of yours? Batak carvers, right? Well, here you are: I am a Batak carver, so you can paint the letters on my new sign, and call it a gift to me. Then you can write all about it in your computer and call it 'research.' Okay?"

I finished the sign (both sides) in English, which Partoho thought made it look especially "refined," and stretched my legs. Yeah, sure, it looked fine. It looked nicer than any other sign in town because Partoho had put *gorga* carving all over it. It was just red, white, and black. Very refined, and very *traditional.* Several of the neighbors found reasons to go down to the lake, to search for fallen *kemiri* nuts in the farthest reaches of their overgrown yards, or to carry some vitally important message to a relative living within eyeshot of the new shop. "Ahhh," one would say with a really nice smile, "that is so *beautiful*, Pak Guru! Wow. Really nice. . . . Hey, I'm making a new sign too. How about helping?" I steadfastly declined them all, saying first, "I am incredibly busy with my research," and second, "Partoho has paid me for the sign by teaching me to carve." That deflated them fast, and they wandered off muttering a polite, "Well, perhaps another time. . . ."

Partoho and I were sitting in his front yard, he perched on a rock that was peaked like a mountain, and I on the disk of log Ito used to split fire-wood. I, at least, was very comfortable. It was a pale lavender dusk. It was the time of day when voices carried very far and the lake breezes slapped up whitecaps. The air between things was so pure and invisible that distances seemed compressed. Partoho and I were sitting in the yard mumbling end-of-the-day pleasantries to each other, smoking cigarettes. Perhaps we were wondering if the *kios* would be a success, if it would be sold out tomorrow, giving Partoho so much money he could buy a motorcycle to rent to the tourists and then *really* become successful—successful enough to send all the kids to college. I was tapping a large *kemiri* leaf on my calf in an idle, brainless way. Partoho stubbed out his *kretek* and happened to look up—through and past the shop's open walls—to see his teenaged nephew Budri, son of Nalom, walking on the path with his eyes downcast. He seemed to be trying to move past us unseen. Tucked under his arm was something very long, wrapped up in fabric. Partoho and I shifted our eyes to each other and seemed to share the same thought: this is very suspicious!

Partoho smiled and called out to Budri, saying, "Where are you going? What have you got there?" Budri tried to bypass the interrogation as he could tell by his uncle's smile that he was going to be teased. Budri replied, "I'm going home . . . have to return this . . ." and started to move off. "Hey!" I said, "not so quick there. What's the hurry?" I entered into this situation as it looked so positively ripe for investigation. I went over to where he was standing with the veiled object and pulled a loose edge of the fabric to the side for a peek. "Wow! What's *this?*" I asked in my sweetest voice. "Look, Pak," I said to Partoho, "it's a carving—it's a *tung-gal panaluan.* Hey, Budri, what happened to it? What's all this stuff on it? Looks like you dropped it in the rice fields!" Budri stopped looking so hangdog and got a laughing sparkle in his eye, saying, "It's a carving we were trying to sell to the big collector from California. He told everyone he's looking for antiques, so we brought this out for him."

With a frown of respect, Partoho reached over to pull the fabric back farther, exposing the carving's filthy surface more fully. He said to me in a grave voice, "This is Very Old. This is an heirloom from the *nenek moyang* (I: ancestors).[23] There's only one left in the village like this"—and then he could hold his serious face no longer. He began laughing, and Budri, blushing and smiling, hid the carving in its shroud again and disengaged himself to hurry home. The dirt on the stick didn't fool me for one second, nor did the act Partoho put on to convince me that the thing was antique. In the few minutes the carving had been disrobed I had seen the unmistakable carving style of Budri's father, Nalom. I also saw the dirt and glue he had hastily put on the carving that, although almost imitating the surface of a Batak antique, could not mask the gaps between the jointed sections of this *tunggal panaluan.*

Partoho and I went into the house chuckling that Nalom would attempt such a halfhearted fake. We sat down on the mat where the children were watching a Japanese robot cartoon on TV and drank our hot sugar tea with Ito. She had watched the whole incident from the doorway and now wanted to hear the details of the story—sound effects, imitations, and all. Partoho knew the story from the beginning, so he started it:

> You know that Sulean has been showing around that big important collector from California all week long, right? Yeah, well, that guy wants to buy antiques—*only* antiques—and he has a *lot* of money to buy things . . . like I said, he's an American. Well, Sulean knows there's nothing for sale around here, but the guy is paying him to help, so he agreed to help. There's just nothing to buy, though—its all been gone for years, you know? First the Dutch came, and our grandparents sold their things, then the tourists came, and people still sold their things—*Bah!*—they even sold other people's things, things they stole. So, now there's nothing left. Well, there are things left, but nobody would want to own them—you know, things too dangerous, too potent and uncontrollable to own unless you know what to do with them.
>
> So, Nalom called Sulean over and hatched a plan. He said, "I'll bet he will buy one of my carvings. What is he looking for?" And Sulean told him he wanted a king's staff, a *tunggal panaluan.* Nalom says, "Okay. Fine. I have a nice *tunggal panaluan* to sell, so just tell him to go to Grandfather Duma's house tomorrow night and we will get millions of rupiah out of him. Millions! We will split it between us: you, me, and Grandfather Duma."

Ito asked why the transaction had to be at Grandfather Duma's house. Partoho looked at her with a mock weary face, a face full of annoyance that she could be so clueless as to their intentions. (She knew perfectly well why they had chosen this backdrop for their plan, but wanted to make sure it was part of Partoho's story.) He said: "Of course, everyone knows why they would want it to happen at Grandfather Duma's! It's this: Grandfather Duma has the biggest, oldest, most beautiful traditional house in town. Also, Grandfather Duma is the oldest man in town. Old, old men who live in old traditional houses, well . . . of *course* they have antiques!" He chuckled again now, and winced and raised his shoulder in defense against Ito's hard slap on the shoulder for telling such a lie. He went on:

> They took this carving to Grandfather Duma, and you should have seen his face. He was obviously disappointed to have to try to sell this thing to a big important collector. He said, "This is supposed to be from my ancestors? I don't think *my* ancestors would have had anything that looked like this!" Grandfather Duma thought the deal would not work because the carving wasn't very good and, in fact, the glue was still damp. But Nalom and Sulean convinced him that they could do it if it was nighttime, if the windows were closed, if he brought the thing down out of the attic wrapped in an old dusty cloth, if he refused to part with it for any amount of money, and so on. So Grandfather Duma said yes, he would do it. He would pretend not to speak much Indonesian and Sulean would translate for him.
>
> Well, it was still light out, right? You can see that it was not even really dark yet and *still* they took the American over there! "Why are the shutters on the windows closed?" asks the American collector. He gets no answer, so he just sits there listening to some story Sulean is telling about how the old man has the only *tunggal panaluan* left on the island. Finally, the old man creeps up the ladder to the attic and brings down the carving in a cloth—very dusty, very old. He brushes the spiderwebs off it. He leans over and says in a very creaky voice, "This is the last heirloom from the *nenek moyang,* and I won't sell it for any price, but I will let you look at it . . . are the shutters closed?"

Partoho now imitated Grandfather Duma (who really is hunched over and walks with a stick), exaggerating his aged, limping gait and holding the cloth-covered carving in tired, outstretched arms as if the thing were so old and heavy that he could barely manage to carry it. Partoho evoked such an outburst of laughter from us that he decided to do it again: "Oh-hhhh, this is very old. This is an *antique.* A real heirloom and very old. It is direct from my *nenek moyang,* and, oh *my* it is so very, very old, I could never *ever* sell it to anyone, not even a collector from California. . . ." We found this even funnier, and each of us, being the hams that we are, decided to try out this new act, to see if we could outdo Partoho. Ito did it with a limp head, looking up at us with one eye like a mournful beggar and added the line, "people have tried to buy this, they have offered millions, but I can't let it go, it is from the *Nenek Moyang!*" I did it too, and got a raucous round of laughter simply because it was so absurd that I should be trying to say I have a Batak king's staff from *my* ancestors. We finally stopped playing around to hear the rest of the story, asking, "So? Well? What happened then?" Partoho went on:

> The American wasn't fooled for one minute. He's clever and Sulean should have known this. He took one look at the thing and could see the dirt was too new, too rough, and said to Grandfather Duma, "O yes, Sir, this is indeed a beautiful old heirloom. See the workmanship! Feel its weight! But I cannot take such a valuable thing from you. This is something that must stay here. I know that no matter how much money I could offer you, you would not sell it, so I won't even begin to bargain. Thank you so much for showing your ancient heirloom from the ancestors to me. And now, I must be off! Please excuse me." And he left! And that was it. Sulean tried to hold him back, saying, "If you really want it you might be able to offer him something . . ." but the guy just said, "I could never take such an amazing thing away from the old man!" Imagine how dimwitted they are trying this trick! *Ha!* ha ha! Whose trick is it now?

Partoho chuckled, and we all clucked and nodded in admiration at how the story had ended. Ito said, "That American was smart. He could see the carving was new even with the shutters closed." Partoho added: "It was very stupid of Nalom to try to sell that thing so close to his own shop. Maybe if Sulean had taken him to a house really isolated, really far away, maybe then it would have worked. But that American, that collector, could tell, couldn't he? He could see that there was nothing left in this town—why would there be anything antique still here? We are so close to Tuk-Tuk and all the tourists—things have been sold and gone for years! Nalom was stupid to have used Grandfather Duma's house." He looked over at me with a sharp, happy twinkle in his eye and said, "Next time you see Nalom you should ask him if he has any old heirlooms. Ask him, 'Do you have any antiques to sell me?' Tell him, 'I hear you have a special deal for Americans!' He'll think you're really funny. Try it." I had no intention of "trying it," and, caught off balance, I failed to conjure up a response and lost the moment. So Partoho won this one.

What I hope the stories told in this chapter show is that, if a carver is to be financially successful in the marketplace of touristic objects, he must try to outmaneuver his competitors in satisfying tourists' preferences. For some carvers this means replicating ancestral forms by the dozen; for some, it means producing objects that are more unique. Other carvers, like Partoho, put their energies into inventing *cipta baru,* hoping for the right combination of form and design—an innovation that tourists will buy yet rivals won't steal. Western tourists on Samosir Island who evaluate, select, and purchase Toba Batak wood carvings do so according to a set of generalized preconceptions, which they then refine and specify using information from guidebooks, other tourists, and Batak salespeople. The notion of an ideal type for "primitive" Asian art, however, is not a static image, but rather a conception whose possible boundaries are in flux, constantly emerging and fading as the tourist makes refinements based on specific new forms of knowledge, such as stories that promise "cultural legitimacy."

This much seems clear: the category "Toba Batak art" does not constitute a static and authoritative text. Rather, if that term means anything at all, it describes a dynamic process consisting of the shuffling of creative narratives and material desires that occurs with particular intensity in the marketplace of touristic objects. Neither Toba Bataks nor Western travelers (nor, for that matter, historians, museum professionals, or visiting anthropologists) have the ability to construct a notion of "Toba Batak art" by themselves, for, clearly, the marketplace is an arena where assumptions, expectations, and "facts" can be contested and manipulated—a venue where the meanings of "real" and "new" are continuously negotiated, fluctuating, like price, according to the bartering skills of the participants.

Tourists state that they are seeking "traditional" or "authentic" Toba Batak carvings, often avoiding (if they are able) those objects they claim are "just made for tourists." What the stories here presented show is that marking boundaries—between what is traditional and what is innovative, between what is authentic and what is touristy, and between what constitutes change and what exhibits continuity—is not a definitive act. Those tourists who apparently assume that what is "traditional" and what is "authentic" are coterminous, and who further assume that what is "authentic" is also "unique," find their expectations confounded by the Toba Bataks. The point is not whether, for example, the Dutch couple ended up buying their ideal "primitive" object or not, for, as Partoho said, "If they don't buy it, *someone* will." The more interesting point, I think, is that the creation they commissioned and then abandoned will be seen, judged, and accepted by some future Western tourist, and will affect *his* or *her* conception of what the local art looks like. Neither Western value judgments nor artistic legacies from the ancestors can construct inalienable borders for what constitutes "Toba Batak art," for the most "traditional" carvings are often those made specifically for tourists, and the most "authentic" ones are often the most innovative.

Conclusion: Someplace in Between

In Huta Mungkap, almost everyone is trying to find a way to tap into the tourism economy. Not everyone has the ability to make wood carvings to sell, so some open up restaurants, *kedai,* bicycle rental shops, or paperback book exchanges. Sulean decided that he would put his efforts into guiding travelers around Samosir Island on his motorcycle. Because his vehicle was constantly in need of repair, and because he depended on word-of-mouth recommendations, Sulean soon discovered that the financial rewards from his enterprise were undependable. He came to me one day and asked for a small loan to pay for supplies for a new venture. "I was always good in the art classes in high school," he told me, "so I think I can make some money making paintings of the island." I asked him if he thought he could compete with the trained artists who sell the large oil-paint landscapes in Parapat, and he answered that he was confident he could. "Westerners don't usually buy those paintings," I reminded him, to which he responded that he would be making very small paintings that could fit in a backpack. I hesitated a moment and then asked him why he thought westerners came to the island—what it was they really wanted to see. "They like the nature, but they also want to see how people live," he said. I suggested that he paint views of Toba Batak life instead of landscapes—for then he would have no competition —then lent him a modest amount of money for the paints and canvas.

Sulean came to my house a few days later, smiling and concealing a paper folder. "I know I can't pay you the money back, Pak Guru, so I want to give you my first four paintings as a trade," he said. One of the small paintings was an imaginary seascape with a foamy green ocean, orange hills, and pink trees. Another depicted a pair of pale-tan animals standing in a field of blue; and the third was a view of a Batak mother nursing her child. The fourth painting was an image of a young woman in some kind of office (plate 16). The first three paintings delighted me with their honest naiveté, and I said I thought he would easily sell these to westerners wanting an unusual souvenir of their visit to Samosir. I picked up the fourth one again and said, "I don't understand this last one, Sulean. I thought you were going to make scenes of Toba Batak life. What is going on in this one?" He replied: "Pak Guru, that one *is* a picture of Toba Batak life! See, it's a young woman who has gone off to the city to find money to send back to her parents, and all she can do is think about the homeland. See, she has all these things to read but still she stops to think of Samosir."

Years before, Sulean's mother had saved up enough money to send him to a small college in Java. She had great hopes that her only son would be a success in the business world and that he would amass enough money to help provide for his extended family in the future. Sulean only lasted a few months in Java before using what was left of his money to buy a bus ticket for the long journey home. "When she saw me coming up the road, I think she was really disappointed . . . but she understood that I can't live out there. I have to live on Samosir." Now, looking at his painting of a Toba Batak woman crushed in on all sides by a confining office, and pressured by the unrelenting grid of florescent lighting and neat stacks of papers and books, I gained an inkling into Sulean's view of what it was like to search for a career outside of the homeland. The imagery in his painting is symbolic of the unhappy condition many rural Toba Bataks find themselves in when they try to live in the city. Trapped by a stark worktable loaded with paperwork, the central figure in the painting takes a wistful moment to ponder her current situation: she is flanked by two lush landscapes of Lake Toba that seem to beckon her away, but she is monitored by the picture of a faceless human being that looms behind her. Perhaps her daydreams will continue to be nurtured by the landscapes that bracket her room, or perhaps she, like Sulean, will make use of the partially open door behind her.

Sulean's painting project didn't last very long. He made a few more paintings and hung them on the wall of his mother's *kedai,* but only one or two ever sold. He became discouraged by this, and put his energies and money back into his guiding activities. Eventually, he discovered that he could make a decent living by ferrying travelers to places where "magic" mushrooms and other such substances could be obtained. I talked with him one day shortly before I was to return home, and asked about the paintings—would he continue to make his images on the side? "Pak Guru," he said, "the tourists don't seem to be interested in my pictures. I think if they have money, they want to spend it on the *antik* carvings and fabrics, not on paintings of Toba Bataks." Maybe I was wrong to think that Western travelers would want a Toba Batak's view of contemporary rural life as an appropriate remembrance of their time on Samosir, or maybe Sulean's work did not suit their tastes in painting, it is not clear. There is no arguing with Sulean, however, on his statement about Western tourist preferences: wood carvings in the style of the ancestors sell well, while paintings that depict the area do not.

This story of Sulean's painting raises many of the issues discussed in this book: constructions and representations of identity that arise in the context of cultural tourism, Toba Bataks' love of the homeland, spaces of intercultural interaction, and Western travelers' notions of the value of traditional art.

It has been shown here that for centuries westerners have constructed an identity for "the Toba Bataks" based on assumptions of pre-Christian cannibalism and animism, and that this enduring image (rather than that of the modernizing Toba Batak, as depicted in Sulean's painting) continues to beckon contemporary travelers looking for "original" "primitives." Many westerners continue to think of Sumatra as being one of the places that epitomizes the designation "exotic corner of the world." For tourists attracted to places and cultures that seem to exist beyond the global rush, Lake Toba and Samosir Island, at the center of North Sumatra's interior, hold great promise. The dream of a pristine environment and an untouched Toba Batak culture draw travelers to interior areas, first from the mainland to Samosir Island, and then from the island's tourist center to its mountainous center. Despite the intense treks ever more interior, however, the "original" "primitives" are not to be found.

Samosir Island, like many sites of tourist interest around the world, is a place that is valued by both locals and visitors, and because of this is a place whose meanings and value are continually being negotiated. For Toba Bataks, the island is primarily the homeland center, and for westerners, it is primarily a center of tourism, yet the two parties have found ways to share it. As shown, Western visitors do not overwhelm the local populace throughout the island; rather, they spend most of their time in the tourist center, where their needs are catered to at the same time as they are provided with glimpses of contemporary Toba Batak life. These glimpses provide travelers with information (added to what they may have heard or read previously) that they put to use in constructing identities for the other. At the same time, the Toba Bataks who live in the tourist center and come in contact with the travelers on a regular basis (the tourate) are active in inventing notions of who they think westerners are. The tourist center of Samosir Island, because it is a kind of territory that is shared by locals and visitors, is not just an idealized homeland such as that longed for by the figure in Sulean's painting, but also a venue for interactions that are often characterized by exuberant explorations of the limits and rules of behavior.

One of the places that best exemplifies these explorations of behavior is the souvenir marketplace. For the tourate, it is a context not so close to their interior and private spaces that they feel invaded, and for the travelers it is far enough away from their Western-style hotel rooms that it still feels, in some way, "exotic." Because the marketplace is an intermediate area between the cultural worlds of westerners and Toba Bataks, it is a space where the two groups can explore possible behaviors and selves that are neither fully constrained by their respective cultures' values nor completely freed from their emotional and material needs (although it must be noted that the Toba Bataks, because they are at the center of their homeland, are usually more tentative in their explorations). In short, the marketplace is a neutral site—specifically of negotiation rather than contestation—a space where traveler and tourate can test behaviors that exist in the gap between their personal desires and their respective cultures' dominant ideologies.

Following Louis Marin, I have suggested that the souvenir marketplace is a "utopic" space, a stagelike site where both traveler and tourate can discover aspects of their identities by exploring the boundaries between the reality they know and the desires they feel. The explorations are made explicit through narratives or story tellings. The narratives erupt on the spot, often shifting between pure invention (outright lies) and explanations (reaffirmations), but are not necessarily pre-scripted: improvisation is paramount. That these marketplaces are referred to here as utopic does not imply that they are ideal, trouble-free spaces of intercultural interaction. As I have shown throughout this book, engagements between Western travelers and Toba Bataks in the marketplaces are fraught with misunderstandings, tensions, and frustrations, as both parties attempt to clarify or dispel previous assumptions about their identities while maximizing their own material gains.

It has been shown here that the tradition of wood carving was nearly extinguished throughout the Batak homeland when great social changes occurred, and that tourism almost single-handedly has kept the art form vital. Western interest in the Toba Bataks' wood carvings is not new, of course: these objects have fascinated, horrified, and attracted collectors for a century or more. Nowadays, however, travelers see the wood carvings, not just as souvenirs to memorialize their trip abroad, but also as investments in "art" whose "authenticity" is of critical importance. That no one group can truly verify what "authenticity" means simply underscores the fact that this value, like so much else in the touristic context, is unendingly negotiable. Western travelers, because of their relative economic freedom and their ability to buy from whomever they wish, seem to have the upper hand when buying wood carvings from Toba Batak carvers and vendors. Nevertheless, it has been shown that carvers and vendors are able to maintain some control over the bargaining interactions by creating inventive narratives with which they promote their wares and innovative carvings made in the traditional style to satisfy Western tastes for the unique and the traditional.

What all of this indicates is that the vitality of the Toba Bataks' wood-carving tradition cannot be separated from the interpersonal interactions that occur in their marketplaces. If wood carvings made on Samosir Island are said to be of a particular "style," it is a style whose changes are the result of a constant interplay between outsider preferences and local creativity. The innovations and manipulations that carvers seem willing to execute on behalf of Western tourists, and that may appear to ignore the styles and forms of the ancestors, perhaps can be better understood as manifestations of an art tradition that is vibrant and transforming. Rather than regarding such changes as cultural degradations, as many collectors and Toba Batak traditionalists do, it may be closer to the truth to see them as indicating a culture that is resilient enough to incorporate innovations with no threat to its integrity.

NOTES

INTRODUCTION

1. *Pak* is the common Indonesian term of address for adult men; it is short for *bapak,* meaning father.

2. Ranier Carle's book *Opera Batak: Wandertheater am Nord Sumatra* (1990) reflects a formal example of the Toba Bataks' predilection toward humor and comedy. However, the humor of their everyday conversation has not, to my knowledge, been discussed by researchers, and indeed does not seem to be an aspect of communication that is celebrated by local spokespeople.

3. Pierre Bourdieu, in his book *Distinction* (1984), focused on similar issues as they are played out in French culture. One of his primary interests is the notion of "taste," which he says is often developed through formal education. In this book, I am interested in the ways that individuals, both Toba Bataks and Western tourists, use a variety of their experiences (that is, not just formal educational experiences) to distinguish one thing from another. While it is possible that both groups may use some kind of "taste" in the process of distinguishing between things, we cannot assume it. In short, many cultural systems may be at play when a person characterizes meaningful boundaries between things, and formal education (and the taste that it teaches) is just one of them.

4. Toba Bataks have a complex system that frames their social relationships. At its simplest, the system sees the social world as being composed of people who share a clan name *(dongan sabutuha),* people from whom their clan obtains wives *(hulahula),* and people to whom their clan provides wives *(boru).* All three are essential for the society to work, and because of this they are likened to the three stones that hold up cooking vessels in the kitchen hearth, called *dalihan na tolu.* Because I had no clan name, I was, in many ways, unidentifiable within the system.

5. A young unmarried male is sometimes referred to as *dolidoli Jerman* (TB: "German guy"). While there are some Toba Batak males with this status, it is unusual. For Bataks, such a state suggests that the individual is still attending university, is a pastor, has something wrong with him (physically or mentally, and this seems to include homosexuality), or that his family is too poor to afford the customary bride price and marriage fees.

6. There were a handful of local people who distrusted me and saw my presence in the area to be suspicious, if not downright threatening. Some thought I was a rich trader of wood carvings, others, a tour guide for the elite. For these people, concern centered around my visa. Though it is not

unusual for westerners to live for long periods of time on Samosir, most had to renew their visas every two months or so, an annoyance from which my research permit freed me. I explained my situation to all, yet a few remained who saw my extended stay as evidence that I was some shady operative of the U.S. government.

7. I distributed sixty copies of a three-page form to a broad sample of individuals and families in the area (heads of households were given one form per person over age sixteen). There were some minor difficulties with the form: it took a long time to complete, and my language was sometimes unclear. The most perplexing problem was defining what "an opinion" meant. While I found the Toba Bataks I met generally have very strong senses of individuality, nevertheless in certain circumstances these are suppressed in favor of group identity and agreement. The Bataks, like many other groups in Southeast Asia, favor decision making by consensus rather than by individual vote. It is for this reason, I suspect, that I would receive a family's forms as a set, each bearing precisely the same answers. Nevertheless, the response to the Batak questionnaire was good: thirty-three forms were returned completed.

8. See Causey 1999c for a more complete discussion of this issue.

CHAPTER 1. ORIENTING THE VIEW

1. This is why the reader will find this chapter in particular annotated with so many notes.

2. Considerable research has addressed this term. See the Introduction to Feld and Basso (1996) for a review of the literature on this topic.

3. Anna Lowenhaupt Tsing problematizes the meaning of the term "out-of-the-way" by refusing to acknowledge a "division of dynamic core and culturally stagnant periphery by showing the importance of analyzing heterogeneity and transcultural dialogue . . ." (1993:10). I use the term here to underline the gist of her analysis: that dominant frameworks (upon which tourists, among others, rely) tend to "create 'primitives' within a medley of interlinked narratives about progress and civilization. Whether as objects of romantic fascination or missionizing zeal, these imagined primitives are a provocative reminder of all that civilized humanity has lost" (ibid.:7).

4. See Casey 1996 for more on this subject.

5. Of course, these claims are of a different caliber, since the indigenous people are usually asserting legal or customary ownership of the land and authority over use rights, whereas the tourist is usually only expecting neutral trespass in and through the place. This is not to imply that in this context other claims are not made (such as those by governments [see McCarthy 1994]), but rather to stress that the primary claims in a touristic encounter are made by the principal parties in the interactions.

6. The development of golf courses in Thailand is aimed specifically at foreign tourists, often displacing indigenous people who have farmed the land for generations (Pleumarom 1992). In Bali, a privately owned development company has been trying to build a tourist resort at Tanah Lot, a sacred Hindu temple on the south coast of the island, a project that has been denounced by the Balinese since 1993 (Holden 1995).

7. The representatives of Asian-Pacific indigenous peoples attending a recent tourism workshop spoke eloquently on this topic: "We affirm our faith to Mother Earth. We form part of the earth. We do not own the lands that Mother Earth bestowed to us, but we belong to them. We do not own our lands, the lands own us" (from "Statement and declaration: Asia-Pacific Workshop on Tourism, Indigenous Peoples, and Land Rights," Sagada, Mountain Province, Philippines 1995).

8. On this topic, Keith H. Basso says that places that "generate their own fields of meaning" do so "animated by the thoughts and feelings of persons who attend to them" (1996:56). These interactions presuppose some kind of personal and communal commitment over time: "Relationships to places may also find expression through the agencies of myth, prayer, music, dance, art, architecture, and, in many communities, recurrent forms of religious and political ritual. Thus represented and enacted—daily, monthly, seasonally, annually—places and their meanings are continually woven into the fabric of social life, anchoring it to features of the landscape and blanketing it with layers of significance that few can fail to appreciate" (ibid.:57). He does not seem to say that others (or "outsiders" as he refers to them) cannot become part of the "interanimation" of a place, but merely that the indigenous groups' connectedness is more tenable in that place because there is a pattern, or history, of contact with it.

9. Paul Gonsalves (1996) notes that the responsibilities are just as strong for the individual traveler as they are for the tourism industry and national governments.

10. Some tourists, of course, are aware of their interaction with place (although they may not articulate it in terms like those used by Basso) and in fact may engage in tourism for exactly this reason. Cohen describes this type of tourist, whom he refers to as being in the "existential mode." He says, "the 'existential' mode in its extreme form is characteristic of the traveller who is fully committed to an 'elective' spiritual centre, i.e. one external to the mainstream of his native society and culture . . . it is not only ex-centric to his daily abode, but beyond the boundaries of the world of his daily existence; it does not hallow his world, hence, he lives in 'exile'" (1979:189-191). See also Yiannakis and Gibson's description of the "seeker" type of tourist (1992:291).

11. Georges Van den Abbeele (1980 and 1992) assumes that travelers have the

desire to leave home, but nevertheless also desire to "domesticate" their voyages from the very beginning by means of various forms of boundary marking and naming.

12. Dennison Nash says, "the leisured person must move outside his or her home community in order to qualify as a tourist. . . . Of course, the tourist's travels do not lead to permanent residence in another society; he or she is not an immigrant" (1981:462). For similar definitions and comments, see Cohen 1974:531; Feifer 1986:2; Urry 1990:3. See Clifford 1997:84–88 for a review of works on the importance of "home" in anthropological research.

13. Edward S. Casey's discussion of place is enlightening on this issue: "(place) is itself *kind of something*, rather than a definite sort of something." Home, then, is an indefinite term for a "*type* or a *style* (rather) than a pure concept or formal universal . . . (one that) connotes an open manifoldness, a unity-in-diversity, and not a self-identical unity." Like his examples "just here," and "in this place," home would seem to be an example of "the open-endedness of place, its typological status as morphologically vague, its *de*-finition, (that) creates the semantic space within which definite demonstrations and exact localizations can arise" (1996:27).

14. In fact, Van den Abbeele states that, despite the fact that a particular "Home" (that relating to a specific individual) is a concrete site, it is nevertheless an indefinite referent, because as soon as the individual has left, she or he can never return unchanged, and can thus never return to the same imagined place (1992:xix).

15. In proposing to use the term "touristic process" rather than "tourism," Nash does recognize that the indigenous people being visited are actively involved, but only insofar as they contribute to the tourist's experience (1981:462).

16. Again, Nash: "At the heart of any definition of tourism is the person we conceive to be a tourist" (1981:461); "Though all aspects of the touristic process are essential for the existence of tourism, that part which concerns the generation of tourists would seem to be most important. This is because without leisured travelers there can be no tourism" (ibid.:462).

17. Here are two brief examples. Indonesian tourist officials and consultants identified the carved traditional houses of the Toraja of Sulawesi Island as "tourist objects," zoning them in ways that prohibited changes being made to them. K. Adams notes that in doing so they reinforced "the tendency of outside planners to approach living villages as dead objects or tourist commodities. The zoning proposals are built upon the assumption that a material site is divorced from its social life. In forbidding people to alter their traditional houses, outside consultants ignore the connection of the living people to these structures" (1990:33). On the Gili Trawangan islands of Lombok, local people have been evicted from their recent set-

tlements by the Indonesian government in order to allow tourism development to proceed (McCarthy 1994:56).

18. This is not a novel proposition. Much more has been written about tourists relating to the moments when they are temporarily stationary (i.e., taking photographs [Cohen et al. 1992], lounging in the hotel [Farver 1984; Errington and Gewertz 1989], and shopping in the marketplace [Bowman 1989]) than about the times when they are in motion (Alder 1989). Casey (1996:39) refers to the intermediate places of travel as "interplaces."

19. Taussig (1993), following Benjamin, speaks of a similar in-between space in which individuals act out. The difference, it appears, is that the space he discusses involves mimetic behavior the intention of which is to become some "Other," whereas the actions I observed fluctuate between imitating the other and exaggerating the self.

20. Tim Edensor (2000) explores in great detail the notion of tourism as a performed act. The contexts described in this paper relate to the places he calls "heterogeneous spaces," which "provide a system of spatial ordering where transitional identities may be sought and performed alongside the everyday enactions of residents, bypassers, and workers" (333).

21. Turner's (1969) use of Van Gennep's (1960) term "liminal," or his own reformulation "liminoid" (1979), could be applied here, but I avoid doing so because both terms tend to focus attention on those individuals in transformation rather than all those in attendance (1969:95). Marin is interested in discussing "utopia" but free from the associations that over time it has come to embrace, wanting instead to affiliate it with his notion of the neutral, the playful in-between. He says, "The neutral can be conveyed by forcing the adjective 'utopian' into a new form, 'utopic,' and using this adjective as a noun to free it from its substantive anchoring" (1984:8).

22. For a more complete discussion of cultural tourism as a utopic space, please see Causey 1997.

23. Despite the fact that the tourist's perceptions of "difference" are often based on the tourist culture's own constructions and are in a continual state of contestation and re-formation (MacCannell 1976), they are nevertheless very real foundations of the tourist's experience (cf. Crick 1989: 329). The term "ethnic tourism" is often used interchangeably with "cultural tourism" (see, e.g., K. Adams 1995; Van den Berghe 1992, 1994; Volkman 1990). Lucy Lippard suggests that "Cultural tourism is what the bureaucrats prefer to call 'arts and heritage tourism,' since the very term *culture* is considered elitist," noting that in the United States the more appropriate term for the kind of tourism discussed in this book is "ethnotourism" (1999:72).

24. Bruner states instead that the parties involved in ethnic tourism are tour-

ists, the indigenous population, and multinational travel corporations and government bureaucracies that construct the infrastructure (1996:158). Van den Berghe (1994), in reference to the specific example of ethnic tourism he studied in the Maya area, proposes that the three sets of actors involved are tourists, the indigenous people, and the ladino bourgeoisie who act as middlemen.

25. See Cohen 1974, 1979; Lowyck et al. 1992; McIntosh 1972; Ryan 1991; Witt 1992.

26. See Dann (1999) for a detailed discussion of travelers defining themselves in opposition to tourists.

27. This has been one of the most persistent criticisms of tourists since the eighteenth century (Feifer 1986:134), and a number of researchers have observed this phenomenon in the present day as well (Foster 1964; MacCannell 1976; Errington and Gewertz 1989; Bruner 1991; Munt 1994).

28. Mieczkowski 1990:171–176. Budianta (perhaps cynically) goes so far as to suggest that tourism might well be considered an *"agama modern"* (modern religion) (1993:13).

29. Bruner (1991) rejects this theory in the context of ethnic tourism, suggesting instead that tourists are looking for interesting yet distanced experiences with real "primitives," a term used by these tourists to refer to the groups who are the focus of their interest. Errington and Gewertz state that the travelers "wished to engage with the 'primitive' as a means of personal development," while the tourists' engagement tended to be used to demonstrate their (already achieved) personal development (1989:45).

30. The work of Bruner (1996) and K. Adams (1995) show that indigenous groups do have considerable agency in the interactions of tourism, and can use these to effect change or wield power for their own benefit.

31. Two of the meanings of the suffix "-ate" come into play here: "a group of persons holding a specified office or rank," and "one acted upon in a specified way" (*Webster's Ninth New Collegiate Dictionary,* 1983).

32. Reliable data on ethnic populations is difficult to find. The first estimate is calculated on a variable of the number of Batak speakers counted in Indonesia's 1997 census (Victoria Beard, University of Wisconsin, personal communication), while the second estimates the number of nonurban individuals living in North Sumatra Province (which contains most of the Batak homeland), assuming that the number of non-Bataks living in rural areas is offset by the number of Bataks living in cities and outside the province (see www.bps.go.id/sector/population/pop2000.htm).

33. The Gayo people are sometimes mentioned as a seventh subgroup (Parkin 1978:1), but they have also been described as an affiliated but separate ethnicity (Bowen 1991:15, 55).

34. It should be noted that some Karo feel they are not actually part of the

same ethnic group as the Toba (Kipp 1993:5). This was made clear to me when I traveled to Brastaggi, in the Karo Batak homeland: I asked to see local wood carvings, and the vendor responded by saying, *"Kalau orang Karo, tidak ada ukiran lagi. Kalau mau ukiran, harus ke orang Batak"* ("We Karo people don't make carvings anymore. If you want carvings, you have to go to the Batak people"). Some Mandailings want to distance themselves from connection with the Batak ethnic group as well (http://www.mandailing.org/mandailinge/columns/mownterms.htm).

35. K. Adams (1995), Bruner (1996), and to a lesser extent V. Adams (1996), however, discuss their own effects on tourism interactions.

36. Bruner (1996) describes a situation that is comparable: "At times, when our tour group approached a new site, the Indonesians would behave toward me as if I were another tourist, and I could rupture that attribution by speaking the Indonesian language.... At times I felt myself becoming a tourist, gaping in awe at Borobodur, rushing from the bus to take photographs . . ." (171).

37. This is comparable to V. Adams' (1996) work on Sherpa mimesis of a Sherpa identity composed by westerners, except that, in this case, Toba Batak identity construction does not derive solely from Western perceptions. Rather, Toba Bataks' conceptions of themselves are based on notions of ethnic difference that are articulated in innumerable ways—from conversations, to magazine and newspaper articles and song lyrics, to name a few. Such things help define the boundaries between them and the neighboring ethnic groups, between them and "Indonesians," and between them and Western others.

38. See Steve Feld (1994) in regard to the interactions between non-Western musicians and those concerned with appropriating their musics under the rubrics "world music" and "world beat."

39. In answer to my questionnaire, a number of Western travelers noted that the Batak carvings looked "like something from the Philippines," that they were "like the rest of Indonesia's wood carvings," or that they were "primitive, almost Pacific-looking." This implies that westerners may observe that objects from such widely dispersed areas share visual qualities, or that they participate in a similar ideal type.

40. Dalton 1995; Bruce 1986.

41. Shelly Errington (1998) describes in more detail how these designations are given meaning in the West.

42. See also Noel Carroll, who writes: ". . . cultural practices need not be static . . . [they] sustain and abet change while remaining the same practices . . . contain[ing] the means, such as modes of reasoning and explanation, which provide for the rational transformation of the practice" (1988:143).

43. Alan Hanson's (1989) work may provide more details. He discusses contemporary Maori who integrate Western constructions of their history and

culture into their conceptions of themselves because they are believable, or possible. Wolfgang Welsch (1996), on the other hand, suggests that there might be different layers of "aestheticization" in a given artistic tradition—"deep-seated" and "surface" (which he likens to microelectronics' "hardware" and "software")—which change at different rates, and under different circumstances. In a society with very strong notions of tradition, changes in what Welsch is calling "deep-seated" would probably not be considered possible.

44. The lack of an "original" or "true" authentic has been discussed with respect to referents other than tourism experiences (Baugh 1988:483; Kasfir 1992; Stewart 1984:92). Kubler, on the other hand, suggests that, when it comes to material entities, there may indeed be authentic originals that serve as the inspiration for later duplicates or replicas. He refers these entities as "prime objects" (1962:39).

45. On this subject Umberto Eco writes: "The current notion of fake presupposes a "true" original with which the fake should be compared. But . . . every criterion for ascertaining whether something is the fake of an original coincides with the criteria for ascertaining whether the original is authentic. Thus, the original cannot be used as a parameter for unmasking its forgeries unless we blindly take for granted that what is presented to us as the original is unchallengeably so" (1994:199).

46. Richard Handler may offer a balance between these two by stating "*all* human experiences are real *and* symbolically mediated . . ." (1990:354; italics added).

47. Arnold Hauser, following Max Weber, discusses art style as a kind of "ideal type," or ideal form. He notes that an ideal form is not composed of an "essence," but rather an "exaggerated, utopian form, an abstraction which, without being in any way better or more complete, never occurs in reality" (1982:66). While it is true that Hauser's description indicates a purely mental image, he nonetheless goes on to state that the "ideal type" is a conceptual amalgamation of all known examples of a particular form that exist: thus, he says, "the" medieval city never existed—"there were only medieval "cities" (ibid.:66).

48. See Errington 1998:142; Graburn 1976; Littrell et al. 1993; Spooner 1986.

49. See Bourdieu 1989; Brown 1992; Csikzentmihalyi and Rochberg-Halton 1981; Gordon 1986; Helms 1993; Hoski 1996; Littrell 1990.

50. Russell Belk et al. state that individuals extract objects from the real world and infuse them with (at times temporary) significance. Because consumption is socially validated in much of the west, consumers "participate in a celebration of their connection to the society as a whole . . ." (1989:31).

51. The fact that evaluations of art are made with reference to qualities such as uniqueness, cultural integrity, and age seems to negate the possibility that an object's value might be intrinsic, as is suggested by Walter Benjamin (1969) and Robert Plant Armstrong (1971). If an art object had, as Csikzentmihalyi and Rochberg-Halton (1981) suggest, a "charge" that was ingrained within it, thus marking it as special, then there would be no need to identify it as being out-of-the-ordinary, much less to further evaluate it, as its energy would be apparent to all. But discussions and evaluations concerning which works are "good" continue to be made (Satov 1997), and much ink is spent in defending the character of such selections. This corroborates the assertion that aesthetics and the associated designation "art" are culturally constructed, a proposal that some theorists (perhaps cynically) elaborate upon, stating that "art" is what circulates in the art market network (Maquet 1971; Dickie 1974) and, consequently, is what the art market network says it is (Carroll 1988; 1994).

52. See McCracken 1990 for a discussion of the importance of patina on material objects as a sign of high status.

CHAPTER 2. LOCATING LAKE TOBA

1. *Masuk angin* is considered by Toba Bataks to be an illness.

2. In mid-1995, while I was doing my research, the body of a Chinese-Indonesian tourist was found floating in the lake at this spot.

3. Local people use the term *orang Cina* (I: Chinese) to mean anyone of Chinese ancestry, whether they are domestic or international tourists. In everyday conversation, this includes Chinese-Indonesians whose families may have migrated to Indonesia decades, or even centuries, ago. While most tourists of non-European ancestry usually stay at hotels in Parapat, during certain busy holidays such as Chinese New Year, they will stay on Samosir Island as well.

4. The phrase used was *"orang yang tinggal di danau,"* which literally means "the people who live in the lake."

5. The Toba Bataks believe that each human being has an essence of being (something like westerners' concept of "soul") called *tondi.* The difference between soul and *tondi,* as I understand it, is that the latter can roam away from the living body under certain circumstances. Ordinarily, when a person dies, I was told, the *tondi* hovers very close to the body for three days. After this, the *tondi* becomes a *begu* (TB: ghost) which stays in the vicinity of the bodily remains; the *begu* can cause trouble for the living if they are disrespectful. As people's descendants continue to revere and respect them after death, the *tondi* can become a more refined level of spirit, one that will not hinder the living, but rather can be summoned to help them (see also Parkin 1978:145; Tobing 1994:97; Vergouwen 1964:64). Appar-

ently, these people in the lake were killed so quickly that either their *tondi* were not able to leave their bodies permanently or, more likely, their *begu* spirits have no descendants to pray them to the next level. Either way, they will never cease trying to cause trouble to the living.

6. The phrase used was *masih hidup,* which in Indonesian literally means "is still living," or "is still alive."

7. The paintings range in size from about 1 × 2 feet to 4 × 8 feet. They range in price from US$8 to US$100, depending on the detail and the buyer's and seller's bargaining skills.

8. A large umbrella-shaped hardwood tree with broad leaves that produces a nut that can be eaten or processed for oil.

9. No accurate measurement of the lake's depth has yet been made, but estimates range from between 1,475 and 1,725 feet deep, making it one of the deepest lakes in the world. The surface of the lake is about 3,000 feet above sea level. Lake Toba is drained by the Asahan River, which until recently was marked by a series of cataracts and rapids as it made its way down to the Straits of Malacca. In 1983, the government of Indonesia, in conjunction with Japanese and American investors, built a hydroelectric dam and aluminum-processing plant at one of the narrow cataracts.

10. This retelling of the origin myth is synthesized from several translated verbatim versions found in both Niessen 1985 and Tobing 1994.

11. Not only was the groom-to-be repulsive, but he was of the same *marga* (TB: clan) as she was, a situation that amounts to incest.

12. This is the most powerful deity in the Toba Bataks' pre-Christian religion.

13. His name means something like "He, Honorable Carved House." It is possible that the name refers to the *rumah adat* of the Toba Batak that is traditionally carved with *gorga* (a kind of surface filigree). Si Deak Parujar was the first woman on earth to weave, and her husband the first man on earth to carve.

14. Pusuk Buhit, as stated, literally means Navel Hill, or "Mount Navel" (Sherman 1990:17), but its meaning is extended metaphorically here to mean something like "most central hill." It is not clear who erected the bronze plaque that says, in essence, "this is the place where Si Deak Parujar first landed on earth. . . ."

15. Folktales about the origins of the lake exist, but they are mostly forgotten by the Toba Batak tourate. A few are printed in books, such as Aman 1988, Joosten 1992, and Sihombing 1985.

16. There is no evidence for human occupation in North Sumatra before about eight thousand years before the present (Maloney 1996:172); as mentioned, the volcano erupted about 74,000 years ago.

17. F. M. Schnitger feels that all Batak subgroups consider Samosir Island the center as well (1989:101).

18. The Toba Batak social historian Sitor Situmorang suggests that, prior to the Dutch colonial administration's outlawing of the Toba Bataks' traditional system of communal law *(bius)* in the early twentieth century, the homeland was "the center of the Toba's spiritual map, the [spiritual beacon] towards which the execution of every important ceremony and ritual [pointed]" (". . . pusat peta spiritual Toba, kiblat dalam setiap penyelenggaraan upacara/ritual penting") (1993:25).

19. This situation is similar to that of the Meratus, described by Anna L. Tsing, where the "groups which in official discourse are marginalized as tribal minorities, outside 'civilization,' are further peripheralized from the projects of governance" (1993:25).

20. This is not a new development, for, as Clark Cunningham notes, the Toba Bataks' tradition of migrating away from Samosir Island has been going on perhaps for centuries (1958:82). It is common for young Toba Batak men (and very often young women too) to move to an urban area to look for work or, even better yet, attend a college or trade school. In common parlance, this kind of migration (exploration outside the homeland with the possibility of returning) is called *"merantau,"* which Mochtar Naim defines as leaving one's cultural territory for a short or long period of time with the intent to return home (1974:18–19). Sherman notes that the Toba Batak language expresses a variety of shades of meaning of this term (TB: *maranto*), which includes those who do not return (1990:197). See Rodenburg (1997) for more information on such migrations.

21. The *peci* is an oblong, brimless hat often worn by Muslim Indonesians who have returned from their pilgrimage to Mecca. This man was neither Muslim nor had he been on a *haj,* so it is not clear why he chose to wear this particular hat.

22. Tobing believes that the goddess is actually just one manifestation of the water monster that originally caused Si Deak Parujar such grief when she was trying to make the original land (1994:116).

23. As noted, there is a large hydroelectric dam on the Asahan River that drains the lake, and there are rumors of a plan to divert a substantial river to the north of the lake directly into it to increase the pressure through the turbines.

24. Apparently, this decree attempts to maintain the natural beauty of the lake's coastline as well as to make the shores accessible to everyone, not just coastal property owners. The decree addresses the entire lake and all adjacent lands, but the way it is worded seems to target the tourist center on the east coast; it is in this relatively small area that land issues are most contentious.

25. Toba Batak land tenure laws are very complex. Much of the land in any particular area may be controlled by members of one *marga,* and while people from other *marga* may live on and work the land, their long-term

rights are limited unless they purchase it, or are given it in repayment of a debt or as a marriage gift (see Vergouwen 1964:113).

26. There is a common belief among rural Toba Bataks that the Indonesian government owns and controls all the land and water within its territory. While there are laws pertaining to explorations and exploitations of its territorial seas (Wasis 1991:22), the Basic Agrarian Law of 1960 seems to ensure that private ownership of land is protected unless the land is set aside by the government for specific purposes (Brewer 1990:128).

27. In March 1995, the inhabitants of three villages in North Tapanuli, North Sumatra, were able to resist the construction of a cement factory that threatened to pollute their land (Tanah kami bukan untuk tempat pabrik semen 1995:14).

28. This is not unusual. Feld (1990, in reference to the Kaluli) and Kahn (1996, in reference to the Wamira) talk of how Papua New Guineans draw on the links between places and social relations to define homeland boundaries; Basso (1996) speaks of the ways in which Western Apaches conceive of their lands in using names derived from stories of past events; Stewart (1996) tells of West Virginians whose notions of their places are sometimes defined by things or actions of which no physical evidence remains.

29. A kind of ficus tree that often grows to immense height and girth.

30. A tart pink, bell-shaped fruit.

31. I did not find Goroga.

32. Similarly, MacCannell says, "Modern international sightseeing possesses its own moral structure, a collective sense that certain sights must be seen. . . . If one goes to Europe, one 'must see' Paris; if one goes to Paris, one 'must see' Notre Dame, the Eiffel Tower, the Louvre . . ." (1976:43).

33. I am using quotation marks around Sumatra to indicate that what I am talking about here is a constructed image of the place that may or may not coincide with any lived reality of that place. This usage is similar to that of John Pemberton, who talks about representations of "Java" that were constructed over time by Dutch colonialists and native Javanese under the rubric "Javanese style" (1994:23).

34. In the introduction to the section on Sumatra, Dalton's guidebook refers to the island as the "Africa of Southeast Asia," the meaning of which is not entirely clear (1996:678).

35. One of the most recent marketing schemes is that created by Starbuck's Coffee, where each kind of bean is iconically conceptualized by a brightly colored graphic logo reminiscent of the decals and stickers that stereotypically covered trunks and suitcases in the 1920s and 1930s. Starbuck's logo for Sumatran coffee is a bright orange and black tiger, rampant.

36. Taprobane is an island nation mentioned in histories by Strabo, Ptolemy, and Pliny. It is generally thought to be the island of Ceylon (Smith 1873:

1091), but there are some interesting similarities with the northern end of Sumatra. Ophir is a place mentioned in the Old Testament from which King Solomon's fleets brought back gold, silver, ivory, apes, and peacocks (Marsden notes that all of these except silver are found in North Sumatra). Other theories suggest that Ophir was located on the east coast of Africa or the west coast of India (Smith 1873:484).

37. *Air* means "water" in Indonesian, but it is not clear what the other word refers to. *Pau* (TB) and *pauh* (I) are formal words for mango. It is possible that she misheard the unaspirated *b* in *bau* (I: smell, odor) that could refer to the sulphur hot springs in the Silindung valley. The word "great" in Toba Batak is *belga;* in Indonesian, *besar* or *agung.*

38. The Dutch linguist van der Tuuk was the first European to see the lake, in 1857.

39. One indication of the rate at which places have become "known" and documented is the increase in the size of tourist guidebooks: in 1977, Lonely Planet's guide for Indonesia was 116 pages (Wheeler 1977) and in 1995 it was 1,002 (Turner et al. 1995); in 1980, Bill Dalton's *Indonesia handbook* was 486 pages; in 1995, it was 1,352.

40. See Rodenburg 1997, chapter 5, for more information on Toba Bataks' complex psychological, social, and legal connections to their homeland.

41. See also Anderson 1971:365; Bickmore 1868:423.

42. It is not uncommon in some areas of Indonesia for heterosexual men talking in a public area to stand very close or to hold hands loosely while talking.

CHAPTER 3. KNOWING WHO IS WHO

1. Unlike some other groups in Indonesia, the Batak eat with the cupped fingers of the right hand.

2. The traditional houses are not partitioned by walls into separate rooms.

3. Cooking is always done inside the house or outside at the back of the house, except in extraordinary situations such as a party that involves preparing large amounts of food. Toba Bataks, like many others in Indonesia, have a strong sense of propriety, in behavior and in place. Cooking food is something that should be done at the "back" of the house.

4. This young woman spoke very good English and hired herself out to both women and men. Most Batak understand her work as a need to make money—indeed, most Batak I met fully accepted the fact that they must compromise their cultural or personal values in order to make money in the tourism business. Nevertheless, many people thought she was very daring (and possibly immoral) to guide single Western men, noting that she had spent so much time with westerners that she might soon become like a Western woman (that is, sexually unrestrained).

5. Gossip (I: *gosip*) and gossiping were a serious problem in Huta Mungkap,

and because of this people were often hesitant to talk about things about which they had no knowledge, or about situations their neighbors might view as gossip.

6. I heard people in Huta Mungkap use this word only occasionally, most often in referring to the indigenous people of Irian Jaya they saw on the national television news.

7. A common euphemism for a man and woman living together out of wedlock is *"kumpul kerbau,"* which means "join/gather like water buffalo."

8. He is referring to the German Protestant missionaries of the Rhenish Missionary Society, who first came to the Batak area in 1861 (see Kipp 1993 and Pedersen 1970 for more information on missionization in the Batak areas).

9. Some were suggesting their own *marga* names, implying that I would become a *dongan sabutuha* to them, making me in some ways responsible for their welfare and future. Others were quickly trying to figure out names that would make me eligible to marry their sisters or daughters, which would put me in a much more subservient position to them.

10. For "become," he used the Indonesian verb *menjadi,* which in its colloquial use in this area of Sumatra has a range of meanings: taking on a new employment position (*menjadi guru:* become a teacher); changing an emotional state temporarily (*menjadi sedih:* to become sad); changing a state of health (*menjadi sakit:* become ill); changing a state of being (*menjadi begu:* become a ghost).

11. Partoho was referring to the fact that Marbada's sight is restricted.

12. The book is called *Sejarah Batak* (1977) by Batara Sangti (Ompu Buntilan Simanjuntak), published in Medan.

13. That this assumption has remained a cherished trope for some can be seen in the following quotation: "Institutionalized cannibalism is found only in those societies we call 'primitive'—simple preliterate cultures that are studied by anthropologists—as distinguished from complex, literate cultures that are studied by sociologists. The Aztecs developed a literate, complex culture, and, yet, they practiced cannibalism to a very limited degree. But they are the only known exception to the rule that cannibalism is practiced only by primitive societies" (Sagan 1974:2).

14. The Renaissance essayist Montaigne's attitude on this topic is not so simplistic. He excused the behavior of recently discovered Brazilian cannibals because they were "pure and simple," having "no kind of traffic, no knowledge of letters, no intelligence of numbers . . . no contracts, no successions . . ." (Crocker 1959:142). Despite his relativism, it seems clear that Montaigne is not saying that all European cultures are "uncivilized," rather that they have the potential to be so; the examples of European tortures and inhumanity he provides are mostly aberrations from the norm, not institutionalized or sanctioned behaviors.

15. Hodgen notes that in the seventeenth century an issue of great philosophical importance in regard to "savages" was whether they actually descended from Noah as did Europeans, for if they did, the only explanation for their degraded cultures was "that the world and man were subject to inevitable and progressive decay. The savage was only a little more corrupt than anybody else" (1964:378).

16. See *The history of Sumatra* 1812:290–291; *Short account of the Battas* 1821:218; *Anthropophagy amongst the Battaks* 1828; Hamilton in Pinkerton 1811:451; Low 1833:47, 49–50; Marsden 1811:390–395

17. In 1812, the Reverend C. Buchanan wrote that Christian proselytizers were needed to help quell the paganism (and especially the cannibalism) supposedly rampant in the area, but he seemed also well aware of the important connection between missionization and trade, writing, "in return for the pepper which the natives give us, it would well become our character as a Christian nation, were we now at length, to offer them the New Testament" (96). Sir Stamford Raffles was not so coy when he made his suggestion that the Batak territories should be the focus of Christian missionization in order to block the Acehnese in the north and the Minangkabau in the south from unifying Sumatra as a Muslim state (Parkin 1978:14).

18. They say: "The well-established fact of their cannibalism has, perhaps, naturally led to the conclusion that they were a remarkable ferocious and daring people. . . . So far from this, however . . . the people of Silindung, in quietness and timidity, are apparently not surpassed even by the Hindus" (Burton and Ward 1827:498). In fact, Burton and his wife lived safely in the coastal town of Tapanooli (present-day Sibolga) for many years, finally leaving only because of illness. John Anderson's 1823 report, while it supports the notion of cannibalistic Bataks, at the same time states that only *certain* Batak tribes engaged in anthropophagy: ". . . [the] tribe Tubbak [i.e., Toba], [are] not cannibals. . . ." (1971:306).

19. Letters from Messrs. Munson and Lyman 1835:103

20. The reports in *The Missionary Herald* were always careful to direct attention away from the cannibalism issue: "The story that their bodies were eaten by their murderers, appears to be a conclusion drawn from the manners of the Battahs, or at most, rests upon mere flying reports. To them it matters not whether savage man or savage beast consumed their bodies; their immortal spirits doubtless found an immediate and blissful entrance into the presence of their Lord" (Mission to the Indian archipelago 1836:17). Nevertheless, popular imagination appears to have been more attracted to the macabre reports.

21. See Pfeiffer 1856:135 and Bastin 1866:118.

22. See, for example, Bickmore 1868:424–425, 445–447; Crawfurd 1848: 249 and 1856:42; Giglioli 1893; Shufeldt 1897:38–42.

23. The first missionary to live in the Toba Batak lands, L. I. Nommensen, arrived in 1861. By 1881, more than six thousand people had converted; and by 1918, 110,000 had done so (Parkin 1978:15). Missionary work and Dutch colonial domination of North Sumatra worked in tandem: Nomenssen's work was undoubtedly facilitated by the Dutch colonial government's consolidation of control over the neighboring Similungen and Asahan Bataks to the east in 1870 (Reid 1969:49), and official annexation of Toba Batak lands was facilitated by the work of Nomenssen's Rheinische Mission and the lack of a strong local leader (Sibeth 1991:24; Barbier 1983:14).

24. See Giglioli 1893:109; Schreiber 1883:113–114; von Brenner 1894.

25. At one point, Hall's car broke down, forcing him to leave his mother behind while he sought assistance. He wrote: "For my mother to be left alone at night in the wilds of a country until recently addicted to cannibalism, while I set out on an indeterminate search for help was an unpleasant prospect. . . ." When he returned to the car several hours later, his mother said: "I am very glad to have you back. I've felt rather 'shivery'; first watching [the Bataks] appear out of the dark, one or two at a time; then hearing them talk in low voices. I didn't know whether they were planning to eat me . . . but for the last half hour they have stood like a row of vultures and haven't made a sound, and that was the worst of all!" (1920:93–95). See also Clark 1943:271; Emerson 1923:427; Miller 1926: 22; Salisbury 1924:276. Robert Moore writes as if a change had just occurred: "They are no longer hostile to the white man and they have long since ceased the practice of the ceremonial eating (a fine distinction from cannibalism) of their elderly relatives and their enemies. They are now a peaceful agricultural and pastoral people" (1930:207).

26. See, for example, H. Arden's *National Geographic* article on Sumatra, where the main reference to the Toba Bataks concerns cannibalism and dog stew (1981:427). A particularly offensive bit of writing is found in Krannich and Krannich's *The treasures and pleasures of Indonesia:* "Samosir Island . . . is the home of the Toba Bataks, once a fierce head-hunting group now Christianized and preying on tourists" (1996:266).

27. See also Oey 1996:86. McGregor discusses the importance of guidebook narratives to travelers' perceptions of other cultures, stating, "Travelers are not the roaming, romantic free agents they are often portrayed as in academic literature, but a subgroup of tourists whose experience and gaze is [*sic*] heavily structured by a restricted number of non-stigmatized, traveler-friendly texts" (2000:46).

28. Sibeth feels that the frequency of cannibalism among the Bataks may be exaggerated (1991:17). Vergouwen, on the other hand, suggests that since the Toba Batak legal system was not necessarily fair prior to Dutch colonial administration, anthropophagy may have happened fairly often (1964:363).

29. Michael Hitchcock et al. note how the "long shelf-life" of photographic images (particularly tourist postcards) can "shape the outlook and expectations of visitors over several decades (1993:13).

30. On a contradictory note, Dalton goes on to add: "No matter what your religion, attend church on Samosir Island; the ardor with which the people worship and sing in praise of Christ is something to see" (1995:788).

31. It is probably true that few westerners pray to their ancestors for assistance in the physical world, as do some Toba Bataks, but to imply that Western Christianity (Protestant or Catholic) lacks references to animist beliefs and rituals would be to ignore the origins of holidays such as Christmas and Halloween. (Some Protestant denominations such as the Jehovah's Witnesses do, in fact, reject such holidays precisely because of their derivation from pagan celebrations.)

32. Although contemporary travelers assume that the old Batak religion was closer to animism, it is interesting to note that the early Western descriptions of Toba Batak religion are unclear on the point. Some sources reported that the Toba Bataks believed in three supreme deities (see, e.g., Miller 1778:165; Marsden 1811:385), which other individuals associated with Hindic influence (Baird 1822:52). Both Sir Stamford Raffles (1816) and Burton and Ward (1827:499), however, state unequivocally that the Toba Bataks' religion was based on *one* supreme god divided into three parts. Although their belief in supreme deities was known, this aspect of their religion was deprecated and all attention directed to their preoccupation with ghosts and magic (see Ennis 1838:403–404 and Crawfurd 1856:42). No doubt this oversight on the part of the early-nineteenth-century missionaries had much to do with the cannibalism they could not comprehend: a culture of "lettered cannibals" was difficult enough for most of them to understand, but a culture of cannibals who believed in one God was too much. The missionary Nommensen, who studied the Toba Batak language and culture before he began his pastoral work with the Toba Bataks, was successful in his work of converting them in part because he understood how to work with the prevailing systems rather than against them, using his knowledge of the Batak notion of a tripartite god to clarify the Christian Trinity (Parkin 1978:267–268). The story of the Toba Bataks' conversion involves a great deal more than the similarity of religious structure, of course, for it emerged from a complex interaction of many events (Parkin 1978).

33. See, for example, Pederson 1970.

34. Western guidebooks are not the only publications that create this image. See Causey 1998 for information on how national and provincial promotions use similar imagery to increase tourism in North Sumatra.

35. None of my friends showed the least bit of chagrin over this, since, as they told me, it is sanctioned by the Fourth Commandment to love and honor one's parents.

36. Toba Bataks' resistance to the Western characterization of them as "primitives" or "animists" is not just theological, however. As Rita Kipp (1993) shows, practicing animism in Indonesia can have political ramifications as well: the government has decreed that, because animism is not monotheistic and has no prophet, nor a "book," it is to be considered a "belief" or "superstition," not a religion. In a country where affiliation with one of five world religions (Islam, Protestantism, Catholicism, Buddhism, or Hinduism) is mandatory, and where official paranoia about communism might easily foster a conflation of the godlessness of animism with atheism, belief in or practice of animism might be construed as a subversive act. So, when many Toba Bataks react so vehemently to being called "primitive" or "animists," as Gusting did in the story above, it is not just because they feel that their morals are being judged, or simply because they feel that their religious honesty is being doubted, but may also be because in their minds such a characterization brings into question the depth of their nationalism.

37. Parmalim is an animist sect associated with the belief that the last great priest-king of the Toba Bataks is a manifestation of the deity. See Pederson 1970 and Parkin 1978:40. Vergouwen (1964:75) also talks about the related Parbaringin sect.

38. See Dorst 1989:149.

39. Another characterization that is rarely spoken of has to do specifically with Western female travelers' attitudes toward Toba Batak men. Several Western women I met let it slip that Toba Batak men on Samosir Island have a reputation for being sweet and gentle. Several Toba Batak male guides told me that they regularly have sex with Western women. A similar situation exists in Goreme, Turkey (Tucker 1997:113).

40. Mary Steedly notes that the Dutch colonialists characterized Karo Bataks in the same way (1993:78).

41. This impression was supported by travelers' responses on the questionnaire, where the Bataks were often described as "aggressive," "pestering," and "pushy."

42. Of course, these characterizations are only representative statements—not all travelers stay on Samosir Island long enough to form opinions, nor are all travelers able to discern a difference between the Toba Bataks and the other indigenous peoples they have met on their travels. In fact, several travelers made comments on the questionnaire similar to the following: "[the Batak are] as everywhere in Indonesia, friendly," and "it is maybe like in each touristic place—touristic friendly people." In general, I have found that westerners who travel alone tend to form more positive characterizations of the Toba Bataks than those who travel in groups or those who readily bond with other travelers. This is probably because solitary travelers often seek out Toba Bataks for their social company and will

thus form their opinions based on a larger group of individuals and on longer periods of interaction, while those who tend to fraternize solely with other westerners are more likely to have only those kinds of superficial encounters that are common in service-industry relationships.

43. Ward Keeler, in reference to central Java, notes that "to seek wealth . . . perverts relations of exchange. In fact, it is a demonic version of asceticism, a negative form of sacrifice that contrasts with asceticism's positive form. Instead of suffering hardship in order to reap eventual rewards, it implies enjoying material pleasure at the expense of [others]" (1987:113).

44. The way I finally began to understand their attitude toward deceptions of this sort was when Partoho compared them to advertisements on television that make unprovable claims. Trickery is admired in certain Toba Batak folktales. One character in particular, Si Johana, always shows his cleverness and benefits from it, although sometimes only temporarily.

45. Speaking of interactions between locals in a marketplace in Java, Clifford Geertz wrote: "Within the *pasar* [market] context 'let the buyer beware' is a challenge rather than a ruthless or amoral attitude, a reasonable and legitimate expectation for a seller to have, and is accepted as such by a buyer . . . (1963:34).

46. Dennison Nash first described in detail the similarity of modern Western travel or tourism to colonial imperialism, in 1977. It is an idea that has been discussed by other authors since then (e.g., La Flamme 1979, O'Grady 1980, and Thomas 1994) to highlight the fact that tourism is closely allied with servile divisions of labor.

47. One of the most common Toba Batak perceptions of Western tourists, including travelers, is that they are all incredibly wealthy. Of course, compared to a rural Toba Batak, travelers do have more expendable income. As I talked with a number of Bataks, I began to realize that there are several factors they don't yet comprehend. First, they do not clearly grasp the fact different national currencies have values whose exchange rates fluctuate. The idea that a British college student can afford to travel more extensively in Southeast Asia than in Great Britain is practically absurd to them. Second, the idea that a westerner would have saved for years specifically to travel in Indonesia seems very peculiar. Because most Toba Bataks ideally save so that they can invest in their children's education, buy a larger house, a car, or expensive ornaments (in that order), they assume that all Western travelers likewise follow this plan. Thus, when they meet up with young travelers carrying backpacks, they assume they have left behind their expensive houses, cars, and trinkets, not to mention their fine jobs, so that they can travel. Third, because most Toba Bataks (even in the distant villages) are able to watch such rerun television programs as *Dallas, Dynasty,* and *Santa Barbara,* they feel they have proof that all westerners are wealthy. It is not that they believe that everyone is as

rich as the characters portrayed, for they know that these television programs represent the extreme. Rather, they suppose that *most* people are
nearly that rich. Partoho once tried to prove to me how rich everyone was
in America by pointing out the "house" of one of the minor characters in
Santa Barbara. When the screen showed an inexpensive car pulling up to
a five-story apartment building, he said: "Look at that! Look. The house
is made out of cement. Everybody knows that's the most expensive [mate-
rial]. And look at how big it is! That's how it is for Americans." I frowned
and told him the building had lots of apartments in it, and he shook his
head at me. When I told him my house in Texas is made of wood like his,
he scoffed loudly, saying, "No, I already know all Americans have concrete
houses. You're just trying to make me feel better." That there are home-
less people in America was an idea so insane to him that he did not deign
to discuss it with me. This perception of all westerners being much
wealthier than they really are creates a great deal of resentment for the
majority of the Toba Batak tourate, since as far as they are concerned there
is no reason why travelers should be so careful with their money, and certainly no reason why they should bargain for objects such as carvings,
which they really don't need. Of course, there is the possibility that
wealthy westerners come to Lake Toba to "slum" with the travelers
(Tucker describes situations in Turkey in which Western tourists actually
take advantage of the local peoples' hospitality so they can spend even less
money than they might otherwise [1997:111]), but my impression is that
these cases are rarities.

48. The identities Toba Bataks develop for themselves are a mix of both outsiders' characterizations and insider constructions of group "personality"
that may have been valued (and sometimes disparaged) for generations.
A similar point is made by Kipp, in reference to the Karo Batak, throughout her book *Dissociated identities* (1993). While this is unlike some other
tourate groups whose "official" cultural identity is actively contested
internally (see Feinberg's 1996 discussion of the process of contestation
and negotiation of a "metaculture" among the Huautla of Oaxaca, Mexico), it is not to say that the Toba Bataks have a monolithic or unchanging culture. The point here is that cultures change and emerge over time,
and that group identity transforms concurrently. Viner (1979) gives evidence that Toba Batak culture was in a process of dramatic change even
before Western contact.

49. Rural Toba Bataks' identification of themselves as "poor farmers" exists
in contradistinction not only to urban Bataks (a group painted as being
uniformly better off financially) but also to other Indonesian ethnic groups
(cf. Bruner 1973a:380), primarily the Javanese, and to Western visitors.
People mutter in the *kedai* about who has more or better land, or more
wealth, but when the conversation begins to include outsiders, petty dif-

ferences evaporate as all agree that, in comparison, they, the rural Toba Bataks, are far worse off. A common trait of the "poor farmer" is believed to be "stupidity" (i.e., lack of a formal education). Because of the cost of education, many people over age thirty living in rural areas have only a few years of formal schooling. Education is highly valued among Toba Bataks and is the first use of expendable income (cf. Rutten, in reference to weavers in the Philippines [1990:115], which is why any evidence of a lack of formal training is so stigmatized. This is perhaps what Marbada meant when he sneered at my research interests: for, the way he saw it, I was a high-status westerner "slumming" it with the dumb farmers.

50. Many rural Toba Bataks identify themselves primarily through language. This may be why many of the older men sitting in the *kedai* were sullenly quiet when it was pronounced that I was "a Batak": the fact that I could not speak the language made Nalom's proposition utterly preposterous. The use and knowledge of the Toba Batak language, despite its regional variations or accents, is one of the most important traits by which most people living in the homeland mark themselves as being different from the other Batak subgroups. Good rhetorical skills are highly regarded in secular as well as ritual settings. Ordinarily, an extensive knowledge of the language and its proper use is a trait with which adult men identify themselves, but women are also expected to be articulate. Words are felt to have qualities and resonances that are supracommunicative, often having a direct connection to supernatural consequences, and their proper use shows astuteness as well as a healthy respect for the power of the words (see Parkin 1978:137; Rodgers Siregar 1979:39).

51. Many local people enjoyed telling me that the derivation of the word "Batak" comes from a joining of the words *BAnyak TAKtik* (I: many tactics), which implies that a person has lots of plans and manipulations that they can put to use when they need to. This joke had been made years before by a Batak comedian performing with the Opera Batak, a traveling variety show (see Carle 1990 for a history and description of the Opera).

52. By phrasing it in this way, I learned, individuals at once distance themselves from the trait, through use of their ethnic identity *(orang Batak)* rather than an inclusive "we," at the same time as they are making a kind of fatalistic commentary on what they see as a pan-Toba Batak characteristic.

53. *Hosum* (or *hosim*) refers to the kind of envy that inspires a desire to see another person fail; *teal* refers to a person who shows off her/his success with pride; *toal* is a more aggressive aspect of *teal,* usually enacted to create intense envy in another person; *elat* (or *elak*) seems to mean the desire to have another's possessions; *late* is a kind of hatred of another person, not because they have more, but because they are excessively proud that they have it. There is another word associated with these states of feeling—

mangapian, which is a kind of wistful longing to have the same as a more fortunate friend. The difference, apparently, between this and the other five is that the emotion is closer to sadness than anger.

54. "Travelers" rarely write about who they are. If they do write about themselves, it is more likely to be a detailed account of their experiences as they transpired (e.g., Keay 1995 and Lewis 1993), or some type of advice-giving report (such as a guidebook), than an objective account of personal identity. Similarly, when asked, travelers are unlikely to talk about who they suppose they are, rather giving such obvious aspects of their identity such as their nationality, age, profession, and the like.

55. Cf. Munt 1994:108. Donald Macleod describes a comparable situation in the Canary Islands, where German tourists consider their actions to be "a reaction against the norm, an opposition to conformity" (1997:136).

56. Part of the freedom to act out in this way may be personal rebelliousness, but a great deal of it seems to be made possible, or allowed, through a diverse variety of previous narratives that "script" their behaviors. These narratives, ranging from suggestions by friends prior to the trip, advice printed in travel guides, and opinions heard from other travelers, among other things, seem to define both the scope of behavior possibilities and the limits of what is acceptable to this loose-knit group. A few travelers I met used their time on Samosir Island as an opportunity to act out post-modern fantasies. More than once I saw twenty-something travelers spending their days at the edge of Lake Toba sitting indoors drinking orange Fanta and eating potato chips while watching reruns of *American Gladiators* (or some other appropriately campy American television show). As far as I can tell, this seems to be an act of rebelliousness against what "everybody else" (i.e., other travelers) is doing, for the demeanor of these individuals was not sheepish or apologetic, but rather aggressively counterinsurgent.

57. This sandal is currently very popular with travelers. It is composed of a black foam sole and black webbing straps that are sewn with woven ribbons decorated with very subtle "ethnic" designs.

58. This is not to say, however, that Western travelers are necessarily conservative. They may tend to follow the beaten path (literally), but because they believe they are acting counter to the dominant ideology, they also tend to participate in risky behavior the likes of which they would probably never engage in at home—for instance, riding in overcrowded, ill-maintained buses on winding mountain roads with no seatbelts, or staying up till the early hours of the morning drinking heavily and singing in bars with local people whose languages and cultural assumptions are unfamiliar to them.

59. Bruner (1991) speaks of this issue as well, noting that "what [travelers] bring to New Guinea, reinforced by the travel brochures, is clearly imag-

NOTES TO PAGES 98–106 : 249

inary, that is, it is not based on any real assessment of the New Guineans, but is rather a projection from western consciousness . . ." (243).

60. This is perfectly expectable if I am right in suggesting that travel is a kind of utopic gap between real-life situations and unrealizable fantasies—a place where contradictions can be enacted and contemplated in order better to understand them.

61. One American traveler I met has returned to Lake Toba every year for six years. Although his limited finances allow him to stay only a few weeks at a time, he makes a steady effort each time he comes to the area to learn a little bit more of the language and culture, and a few more local songs, because he appreciates the qualities of the people he knows there. Another traveler, a young German, stayed at one of the least expensive *losmen* and walked to an isolated village each day in order to help families reap or plant their fields. He stayed on Samosir Island for four months doing this, living with the families he helped if they happened to have room for him, and at the *losmen* if they did not. I never spoke directly with this traveler, but heard from the hotel owner that every year he spends all of his vacation time in the Toba Batak area precisely in order to live with, and help, the local people.

62. Cf. Picard 1990.

CHAPTER 4. CARVING A LIFE IN BATAKLAND

1. Because Partoho's phrase is based on the Indonesian term usually rendered as "o'clock" (*jam tiga* means "three o'clock"; a more literal translation might be "pig-hitting o'clock").

2. Local blacksmiths make carving knives and adzes from recycled iron or steel purchased from car repair shops in larger towns. Blacksmithing is one of the local arts that has not foundered over the years, since there is a constant demand for practical and specialty tools, in addition to a need for agricultural tool repair. In Huta Mungkap, locally famous for its ironwork, there are three expert blacksmiths who produce their goods when enough contract orders have accumulated enough to make it viable for them to purchase the charcoal and have the bellows manned for an extended period of time. The best carving knives are made from the steel suspension springs of buses, and the challenge for the smith is to straighten the curved metal while also tempering it repeatedly in water. The knife's handle is made by flattening one end of the piece and forming it into a cylinder. Adzes and axes are mounted on hardwood handles with water-buffalo skin holding them in place.

3. In the past, wood carving was strictly a male occupation, but there is no longer a cultural stigma against women carving, even though the idea of a woman using a knife (considered by many to be a male-oriented tool) for such work is unusual. I know several women who produce carvings on

a regular basis in order to augment the family income, and if Ito had shown any desire to carve she could have worked at home as well. The attitude about this seems to have less to do with gender-specified work (because almost any work that brings money into the household is encouraged) than with personal interest or aptitude.

4. *Gorga* carving, which often ornaments the surfaces of figural carvings and the traditional houses, is made by tapping a carving knife along by means of a mallet. In *gorga* work, the outlines of flourishes and undulations are drawn on the wood and the knife edge is placed at a cant, with the hammer tapping it along the line. A similar cut is made with the knife and hammer canted in the opposite direction, which leaves a fine groove. Most *gorga* work consists of three parallel grooves. In order to carve *gorga* properly, the knife blade must be razor sharp, and must be repeatedly resharpened while the work is in process. Because *gorga* carving is difficult to do well, a thorough knowledge and understanding of its techniques and designs is the mark of a master carver.

5. Carvers feel that unless the hammer is used to guide the knife over the wood, one will never be able to control the balance and symmetry of an object. Whittling, or carving by hand (that is, without the mallet), is used only to clean up the surface nicks or deep corners of a work, and is considered to be a kind of play rather than "serious" work.

6. This section gives only a cursory view of a typical Toba Batak family. More complete discussions about extended family relationships and *marga* alliances can be found in Cunningham 1958, Niessen 1985, Rodenburg 1997, Sherman 1990, and Vergouwen 1964.

7. Wood continues to be expensive, so much so that many families cannot repair the old *adat* houses they inherit. It is for this reason that most contemporary wood-carvers freely admit their indebtedness to the relatively new industry of tourism in helping to keep their traditions alive.

8. Timothy and Wall (1997) describe a comparable situation in the urban context of Yogyakarta, Java.

9. This is a term coined by Nicholas Thomas to refer to traditional arts that are reconfigured by contemporary artists (1995:chap. 8).

10. It was commonly agreed that there were more master carvers living near the tourist center on Samosir Island than in the rest of the Batak homeland, although I was not able to corroborate this with government statistics. This was not always the case. When his father was young, Nalom told me, every Toba Batak man had some knowledge of wood carving. In the past, each male Batak was a carver with enough skill to make everyday utensils and tools, and every large village had a master carver who could produce elaborately decorated personal possessions and religious paraphernalia, as well as the complicated house facades of the wealthy.

11. Local markets (that is, non-souvenir markets) are composed primarily of

women as both buyers and sellers. Extra-local and long-distance trade are generally carried on by men (cf. Rodenburg 1997:45; and Sherman 1990: 161).

12. Many think that Pak Sisinga does the best faking in the area, for he is able to create surfaces that are so similar to real antiques that even collectors and museum curators from the West are said to be unable to distinguish between the two. It was noted in the first chapter that one of the primary differences between new carvings and old ones is that the latter have patinas that have accumulated over time. Though fake antique objects are occasionally made and sold, this does not mean that successful surface treatments are easy to produce. The faker's task is understanding how to re-create the surface appearance of age that is made by both wear and encrustation; that is, he must know how to reproduce visual effects that are both subtractive (wear) and additive (encrustation). Unfortunately, I never witnessed imitation patina being applied to a carving by Pak Sisinga or any other such master.

13. The most sought-after wood for most carving projects, *umbang,* is one of the most difficult to obtain, not so much because it is rare or endangered, but rather because public access to the wood is made nearly impossible by government regulations that restrict entry into national forest lands where it grows naturally.

14. This object has carvings that depict seven stacked figures (some on horseback, others adjacent to dogs or serpents); the top figure is the largest and ordinarily is wrapped with strips of fabric out of which a shock of black hair emerges. The carvings represent a myth that concerns an incestuous couple who became trapped in a tree because of their misdeeds, and who were joined in their entrapment by five important, but magically impotent, *datu.* See Lubis 1992:19, Schnitger 1989:84, and Sibeth 1991:133 for several versions of the story behind the object; see Prager and ter Keurs 1998 for more theoretical readings of it.

15. Cunningham had a similar experience in a village on the mainland shore of Lake Toba in 1956–1957 (1958:65).

16. See Causey 2000.

17. None of the carvers were comfortable criticizing another's work. Critical comments, only given when asked for, were usually terse. See Causey 1997 for more information on carvers' critiques of each others' craftsmanship.

CHAPTER 5. CREATING VALUE AND MEANING

1. Partoho called these fish "thorns" because of their appearance (the fish are narrow and pointed), but also because he said it was proof of how poor the Toba Batak are—so poor they have only thorns to eat each day.

2. Florina Capistrano-Baker 1994b.

3. *Sigalegale* is a near life-sized "marionette" of a human. In this case, the strings that move the marionette are hidden inside the figure's limbs and body, and are worked by a puppeteer sitting to the side of the box on which it is mounted.

4. Florina Capistrano-Baker, Divine protection: Batak art of North Sumatra, *The world of tribal arts* 2 (June 1994): 16–22.

5. The stopper's owners gave a photograph of it to a close friend of mine who, since he could not identify the object, sent it on to me. Although I had met the couple in passing once, I was not sure whether they had authorized him to send me the image or not. My hesitation in giving the photo resulted from my trying quickly to imagine how this event would affect their relationship.

6. See Thomas 1991:127.

7. Burton and Ward 1827:501; Pfeiffer 1856:151; Buchanan 1812:96.

8. Sibeth notes that, in 1854, von Rosenburg came to know (and to disseminate) that certain Batak ritual objects were energized, or activated, by including in them this potion, which was made from the fluids rendered from the body of a child kidnapped and killed for this purpose (1992:18).

9. See Anderson 1991:185. Perhaps the extensive collection of objects by individuals (as opposed to institutions such as museums) immediately after pacification of a group occurs not only because that group has been rendered more accessible, but also because the objects' powers (as political insignia, religious icons, as loci of magical power) have been neutralized.

10. See Veldhuisen-Djajasoebrata 1988:175–177; Van Brakel and van Duuren 1996.

11. See Moore 1930:210.

12. Another way to look at this issue is articulated by Carol Breckenridge in reference to British collections of things Indian: "A collection ordered India's unruly and disorderly *past,* at the same time that it pointed towards India's *present* by ordering her unruly and disorderly practices" (1989:209).

13. McCracken, discussing Williams' research on the development of the department store in the late nineteenth century, notes that one of the ways modern Western objects were merchandized was to put them in juxtaposition with ethnographic artifacts in order to evoke a sense of eccentricity and diverse taste, thus indexing the style of the elite (1990:25).

14. See Clifford 1988; Holst 1967; Kaplan 1993; Miller 1992; Morphy 1991; Mullin 1995; Price 1989; Steiner 1994; Torgovnick 1990.

15. Errington 1998; Holst 1967:361; Janson 1970:524.

16. See Steiner 1994:109; Locke 1925:2.

17. While the Dutch may have considered Indonesian material culture "art"

earlier than this, it was underappreciated by other Europeans and Americans. It was not until the 1948 traveling exhibition organized by the Royal Indies Institute of Amsterdam, for example, that an extensive collection of Indonesian artifacts was showcased in the United States (Asia Institute 1948). Several objects from the Toba Bataks were featured in this show, including a shaman's magic staff, a medicine storage horn, and several fabrics.

18. Price 1989:101; Torgovnick 1990:82.

19. See Belk 1995:45; Bordieu 1984; Errington 1998; Pearce 1995:379; Price 1989:90–93; Spooner 1995; Torgovnick 1990:83.

20. Blocker 1994:173,194; McCracken 1990:113; Taylor 1994:19

21. The term "masterpiece" (cf. Torgovnick 1990:83) applied to non-Western art first appeared in museum exhibition catalogs in the late 1950s. It continues to be used (see Grueb 1988) to indicate those objects that are representative of what Western scholars or connoisseurs consider to be the best crafted and most aesthetically pleasing.

22. The question of how objects are defined to be either "art" or "artifact," and whether that definition comes from the context in which the objects move (e.g., the art world) or from within the objects themselves (what I am calling "spiritual" here), is addressed in detail in Myers, ed. 2001.

23. Cf. Marcus and Myers 1995:15.

24. See Belk 1995:60–62. Neotraditional carvings made for tourists depend to a much greater extent on sacred forms than on everyday, or profane, forms. This may be because Western tourists tend to believe that sacred objects and their replicas somehow resonate with a more crucial stratum of tradition than do everyday objects.

25. See Hoski (1996) for a discussion of the ways in which collectors of non-Western objects imbue them with personal meaning.

26. See Perret 1995, who discusses the Western construction of a dialectic between the Malays on the coasts as being more civilized and the Batak in the interior mountains as being more original.

27. It is not entirely clear, however, whether the interest in entering the interior areas was based on a desire to make the "first" contact or whether it was based on a desire to contact the "pristine" primitive.

28. Giglioli notes that Modigliani was able to make plaster casts from life of both Toba Batak men and women (1893:114), another indication of the desire to have contact with "real" Bataks.

29. Mary Helms refers to a very similar phenomenon, but discusses it in terms of things coming to a center from the farthest distance away (1993: 46–51). My use of the term "interior" has to do with the fact that I am considering the "farthest distance away" from the other's point of view— that is, my "interior" is her "farthest distance away."

30. Provenance can also refer to previous owners in the case of antiques (see Pearce 1995:379).

31. This is an issue of some importance for many travelers because, as was noted in Chapter 1, they come to the Toba Batak area with little previous knowledge about local art styles. One of the most basic assumptions they tend to make is that when they are in a given cultural area (excluding metropolitan zones) they will find for sale that culture's art, and only that culture's art. Armed with this assumption, some individuals have been (and will continue to be) disappointed, for many Toba Batak sellers in the marketplaces have carvings from other Indonesian islands, particularly Bali, which they display right next to the local ones. While it is unlikely that Batak sellers purposely misrepresent a Balinese carving as being from the area, they are just as unlikely to volunteer information about the carving's origins if a buyer is interested in making a purchase.

32. Of the 104 tourists who responded to the questionnaire's query "Are you more likely to buy an object of Batak art/craft if you see the artist working on the piece?" 67 answered yes, 37 no. Nevertheless, my observations did not corroborate these numbers, for I found that a far larger number of individuals who browsed in carver studios actually ended up purchasing carvings in the marketplace.

33. Helms talks in general about some of the cultural or psychical difficulties that can accrue to individuals who acquire foreign-derived goods, noting that they are leaving their own "known" and "ordered" society in order to obtain transformative ("energized") objects (1993:128). Contact with the artisans who make these transformative objects may be uncomfortable for some people.

34. Cf. Jules-Rosette 1984:10.

35. See Price 1989 in reference to "anonymous" primitive artists.

36. Hoskins (1998) discusses at length how Kodi objects (Sumba Island, Indonesia), particularly exchange objects, become invested with meanings not only through use but also by means of narratives that are woven around them. In the Toba Batak situation, these sorts of stories rarely accompany objects when they are traded to outsiders, except perhaps in a most rudimentary form.

37. The Indonesian word used here is *antik*. Perhaps borrowed from English, the only difference in the sound of the word is that the Indonesian version is stressed on the first syllable. There are various meanings of the word in standard Indonesian, however: "1. antique. 2. ornate, highly embellished (of furnishings, etc.). 3. eccentric . . . 1. lively. 2. cute (esp. of children)" (Echols and Shadily 1989). In Java, the word is sometimes spelled *antiek*, perhaps to indicate a pronunciation closer to that of English.

38. He was repeating the word I had used inappropriately. In this area of Sumatra, the word *kotoran* is used to refer to animal or human "excrement"

but has implications more like the word "shit." The word I should have used is *tanah,* soil.

39. In 1977, Tony Wheeler's *South-East Asia on a shoestring* guidebook did not mention Toba Batak souvenirs at all, but by 1986 he wrote: "There's a lot of junk for sale on Samosir Island, so be careful about what you buy . . ." (448). Bill Dalton's 1980 edition of *Indonesia handbook* describes the great deals that can be had at the souvenir stalls on Samosir Island, but does not mention fakes (cf. Fodor 1985); but his latest edition (1995) notes that "'antiques' (are) made while you wait" (791). See also Barbier 1983:190 and Maurer 1989 for more information on Toba Batak fakes.

40. Cf. Barbier 1983:194.

41. While Toba Bataks recognize the beauty and historical importance reflected by age and patina, noting as they do that a particularly ancient *tunggal panaluan* or footed bowl is *licin tua* (I: slick from age), one cannot necessarily assume that age or patina equate with higher value. Certain objects of daily use (such as betel or lime containers) that have a heavy patina may actually represent an individual's or a family's inability to replace a worn-out utensil.

42. Numerous other examples of the loss of cultural patrimony in Indonesia are found in Taylor, ed. 1994.

43. The entrance fee for the dance/museum complex in 1995 was the equivalent of US$1.50, and the bus ride was about 50 cents. Some carvers make as little as US$100 a month, so this trip could cost more than half a day's wages, not to mention the time it would take away from productive work.

44. One in particular, *The Batak* (1991) by Achim Sibeth, is clearly a prized possession for carvers, as it contains clear color photographs depicting an encyclopedic variety of antique objects. Its price, about US$80, puts it out of the reach of most people. One carver in Huta Mungkap had been given a copy by a Danish friend, and he kindly allowed others to examine it.

45. Pak Sisinga is a close friend of a European collector and has assisted (and perhaps collaborated) in producing several of these books.

46. Partoho later told me that Pak Sisinga never let him browse through the book, but rather would turn to a page, indicate an object, instruct him how many to make, and then close the book and replace it on the shelf.

47. See Causey 1999b for more information about competition among carvers.

48. See Causey 2000a for more details on the importance of photocopies.

CHAPTER 6. LOCATING SPACES OF INTERACTION

1. Toba Bataks do have stories of the sort called *ceritera rakyat* (I: folktales) or *dongeng* (I: fairy tale; legend), but no one I knew on Samosir Island seemed to know them. Called *torsatorsa* in Batak, these stories consist of origin tales, fables, and legends. A similar genre of story is called *tarombo*

(TB: genealogy), which are recountings of Toba Batak *marga* often mixed with intervals of *turiturian* (TB: stories) that describe the ancestral characters and their activities in more detail (Hutagalung 1991; Siagian 1990; Tappubolon 1985; Tobing 1972).

2. I was told that Sumatran tigers cannot bear their own weight while climbing in the high branches of trees and are thus ground dwellers. Mazak (1981:5) notes that tigers are able to but do not usually climb trees.

3. The kerosene burners used in most hotel kitchens have the problem of flaring up unpredictably.

4. The "big room" was the living space shared by the entire family. One doorway led to the kitchen, another to the outside, and one other to the two small bedrooms. This room was furnished with the blue *lemari,* a table holding the television, a pedal sewing machine, and a large wood-framed bed-couch. Usually, guests and family sat on mats laid out on the floor, but occasionally, in the daytime, hosts and visitors would sit on the bed-couch to have their tea.

5. It is inconceivable, not only in the Toba Batak area but in other areas of Indonesia as well, to receive guests in one's house without serving them sweet tea. A polite visitor knows that, regardless of thirst, some portion of the tea must be imbibed. To neglect doing so is a refusal of the host's hospitality. See Forshee (2001:153–154) for a story about a similarly unworkable situation.

6. What she said was, "Susah, ya? kalau ada tamu begitu dekat ke dalam rumahnya, kan?" The word *dalam* is ordinarily a preposition meaning "in; inside," but she used it as a noun in this sentence.

7. See Urry 1990.

8. My friend Inang could bargain in Batak, Indonesian, Cantonese, Japanese, English, German, French, Italian, and Dutch.

9. On Samosir Island, English words such as "hello," "go," "how much," "hotel," and cognate words such as "ice" *(es),* "soup" *(sup),* "coffee" *(kopi),* and "tea," *(teh,* or *tes),* are used and understood even by rural people outside the tourist center.

10. The suffix *"-lah"* is a typical part of the way Toba Bataks speak Indonesian. It has the meaning of expectation or finality. In the expression *"itu-lah"* (that's the way it is) it implies an attitude that in English might be rendered as "of course!" When the Batak say *"duduklah"* (just go ahead and have a seat), it expresses the meaning of familiarity. The vendor here was using it to express a kind of happiness to be at the end of bargaining, as if to mean, "Okay, great! That'll do!"

11. When I originally heard about the "arrogant" travelers, it was through some friends who worked at a fairly expensive hotel in Tuktuk. I decided to poll (through a questionnaire written in Indonesian) the Toba Bataks I knew to see what their general attitudes were concerning Western tour-

ists' character: of the thirty-three that answered the question "According to you, in general, if you met up with a tourist in a shop, a hotel, or on the street, they would have what sort of character?" fifteen said "good-hearted," fifteen said "friendly," two said "arrogant," and one said "strange."

12. Domestic tourists, in this case, would include tourists from Malaysia and Singapore as well as those from Indonesia.

13. The effect tourists have had in the vegetable market did not pass unnoticed by one young Toba Batak woman who said, when asked if tourism had any impact on local life: "Before tourists came to Indonesia, everyone worked in the rice fields or in the mango, banana, papaya, or orange orchards. The prices for fruits were very cheap. But now, because tourists have come here, many of us work in hotels. Now, the prices for fruits are expensive."

14. This was the most common complaint of travelers who responded to the questionnaire. They said, among other things: "the stall holders are too pushy, they try too hard to get you inside the stall, this has the opposite effect and drives you away."

15. When asked on the questionnaire why they chose what they did, travelers most often answered "attractiveness/beauty." These are very fuzzy words whose meanings are not completely clear. Nevertheless, because a great many travelers subsequently described Toba Batak carvings using words like "primitive," "traditional," and "interesting," rather than, say, "beautiful," "pretty," or "elegant," I suspect that the term "attractive" implies that the things they purchased were somehow fitting, or appropriate, to their expectations of what the Toba Batak culture should produce.

16. These are all towns and cities in the northern half of Sumatra that are popular with Western tourists.

17. Italicized words are those she says in English.

CHAPTER 7. INNOVATING TRADITIONS

1. According to the province of North Sumatra's tourism planning report, 25,688 foreign tourists traveled to Tapanuli Utara (the regency within which Lake Toba lies) in 1989 (Infra Architechs Consultant 1994). Nevertheless, the local people assure me that tourism has dropped off dramatically since the early 1990s.

2. Henrici notes that sellers in the marketplace in Pisaq, Peru, use similar techniques for selling their wares, using words such as "authentic," "real," and "ancient" (1996:99).

3. Forshee (2001:64) discusses a Sumbanese weaver who also combines traditional elements with new forms. In that case, however, the artist is apparently fully aware of the juxtaposition of old and new.

4. My complicity in such interactions no doubt affected the way they

unfolded. Nevertheless, the story told here may not be especially unusual, as I was not Ito's only mediator and translator: three of her seven children have fairly good English vocabularies and communication skills.

5. Ito may have been criticizing Western tourists in general by saying this, since one of the main complaints the Toba Bataks have about tourists in the area is that they do not dress "politely"—that is, do not wear garments that properly cover their bodies. The majority of Toba Bataks I spoke with consider the Dutch to be the most circumspect in this regard, but because this young woman was dressed in a tight-fitting tank top and very short hiking pants, Ito may have been making a humorous ad hominem critique.

6. In anthropological research this form is sometimes referred to simply as "*singa*," but I was told by all the Toba Batak carvers that this is incorrect. In both Indonesian and Toba Batak *singa* means lion; the carvers made a point of saying that this humanoid face form is not a lion.

7. On the questionnaire, the souvenir marketplace was ranked fourth out of eight in response to the question "Where would you say you saw the most traditional Batak culture?"

8. See Causey 1999a for more information on how travelers make their purchase decisions.

9. In formal interviews with travelers, the adjective "primitive" was commonly used to describe the Toba Bataks and their art. Based on this and many other conversations, I suggest that Western tourists' ideal type for rural Asian art seems to be outlined with the concepts "primitive, black, unusual, traditional."

10. Hauser says an art style is "a dynamic, dialectical, relational category which is constantly changing according to its content, scope, and sphere of validity, and this is modified by every important work. . . . A style never materializes in the consciousness of its originator more than a step at a time; in other words, it does not enter the consciousness of the individuals from whose products it arises" (1982:68). Here, he is specifically addressing the consciousness of the creators of objects. Nevertheless, a similar condition must take place in the minds of those who conceive of the art style objectively. See also Shelly Errington 1994.

11. See Causey 1998 for more information on the absence of carvings in official tourist promotions.

12. The Lonely Planet's *Travel survival kit: Indonesia* (Turner et al. 1995), perhaps the most commonly used guide published in English, devotes five paragraphs to describing Batak material culture, and while it is more balanced than the above (including reference to musical instruments), it nevertheless stresses those items related to pre-Christian history and magic (522). An example of guidebook writing that plays down the

Bataks' mystery, portraying them in a perhaps overly harsh light as aggressive capitalists, is Impact Guide's *The pleasures and treasures of Indonesia: The best of the best,* which describes the Toba Bataks as being "once a fierce head-hunting group now Christianized and preying on tourists. . . . If you go here to shop, you will be assaulted by numerous open-air stalls [*sic*] primarily selling identical handicrafts. Most are wood carvings recently made for tourists. The horn containers are often said to be old, but don't believe it. Most likely they were recently made and drug through the mud to look old. . . . Surprisingly, you may find some worthwhile wood carvings in the midst of the junk!"(Krannich 1996:266).

13. It is important to note that others besides carvers are innovating. Niessen (1999) shows that Toba Batak weavers have a long history of creating new forms within an ancient tradition.

14. For an overview of the various stimuli for innovations in such arts, see Graburn 1976.

15. Silverman (1999) describes a similar situation, detailing how Sepik River (Papua New Guinea) carvings change because of Western tourism.

16. The literature on material culture provides a variety of terms to describe transforming or integrative art: "adaptive art," "novelty art," "heterogenetic art," among others, but each of these terms is somehow inadequate, either because it obscures artistic agency or because it implies subjective judgment. Benetta Jules-Rosette criticizes at length the terms "pidgen" or "creole" when applied to such arts, for similar reasons (1984:219).

17. See Causey 1999c for a more thorough discussion of this issue.

18. See Jules-Rosette 1984.

19. On a few occasions, the sale of an object involved thoughtful care on the part of the seller: Ito would occasionally choose a carving from the shelves and hand it to a tourist who seemed to be confused—not because it was the most expensive, and not because she wanted to get rid of the tourist, but because the carving seemed to *"cocok"* (I: fit/be appropriate for) the tourist.

20. See Oberholtzer in reference to the so-called dream catchers sold by many Native American groups (1995:143).

21. See Carroll 1994 in regard to the way innovative art in the West is legitimized through narratives.

22. See Bendix's (1989) discussion of a similar situation in Interlaken, Switzerland.

23. This term is used in the Toba Batak area with the implication that the ancestor is so far back in time that his specific relationship designation (i.e., "great-great-grandfather") is not entirely clear.

GLOSSARY

All words are Indonesian unless marked (TB).

abang—older brother
adat—traditional law, morals, values
adik—younger brother
"Aduh!"—expression of worry or concern
agresif (TB)—aggressive
Ambarita—local government's administrative center, within which much
    of the tourist center lies
antik (TB)—antique; things made in the old style; also written *barang antik*
apok (TB)—(*Megalaima haemacephala,* "Coppersmith Barbet") a small
    woodpecker-like bird whose "tok-tok-tok" call is commonly heard on
    Samosir Island
asli—original, authentic, primary
baik—fine, appropriate, okay
baik hati—good-hearted
banchi—transsexual
bapak—father, sir, "Mr."
barang antik palsu—fake antiques
barang tua—old things
baringin—a kind of ficus tree that often grows to immense height and
    girth. A *baringin* tree is traditionally planted in the center of every
    Toba Batak village.
begu (TB)—ghost
bius (TB)—a traditional bonding feast among members of a clan
boru (TB)—one of three formal relationships recognized by the Toba Batak;
    wife receivers. See *dalihan na tolu.*
"Buh!"—expression of surprise
cankir mewah—fancy cup
cemburu—jealousy; one of five or six forms of the emotion that Toba Bataks
    recognize
cipta baru—"new ideas": Partoho's term for his innovative carvings
dalihan na tolu (TB)—phrase meaning "the three hearthstones." A
    metaphorical term for the three formal relationships recognized by the
    Toba Batak, it refers to the fact that a cooking pot in the fireplace can
    stand upright only if there are three stones to support it, implying that,
    for Toba Batak social relations to work, all three relationships must be
    in evidence. See *boru, hulahula, dongan sabutuha.*

datu (TB)—medical-spiritual practitioner; shaman

debata idup (TB)—name for a pair of figural carvings representing revered ancestors

dolidoli Jerman (TB)—"German guy," a term used to refer to Western males of marriageable age who are unmarried

dongan sabutuha (TB)—one of three formal relationships recognized by the Toba Batak; members of same clan name

gondang (TB)—traditional Toba Batak music played by an ensemble composed of gongs, drums, and an oboe-like instrument

gorga (TB)—kind of decorative wood carving that is a specialty of the Toba Batak; intaglio-carved foliate designs

gulamo (TB)—a side dish made of small dried fish that are fried with chilies and other seasonings

guru—teacher

halus—fine, refined

hasapi (TB)—two-stringed, plucked instrument

hulahula (TB)—one of the three formal relationships recognized by the Toba Batak; wife givers

Huta Mungkap—pseudonym for a village between Tuktuk and Ambarita where several wood-carvers lived, and the setting of many events in this book

ingol (TB)—*(Toona sureni Merr)* a light, fragrant wood commonly used for carving

"Itulah"—expression meaning something like "That's how it is!" or "What more can I say?"

jam pukul babi—pig-hitting hour

jambu—a bell-shaped pink fruit with a watery, tart flavor

kamput—an inexpensive liquor

kedai—small roadside cafe serving beverages and simple meals

kemaluan—lit. "shameful parts"; genitals

kemiri—*(Aleurites moluccana* Willd) a kind of shady tree that produces a fruit whose oily nut is used in certain traditional foods; nut from which "Tung" oil is obtained

kepandaian—cleverness

kerajinan tangan—"hand's diligence"; works made by hand, handicrafts

kerbau—water buffalo

kios—kiosk; small shop

kotoran—dirt; excrement

kretek—cigarette made of tobacco mixed with cloves

kumpul kerbau—"to couple like water buffalos": a phrase of disdain referring to an unmarried, sexually active male and female pair of humans

lae (TB)—brother; social relationship of *marga* name

lemari—cupboard, sideboard

licin tua—"slick from age": a term used to describe old, very polished wood

losmen—home-stay style hotel; cheap tourist hotel

majik—magic

mandi—to bathe; bathing room

marga (TB)—clan; clan name

masuk angin—"the wind enters": an illness believed to result when a wind blows directly on a person

Medan—Indonesia's third largest city, which lies on the east coast of Sumatra about four hours drive away from Lake Toba

merantau—to leave the homeland temporarily in order to find work, attend school, or "have experiences"

miring—crooked, tilted

nenek moyang—ancestors

oplet—A small van-like bus used in many areas of Indonesia as local transportation

orang barat—westerner

orang malu—"Shy Man"

orang putih—"white person": westerner.

pak—polite Indonesian term of address for an adult male

pandai—clever

Parapat—the mainland town on the lakeshore from which most ferries to Samosir Island leave

parau (TB)—canoe

peci—an oblong, brimless hat often worn by Muslim men who have returned from a *haj* to Mecca

pendeta—priest

penipu—trickster, cheater

primitif—primitive

pukkor unte (TB)—an implement used by shamans in pre-Christian days to squeeze the juice from a special citrus fruit for ritual purposes

pupuk—a kind of potion made in the old days by Toba Batak *datu* for magical purposes; supposedly composed of the rendered body of a stolen child

pusaka—heirlooms

rakus—greedy

ramah-tamah—friendly, outgoing

roh—life spirit, soul

ruang tamu—"guest room": parlour, front room.

rumah adat—traditional house; in the Toba Batak area, this house stands on stilts, has a tall facade that is often decorated with figural carvings and *gorga,* and has a saddle-shaped roof

rumbi (TB)—a traditional lidded container of vase shape

rupiah—Indonesian currency

sahan (TB)—water-buffalo horn container for dry storage, often carved with *singasinga* images and *gorga* designs

sarong—length of fabric used as a wraparound skirt

sawah—wet rice fields

seni—art

seniman—artist

Siallagan—village on the east coast of Samosir Island within the tourist center where the "King's Stone Chairs" are found; site of one of the souvenir marketplaces; adjacent to Ambarita

Sibolga—the town (old name: Tapanooli) on the west coast of Sumatra where some of the earliest contacts between Toba Bataks and westerners took place

sigalegale (TB)—life-sized wooden puppet made to dance with human dancers by means of an intricate system of strings and pulleys hidden inside its body

silat—a kind of martial art

singasinga (TB)—symbolic motif found on many kinds of Toba Batak material culture; the name means something like "lion-like," and is believed by many Toba Batak to have protective qualities.

sirih—betel nut chaw

sombong—arrogant, snobbish

Tano Batak (TB)—Batakland

terus terang—to speak clearly, straightforwardly, frankly

tes (TB)—hot tea, or just hot water; always mixed with refined sugar

Tomok—a town in the tourist center on the east coast of Samosir Island where the "Stone Tombs of the Sidabutar Kings" are located; site of one of the souvenir marketplaces

tondi (TB)—a person's life spirit or soul, which Toba Bataks believe can have levels of strength and can at times (such as grave illness) become detached

tradisi—tradition

tuak—slightly alcoholic and effervescent beverage made from the milky sap of a particular kind of palm tree known by the same name. The *tuak* palm also produces a nut that can be carved.

Tuktuk—the knob-shaped peninsula on the east coast of Samosir Island in the midst of the tourist center; location of most tourist hotels

tunggal panaluan (TB)—"great staff"; a tall wand carved with seven sets of figures and often topped with a shock of black horse hair; also called "king's staff," or the "magic staff"

ulos (TB)—traditional fabric shawl

REFERENCES

Adams, Kathleen
  1990   Cultural commoditization in Tana Toraja, Indonesia. *Cultural Survival Quarterly* 14 (1): 31–34.
  1995   Making-up the Toraja? The appropriation of tourism, anthropology, and museums for politics in Upland Sulawesi, Indonesia. *Ethnology* 34(2):143–153.
Adams, Vincanne
  1996   *Tigers of the snow and other virtual sherpas: An ethnography of Himalayan encounters.* Princeton, N.J.: Princeton University Press.
Aman, S.D.B.
  1988   *Folk tales from Indonesia.* Jakarta: Penerbit Djambatan.
Anderson, Benedict
  1991   *Imagined communities.* London: Verso Publishers.
Anderson, John
  1971   *Mission to the east coast of Sumatra in 1823.* Kuala Lumpur: Oxford University Press.
Anthropophagy amongst the Battaks
  1828   *Asiatic Journal and Monthly Register* (London) 25:448–451.
Appadurai, Arjun
  1986   Introduction. In *The social life of things: Commodities in cultural perspective.* Cambridge: Cambridge University Press.
Arden, Harvey
  1981   A Sumatran journey. *National Geographic* 159(3):406–430.
Armstrong, Robert Plant
  1971   *The affecting presence: An essay in humantistic anthropology.* Urbana: University of Illinois Press.
The Asia Institute
  1948   *Indonesian art: A loan exhibition from the Royal Indies Institute, Amsterdam, The Netherlands.* New York: Gallery Press.
Asia-Pacific Workshop on Tourism, Indigenous Peoples and Land Rights
  1995   Statement and declaration. *Contours* 7(1):11–12. Bangkok: Ecumenical Council on Third World Tourism.
Baird, John
  1822   Notice of a species of cannibalism, practice in the interior of Sumatra. . . . *The Museum of Foreign Literature and Science* (London) 1:51–54.
Barbier, Jean Paul
  1983   *Tobaland: The shreds of tradition.* Geneva: Musée Barbier-Muller.

Basso, Keith H.
1996 Wisdom sits in places: Notes on a Western Apache landscape. In *Senses of Place,* ed. S. Feld and K. H. Basso. Santa Fe: School of American Research.

Bateson, Gregory
1981 *Naven: A survey of the problems suggested by a composite picture of the culture of a New Guinea tribe drawn from three points of view.* Stanford, Calif.: Stanford University Press.

Baugh, Bruce
1988 Authenticity revisited. *Journal of Aesthetics and Art Criticism* 46(4):477–488

Belk, Russell W.
1987 Symbolic consumption of art and culture. In *Artists and cultural consumers,* ed. D. V. Shaw et al. New York: Association for Cultural Economics.
1995 *Collecting in a consumer society.* London: Routledge.

Belk, Russell W., et al.
1989 The sacred and the profane in consumer behavior: Theodicy on the Odyssey. *Journal of Consumer Research* 16(1):1–38.

Bendix, Regina
1989 Tourism and cultural displays: Inventing traditions for whom? *Journal of American Folklore* 102(404):131–146.

Benjamin, Walter (Harry Zohn, trans.)
1969 The work of art in the age of mechanical reproduction. In *Illuminations,* ed. H. Arendt. New York: Schocken Books.

Bickmore, Albert S., M.A.
1868 *Travels in the East Indian Archipelago.* London: John Murray Publishers.

Blocker, H. Gene
1994 *The aesthetics of primitive art.* Lanham, Md.: University Press of America.

Bourdieu, Pierre (R. Nice, trans.)
1984 *Distinction: A social critique of the judgement of taste.* Cambridge, Mass.: Harvard University Press.
1989 *Outline of a theory of practice.* Cambridge: Cambridge University Press.

Bowen, John R.
1991 *Sumatran politics and poetics: Gayo history, 1900–1989.* New Haven, Conn.: Yale University Press.

Bowman, Glenn
1989 Fucking tourists: Sexual relations and tourism in Jerusalem's Old City. *Critique of Anthropology* 9(2):77–93.

Breckenridge, Carol A.
　1989　The aesthetics and politics of colonial collecting: India at world
　　　　fairs. *Society for Comparative Study of Society and History*
　　　　31(2):195–216.
Brewer, Jeffrey C.
　1990　Traditional land use and government policy in Bima, East
　　　　Sumbawa. In *The real and imagined role of culture in development,*
　　　　ed. M. R. Dove. Honolulu: University of Hawai'i Press.
Brown, Graham
　1992　Tourism and symbolic consumption. In *Choice and demand in*
　　　　tourism, ed. P. Johnson and B. Thomas. London: Mansell Publishers.
Bruce, Ginny
　1986　*Indonesia: Travel survival kit.* Victoria, Australia: Lonely Planet
　　　　Publications.
Bruner, Edward M.
　1973　Kin and non-kin. In *Urban anthropology: Cross-cultural studies in*
　　　　urbanization, ed. A. Southall. Oxford: Oxford University Press.
　1991　The transformation of self in tourism. *Annals of Tourism Research*
　　　　18(2):238–251.
　1996　Tourism in the Balinese borderzone. In *Displacement, diaspora, and*
　　　　geographies of identity, ed. S. Lavie and T. Swedenburg. Durham,
　　　　N.C.: Duke University Press.
Buchanan, Rev. Claudius, D. D.
　1812　*Christian researches in Asia: With notices of the translation of the*
　　　　Scriptures into Oriental languages. Edinburgh.
Budianta, Eka
　1993　*Menggebrak dunia wisata.* Jakarta: Puspa Swara.
Burton, Richard, and Nathaniel Ward
　1827　Report of a journey into the Batak country, in the interior of
　　　　Sumatra, in the year 1824. *Transactions of the Royal Asiatic Society of*
　　　　Great Britain and Ireland (London) 1:485–513.
Capistrano-Baker, Florina H.
　1994a　Divine protection: Batak art of North Sumatra. *The World of*
　　　　Tribal Arts 2 (June):16–22.
　1994b　Divine protection: Batak art of North Sumatra (brochure). The
　　　　Metropolitan Museum of Art, The Michael C. Rockefeller Wing.
　　　　New York, April 22–December 31.
Carle, Ranier
　1990　*Opera Batak: Das Wandertheater der Toba-Batak in Nord-Sumatra.*
　　　　2 vols. Berlin: Dietrich Reimaer Verlag.
Carroll, Noel
　1988　Art, practice, and narrative. *The Monist* 71(2):140–157.

1994 Identifying art. In *Institutions of Art: Reconsiderations of George Dickie's Philosophy*, ed. R. J. Yanal. Philadelphia: Pennsylvania State University Press.

Casey, Edward S.

1996 How to get from space to place in a fairly short stretch of time: Phenomenological prolegomena. In *Senses of place*, ed. S. Feld and K. H. Basso. Santa Fe: School of American Research Press.

Causey, C. Andrew

1997 Getting more than they bargain for: Toba Batak carvers and Western travellers in a utopic marketplace. Ph.D. diss., University of Texas, Austin.

1998 *Ulos or saham?:* Presentations of Toba Batak material culture in official tourism promotions. *Indonesia and the Malay World* 26(75):97–106.

1999a Making an *Orang Malu:* Aesthetic and economic dialogues between Western tourists and Toba Bataks in the souvenir marketplace. In *Converging interests: Traders, travelers, and tourists in Southeast Asia (279–292),* ed. J. Forshee, et al., Berkeley: University of California Press.

1999b Stealing a good idea: Innovation and competition among Toba Batak woodcarvers. *Museum Anthropology* 23(1):3–20.

1999c The singasinga table lamp and the Toba Batak's art of conflation. *Journal of American Folklore* 112(445):424–436.

2000 The folder in the drawer of the sky blue *lemari:* A Toba Batak carver's secrets. *Crossroads: an Interdisciplinary Journal of Southeast Asian Studies,* 14(1):1–34.

Chesner, C. A., W. I. Rose, A. Deino, R. Drake, and J. A. Westgate

1991 Eruptive history of Earth's largest quaternary caldera (Toba, Indonesia) clarified. *Geology* 19:200–203.

Clark, Elizabeth Allerton

1943 The Batak bridges two worlds. *Asia and the Americas* 43(5):271–277.

Clifford, James

1988 *The predicament of culture: Twentieth-century ethnography, literature, and art.* Cambridge, Mass.: Harvard University Press.

1997 *Routes: Travel and translation in the late twentieth century.* Cambridge, Mass.: Harvard University Press.

Cohen, Eric

1974 Who is a tourist: A conceptual classification. *Sociological Review* 22(4):527–555.

1979 A phenomenology of tourist experiences. *Sociology* 13:179–201.

1984 The sociology of tourism: Approaches, issues, and findings. *Annual Review of Sociology* 10:373–392.

Cohen, Eric, Yeshayahu Nir, and Uri Almagor
   1992   Stranger-local interaction in photography. *Annals of Tourism Research* 19(2):213–235.
Crawfurd, John
   1848   On the alphabets of the Indian Archipelago. *Journal of the Ethnological Society of London* 2:246–261.
   1856   *A descriptive dictionary of the Indian Islands and adjacent countries.* London: Bradbury and Evans.
   1866   On cannibalism in relation to ethnology. *Transactions of the Ethnological Society of London* 4:105–124.
Crick, Malcolm
   1989   Representation of international tourism in the social sciences: Sun, sex, sights, savings, and servility. *Annual Review of Anthropology* (Palo Alto), ed. B. J. Siegel et al.
Crocker, Lester G.
   1959   *The selected essays of Montaigne.* New York: Pocket Library.
Csikzentmihalyi, M. and E. Rochberg-Halton
   1981   *The meaning of things: Domestic symbols and the self.* Cambridge: Cambridge University Press.
Culler, Jonathan
   1981   Semiotics of tourism. *American Journal of Semiotics* 1(1/2):127–140.
Cunningham, Clark E.
   1958   *The postwar migration of the Toba-Bataks to East Sumatra.* New Haven, Conn.: Yale University Press.
Dalton, Bill
   1980   *Indonesia Handbook,* 2d ed. Chico, Calif.: Moon Publications.
   1995   *Indonesia Handbook,* 6th ed. Chico, Calif.: Moon Publications.
Dann, Graham
   1999   Writing out the tourist in space and time. *Annals of Tourism Research* 26(1):159–187.
DeKadt, Emanuel
   1979   *Tourism: Passport to development? Perspectives on the social and cultural effects of tourism in developing countries.* Oxford: Oxford University Press (for the World Bank and UNESCO).
Diamondstein, Morton, and James Willis
   1979   *Sculpture of the Batak.* San Francisco: James Willis Gallery.
Dickie, George
   1974   *Art and the Aesthetic.* Ithaca, N.Y.: Cornell University Press.
Dorst, John D.
   1989   *The written suburb: An American site, an ethnographic dilemma.* Philadelphia: University of Pennsylvania Press.

Draper, Dianne, and Herbert G. Kariel

    1990   Metatourism: Dealing critically with the future of tourism environments. *Journal of Cultural Geography* 11(1):139–155.

Echols, John, and Hassan Shadily

    1989   *An Indonesian-English dictionary.* Ithaca, N.Y.: Cornell University Press.

Eco, Umberto

    1994   Fakes and forgeries. In *The limits of interpretation.* Bloomington: Indiana University Press.

Edensor, Tim

    2000   Staging tourism: Tourists as performers. *Annals of Tourism Research* 27(2):322–344.

Emerson, Gertrude

    1923   Across the Sumatran highlands. *Asia* 23(6):425–429.

Ennis, Mr.

    1838   Journal of Mr. Ennis on a tour in Sumatra. *The Missionary Herald* 34(1):364–408.

Errington, Frederick, and Deborah Gewertz

    1989   Tourism and anthropology in a post-modern world. *Oceania* 60:37–54.

Errington, Shelly

    1994   What became of authentic primitive art? *Cultural Anthropology* 9(2):201–226.

    1998   *The death of authentic primitive art and other tales of progress.* Berkeley: University of California Press.

Extracts from instructions to missionaries

    1833   *The Missionary Herald* 29:271–275. Boston: American Board of Commissioners for Foreign Missions.

Farver, Jo Ann M.

    1984   Tourism and employment in the Gambia. *Annals of Tourism Research* 11:249–265.

Feifer, Maxine

    1986   *Tourism in history: From Imperial Rome to the present.* New York: Stein and Day Publishers.

Feinberg, Benjamin

    1996   A Toyota in Huautla: Metacultural discourse in the Sierra Mazateca of Oaxaca, Mexico. Ph.D. diss., University of Texas, Austin.

Feld, Steven

    1990   *Sound and sentiment: Birds, weeping, poetics, and song in Kaluli expression.* Philadelphia: University of Pennsylvania Press.

    1994   From schizophonia to schismogenesis: On the discourses and

commodification practices of "World Music" and "World Beat."
In *Music Grooves*, Charles Keil and Steve Feld. Chicago: University
of Chicago Press.

Feld, Steven, and Keith H. Basso
1996   Introduction. In *Senses of Place*. Santa Fe: American School of
Research.

Fodor, Eugene
1985   *Southeast Asia*. New York: Fodor's Travel Guides.

Forshee, Jill
2001   *Between the folds: Stories of cloth, lives, and travels from Sumba*.
Honolulu: University of Hawai'i Press.

Foster, John
1964   The sociological consequences of tourism. *International Journal of
Comparative Sociology* 5(2):217–227.

Frow, John
1991   Tourism and the semiotics of nostalgia. *October* 57:123–151.

Geary, Patrick
1986   Sacred commodities: The circulation of Medieval relics. In *The
social life of things,* ed. A. Appadurai. Cambridge: Cambridge
University Press.

Geertz, Clifford
1963   *Peddlers and princes: Social change and economic modernization in two
Indonesian towns*. Chicago: University of Chicago Press.
1973   Person, time, and conduct in Bali. In *The interpretation of cultures*.
New York: Basic Books.

Giglioli, Henry
1893   The ethnographical collections formed by Elio Modigliani
during his recent explorations in central Sumatra and Enggano.
Internationales Archiv für Ethnographie 6:109–12.

Gonsalves, Paul
1996   Is there a right to travel? *Contours* 7(5):45–49. Bangkok:
Ecumenical Council on Third World Tourism.

Gordon, Beverly
1986   The souvenir: Messenger of the extraordinary. *Journal of Popular
Culture* 20(3):135–146.

Gove, Philip B., editor-in-chief
1971   *Webster's Seventh Collegiate Dictionary*. New York: G. and C. Merriam
Company, Publishers.

Graburn, Nelson H. H.
1976   Introduction: The arts of the Fourth World. In *Ethnic and tourist
arts: Cultural expressions from the Fourth World,* ed. N.H.H. Graburn.
Berkeley: University of California Press.

Hall, Melvin A.

1920 By motor through the east coast and Batak highlands of Sumatra. *National Geographic* 37(1):69–102.

Hamilton, Capt. Alexander

1727 A New Account of the East Indies. In John Pinkerton, *A general collection of the best and most interesting voyages and travels in all parts of the world.* London: Longman, Hurst, Rees, Orme, and Brown.

Handler, Richard

1990 Consuming culture. *Cultural Anthropology* 5(3):346–357.

Hanson, Alan

1989 The making of the Maori: Culture invention and its logic. *American Anthropologist* 91(4):890–902.

Hauser, Arnold (K. J. Northcote, trans.)

1982 *The sociology of art.* Chicago: University of Chicago Press.

Helms, Mary

1993 *Craft and the kingly ideal: Art, trade, and power.* Austin: University of Texas Press.

Henrici, Jane M.

1996 The artisanal and the touristic in Pisaq, Peru. Ph.D. diss., University of Texas, Austin.

History of Sumatra, The

1812 Book review. *The Eclectic Review* 3(1):290–295.

Hitchcock, Michael, et al.

1993 Tourism in South-East Asia: Introduction. In *Tourism in South-East Asia,* ed. M. Hitchcock, V. T. King, and M.J.G. Parnwell. New York: Routledge.

Hodgen, Margaret T.

1964 *Early anthropology in the 16th and 17th Centuries.* Philadelphia: University of Pennsylvania Press.

Holden, Peter

1995 Balinese seek support to halt development at *Tanah Lot* temple. *Contours* 7(2):4–5. Bangkok: Ecumenical Coalition on Third World Tourism.

Holst, Niels von

1967 *Creators, collectors, and connoisseurs: The anatomy of artistic taste from antiquity to the present day.* New York: G. P. Putnam's Sons.

Hoski, Kathleen Mary

1996 Furnishing desires: Narratives of the real and the appropriation of the other. M.A. thesis, University of Texas, Austin.

Hoskins, Janet

1998 *Biographical objects: How things tell the stories of people's lives.* New York: Routledge.

Indian Archipelago: Baptist Missionary Society
  1828 *Missionary Register*, p. 125. London: L. B. Seeley and Sons.
Indian Archipelago: Various fields for missionary labor
  1833 *The Missionary Herald* 29:407–409. Boston: American Board of
         Commissioners for Foreign Missions.
Infra Architech's Consultant
  1992 *Rencana induk pengembangan pariwisata Sumatera Utara.* Medan,
         Indonesia.
Janson, H. W.
  1970 *History of art: A survey of the major visual arts from the dawn of
         history to the present day.* New York: Prentice-Hall and Harry
         Abrams.
Jones, Mark
  1992 Do fakes matter? In *Why Fakes Matter: Essays on Problems of
         Authenticity,* ed. M. Jones. London: British Museum Press.
Joosten, P. Leo
  1992 *Samosir: The Old-Batak society.* Pematang Siantar, North Sumatra,
         Indonesia.
Jules-Rosette, Benetta
  1984 *The messages of tourist art: An African semiotic system in comparative
         perspective.* New York: Plenum Press.
Kahn, Miriam
  1996 Your place and mine: Sharing emotional landscapes in Wamira.
         In *Senses of place.* Santa Fe: School of American Research.
  2000 Tahiti intertwined: Ancestral land, tourist postcard, and nuclear
         test site. *American Anthropologist* 102(1): 7–26.
Kaplan, Flora S.
  1993 Mexican museums in the creation of a national image in world
         tourism. In *Crafts in the world market: The impact of global exchange
         on Middle American artisans,* ed. J. Nash. Albany: State University
         of New York Press.
Kasfir, Sidney Littlefield
  1992 African art and authenticity: A text with a shadow. *African Arts*
         25(2):40–53.
Keay, John
  1995 *Indonesia: From Sabang to Merauke.* London: Boxtree Ltd.
Keeler, Ward
  1987 *Javanese shadow plays, Javanese selves.* Princeton, N.J.: Princeton
         University Press.
Keuning, Johannes (Claire Holt, trans.)
  1958 *The Toba Batak, formerly and now.* Ithaca, N.Y.: Modern Indonesia
         Project, Cornell University.

Kipp, Rita Smith

1993 *Dissociated identities: Ethnicity, religion, and class in an Indonesian society.* Ann Arbor: University of Michigan Press.

Krannich, Ron, and Caryl Krannich

1996 *The treasures and pleasures of Indonesia: Best of the best.* Manassus Park, Va.: Impact Publications.

Kubler, George

1962 *The shape of time: Remarks on the history of things.* New Haven, Conn.: Yale University Press.

La Flamme, A.

1979 The impact of tourism: A case from the Bahama Islands. *Annals of Tourism Research* 6:137–148.

Letters from Messrs. Munson and Lyman

1835 *The Missionary Herald* 31:17. Boston: American Board of Commissioners for Foreign Missions.

Lewis, Norman

1993 *An empire of the East: Travels in Indonesia.* London: Jonathan Cape.

Leyden, J., M.D.

1811 On the languages and literature of the Indo-Chinese nations. *Asiatic Researches* 10(3):158–207.

Lippard, Lucy R.

1999 *On the beaten track: Tourism, art, and place.* New York: The New Press.

Littrell, Mary Ann

1990 Symbolic significance of textile crafts for tourists. *Annals of Tourism Research* 17:2.

Littrell, Mary Ann, Luella F. Anderson, and Pamela J. Brown

1993 What makes a craft souvenir authentic? *Annals of Tourism Research* 20(1):197–215.

Locke, Alain

1925 Blondiau-Theatre Arts Collection of Primitive African Art. On exhibition at the New Art Circle, New York.

Low, Capt. James

1833 An account of the Batta race in Sumatra. *Journal of the Royal Geographical Society of Great Britain and Ireland* (London) 1(3):43–50.

Lowyck, Els, Luk Van Langehove, and Livin Bollaert

1992 Typologies of tourist roles. In *Choice and demand in tourism,* ed. P. Johnson and B. Thomas. London: Mansell Publications.

Lubis, Z. Pangaduan

1992 *Cerita Rakyat dari Sumatera Utara.* Jakarta: Rasindo Gramedia Widiasarana.

MacCannell, Dean
1976   *The tourist: A new theory of the leisure class.* New York: Schocken
       Books.
1992   *Empty meeting grounds: The tourist papers.* London: Routledge.
Macleod, Donald V. L.
1997   "Alternative" tourists on a Canary Island. In *Tourists and tourism:
       Identifying with people and places,* ed. S. Abram, J. Waldren, and
       D.V.L. Macleod. Oxford: Berg.
Maloney, Bernard K.
1996   Possible early dry-land and wet-land rice cultivation in Highland
       North Sumatra. *Asian Perspectives* 35(2)165–192.
Mannheim, Karl
1953   *Ideology and Utopia.* New York: Harvest Books.
Maquet, Jacques
1971   *Introduction to aesthetic anthropology.* Reading, Mass.:
       Addison-Wesley Publishing.
Marcus, George E., and Fred R. Myers
1995   The traffic in art and culture: An introduction. In *The traffic in
       culture: Refiguring art and anthropology,* ed. G. Marcus and F. Myers.
       Berkeley: University of California Press.
Marin, Louis (R. A. Vollrath, trans.)
1984   *Utopics: Spatial play.* New York: Macmillan Humanities.
Marsden, William
1783   *The History of Sumatra, containing an account of the government, laws,
       customs, and manners of the native inhabitants, with a description of the
       natural productions, and a relation of the ancient political state of that
       island.* 1st ed. London: Thomas Payne and Son; 2d ed. 1811.
1966   *The History of Sumatra. . . .* 3d ed. Kuala Lumpur: Oxford
       University Press.
Maurer, Evan M.
1989   Art and imitation: Original works and forgeries of tribal art.
       Antiques and Fine Art 7(1):45–52.
Mazak, Vratislave
1981   Pantera Tigris. In *Mammalian Species,* no. 152, pp. 1–8.
       http://www.science.smith.edu/departments/Biology/
       VHAYSSEN/msi/pdf/152_Panthera_tigris.pdf
McCarthy, John
1994   *Are sweet dreams made of this? Tourism in Bali and eastern Indonesia.*
       Northcote, Australia: Indonesian Resources and Information
       Program.
McCracken, Grant
1990   *Culture and consumption: New approaches to the symbolic character of
       consumer goods and activities.* Bloomington: Indiana University Press.

McGregor, Andrew

2000   Dynamic texts and tourist gaze: Death, bones and buffalo. *Annals of Tourism Research* 27(1):27–50.

McIntosh, Robert W.

1972   *Tourism principles, practices and philosophies.* Columbus: Grid Inc.

Metcalf, Bruce

1997   Craft and art, culture and biology. In *The culture of craft,* ed. Peter Dormer. Manchester: Manchester University Press.

Mieczkowski, Zbigniew

1990   *World trends in tourism and recreation.* New York: American University Studies, Series 25, Peter Lang Publications.

Miller, Charles

1778   An account of the island of Sumatra. *Philosophical Transactions of the Royal Society of London* 68:160–179.

Miller, Daniel

1992   Primitive art and the necessity of primitivism to art. In *The Myth of Primitivism: Perspectives on Art,* ed. S. Hiller. London: Routledge.

Miller, Warren Hastings

1926   A land where factories are taboo. *Travel* 47, no. 3 (July): 22–26.

Mission to the east coast of Sumatra in 1823

1826   Book review. *Quarterly Review* 34:99–110.

Mission to the Indian archipelago

1836   *Missionary Herald* 33:17. Boston: The American Board of Commissioners for Foreign Missions.

Moore, W. Robert

1930   Among the hill tribes of Sumatra. *National Geographic* 57(2):187–227.

Morphy, Howard

1991   *Ancestral connections: Art and an aboriginal system of knowledge.* Chicago: University of Chicago Press.

Muller, Molly H.

1995   The patronage of difference: Making Indian art "art, not ethnology." In *The traffic in culture: Refiguring art and anthropology,* ed. G. E. Marcus and F. R. Myers. Berkeley: University of California Press.

Munt, Ian

1994   The 'other' postmodern tourism: Culture, travel, and the new middle classes. *Theory, Culture, and Society* 11(3):101–124.

Myers, Fred R., ed.

2001   *The empire of things: Regimes of value and material culture.* Santa Fe: School of American Research Press.

Naim, Mochtar
    1974   Merantau: Minangkabau voluntary migration. Ph.D. diss.,
            University of Singapore.

Nash, Dennison
    1977   Tourism as a form of imperialism. In *Hosts and guests,* ed. V. Smith.
            Philadelphia: University of Pennsylvania Press.
    1981   Tourism as an anthropological subject. *Current Anthropology*
            22(5):461–481.

Niessen, Sandra
    1985   *Motifs of life in Toba Batak texts and textiles.* Dordrecht: Foris
            Publications.
    1999   Threads of tradition, threads of invention: Unraveling Toba Batak
            women's expressions of social change. In *Unpacking culture: Art and*
            commodity in colonial and postcolonial worlds, ed. Ruth B. Phillips
            and Christopher B. Steiner. Berkeley: University of California
            Press.

Oberholtzer, Cath
    1995   The *re*-invention of tradition and the marketing of cultural values.
            Anthropologica 37:141–153.

Oey, Eric M., ed.
    1996   *Sumatra: Island of adventure.* Lincolnwood: Passport Books.

O'Grady, R., ed.
    1980   *Tourism in the Third World: Christian reflections.* New York: Orbis
            Books.

Okatai, Temu, et al.
    1982   The cultural impact of tourism, art forms—revival or degradation?
            In *The impact of tourism development in the Pacific.* Trent University:
            Environmental and Resource Studies Programme.

Parkin, Harry
    1978   *Batak fruit of Hindu thought.* Madras: Christian Literature Society.

Pearce, Susan
    1995   *On collecting: An investigation into collecting in the European tradition.*
            London: Routledge.

Pedersen, Paul Bodholdt
    1970   *Batak blood and Protestant soul: The development of national Batak*
            churches in North Sumatra. Grand Rapids, Mich.: Eerdmans
            Publishing Co.

Pemberton, John
    1994   *On the subject of "Java."* Ithaca, N.Y.: Cornell University Press.

Perret, Daniel
    1995   *La formation d'un paysage ethnique Batak et Malais de Sumatra*
            Nord-Est. Paris: Presses de l'École Française d'Extrême-Orient.

Pfeiffer, Ida
   1856   *Lady's second journey round the world.* New York: Harper and Bros.
Phillips, Ruth B., and Christopher B. Steiner
   1999   Art, authenticity, and the baggage of cultural encounter. In
          *Unpacking culture: Art and commodity in colonial and postcolonial
          worlds,* ed. Ruth B. Phillips and Christopher B. Steiner. Berkeley:
          University of California Press.
Picard, Michel
   1990   "Cultural tourism" in Bali: Cultural performances as tourist
          attraction. *Indonesia* 49:37–74.
   1990   Kebalian Orang Bali: Tourism and the uses of Balinese culture in
          new order Indonesia. *RIMA (Review of Indo-Malay Affairs)*
          24:1–38.
Pinkerton, John
   1811   *A general collection of the best and most interesting voyages and travels in
          all parts of the world.* London: Longman, Hurst, Rees, Orme, and
          Brown.
Pleumarom, Anita
   1992   Course and effect: Golf tourism in Thailand. *Contours* 5(7): 23–28.
          Bangkok: Ecumenical Coalition on Third World Tourism.
Pommerehne, W., and J. M. Granica
   1995   Perfect reproductions of works of art: Substitutes or heresy?
          Journal of Cultural Economics 19:237–249.
Pospos, P. (Susan Rodgers, trans.)
   1995   *Me and Toba: A childhood world in a Batak memoir.* In *Telling lives,
          telling history: Autobiography and historical imagination in modern
          Indonesia,* ed. S. Rodgers. Berkeley: University of California Press.
Prager, Michael, and Pieter ter Keurs
   1998   *W. H. Rassers and the Batak magic staff.* Leiden: Rijksmuseum voor
          Volkenkunde.
Price, Sally
   1989   *Primitive art in civilized places.* Chicago: University of Chicago Press.
Raffles, Stamford
   1816   Discourse of the Honorable President Tho. Stamford Raffles. In
          *Verhandleingen van het Bataviaasch Genootschap der Kunsten en
          Wetenschappen,* 8 Deel. Batavia.
Rampino, M. R., and S. Self
   1992   Volcanic winter and accelerated glaciation following the Toba
          super-eruption. *Nature* 359:50–52.
Recent intelligence: Sumatra
   1838   *Missionary Herald* 34:188–189. Boston: American Board of
          Commissioners for Foreign Missions.

Reid, Anthony
   1969   *The contest for North Sumatra: Atjeh, the Netherlands, and Britain
           1858–1898.* Kuala Lumpur: Oxford University Press.
Ricoeur, Paul
   1984   *Lectures on Utopia and ideology.* Ed. G. H. Taylor. New York:
           Columbia University Press.
Rodenburg, Janet
   1997   *In the shadow of migration.* Leiden: KITLV Press.
Rodgers, Susan
   1979   Advice to newlyweds: Sipirok Batak wedding speeches—adat or
           art? *Art, ritual, and society in Indonesia,* ed. E. Bruner and E. Becker.
           Athens: Ohio University Southeast Asia Series No. 53.
   1995   *Telling lives, telling history: Autobiography and historical imagination
           in modern Indonesia.* Berkeley: University of California Press.
Rutten, Rosanne
   1990   *Artisans and entrepreneurs in the rural Philippines: Making a living
           and gaining wealth in two commercialized crafts.* Quezon City: New
           Day Publishers.
Ryan, Chris
   1991   *Recreational tourism: A social science perspective.* New York: Chapman
           and Hall.
Sagan, Eli
   1974   *Cannibalism: Human aggression and cultural form.* New York: Harper
           and Row.
Salisbury, Edward A.
   1924   A mountain people with sea-memories. *Asia* 24:274–278.
Sangti, Batara (also known as Ompu Buntilan Simanjuntak)
   1977   *Sejarah Batak.* Medan, Indonesia: Karl Sianipar Company.
Satov, Murray
   1997   *"Catalogues, Collectors, Curators: The Tribal Art Market and
           Anthropology," Contesting art: Art, politics and identity in the modern
           world.* Ed. Jeremy MacClancy. Oxford: Berg.
Schnitger, F. M.
   1989   *Forgotten kingdoms in Sumatra.* Oxford: Oxford University Press.
Schreiber, Dr. A.
   1883   Life among the Battas of Sumatra. In *The Popular Science Monthly.*
           New York: D. Appleton and Co.
Sherman, D. George
   1990   *Rice, rupees, and ritual: Economy and society among the Samosir Batak
           of Sumatra.* Stanford, Calif.: Stanford University Press.
Shils, Edward
   1971   Tradition. *Comparative Studies in Society and History* 13(2):122–159.

Short account of the Battas

1821   *Asiatic Journal and Monthly Register* (London) 12:215–219.
       Reprinted from the *Malayan Miscellanies.* Bencoolen, Sumatra:
       Sumatran Mission Press.

Shufeldt, Dr. R. W.

1897   Notes on Bhils, Burmese, and Battaks. *Popular Science Monthly*
       50:34–42.

Siagian, Prof. L. D.

1990   *Turi-turian Ni Halak Batak.* Medan: Penerbit Linggom.

Sibeth, Achim

1991   *The Batak: Peoples of the island of Sumatra.* London: Thames and
       Hudson.

Sihombing, Dr. T. M.

1985   *Si Jonaha: Dan Cerita-cerita Dongeng yang Lain.* Jakarta: PN Balai
       Pustaka.

Silverman, Eric Kline

1999   Tourist art as the crafting of identity in the Sepik River (Papua
       New Guinea). In *Unpacking culture: Art and commodity in colonial
       and postcolonial worlds,* ed. Ruth B. Phillips and Christopher B.
       Steiner. Berkeley: University of California Press.

Situmorang, Sitor

1993   *Toba na Sae: Sejarah Ringkas Lahirnya Institusi-institusi Organisasi
       Parbaringin dan Dinasti Singamangaraja dalam Sejarah Suku Bangsa
       Batak-Toba.* Jakarta: Pustaka Sinar Harapan.

Smith, Valene

1989   Introduction. In *Hosts and guests: The anthropology of tourism,* 2d ed.
       Ed. V. Smith. Philadelphia: University of Pennsylvania Press.

Smith, William, ed.

1873   *A dictionary of Greek and Roman geography by various writers.*
       London: John Murray.

Spooner, Brian

1986   Weavers and dealers: The authenticity of an Oriental carpet. In
       The social life of things, ed. A. Appadurai. Cambridge: Cambridge
       University Press.

Steedly, Mary M.

1993   *Hanging without a rope: Narrative experience in colonial and postcolonial
       Karoland.* Princeton, N.J.: Princeton University Press.

Steiner, Christopher B.

1994   *African art in transit.* Cambridge: Cambridge University Press.

Stewart, Kathleen

1995   *A space on the side of the road: Cultural poetics in an "other" America.*
       Princeton, N.J.: Princeton University Press.

1996   An occupied place. In *Senses of place*. Santa Fe: School of American
       Research.

Stewart, Susan
   1984   *On longing: Narratives of the miniature, the gigantic, the souvenir, the
          collection*. Baltimore: Johns Hopkins Press.

Swift, Jonathan (Lemuel Gulliver)
   1726   *Travels into several remote nations of the world*. Dublin: P. Wogen.

Tambiah, Stanley
   1979   A performative approach to ritual. *Proceedings of the British Academy*
          65:113–169. Tanah kami bukan untuk tempat pabrik semen.
          Prakarsa 53(1995):14–16.

Tappubolon, Oppu Ijolo
   1985   *Torsatorsa Batak*. Medan: Lemari Batak.

Taussig, Michael
   1993   *Mimesis and alterity: A particular history of the senses*. London:
          Routledge.

Taylor, Paul Michael, ed.
   1994   *Fragile traditions: Indonesian art in jeopardy*. Honolulu: University
          of Hawai'i Press.

Thomas, Nicholas
   1991   *Entangled objects: Exchange, material culture and colonialism in the
          Pacific*. Cambridge, Mass.: Harvard University Press.
   1994   *Colonialism's culture: Anthropology, travel, and government*.
          Cambridge: Polity Press.
   1995   *Oceanic art*. London: Thames and Hudson.

Timothy, Dallen J., and Geoffrey Wall
   1997   Selling to Tourists: Indonesian Street Vendors. In *Annals of
          Tourism Research* 24(2):322–340.

Tobing, B.A.S.
   1972   *Djambar Hata: Tarombo Adat Batak*. Jakarta: privately printed.

Tobing, Ph. O. L.
   1994   *The Toba Batak belief in the High God*. 3d ed. Jakarta.

Torgovnick, Marianna
   1990   *Gone primitive: Savage intellects, modern lives*. Chicago: University of
          Chicago Press.

Tsing, Anna Lowenhaupt
   1993   *In the realm of the Diamond Queen*. Princeton, N.J.: Princeton
          University Press.

Tucker, Hazel
   1997   The ideal village: Interactions through tourism in central
          Anatolia. In *Tourists and tourism: Identifying with people and places*,
          ed. S. Abram, J. Waldren, and D.V.L. Macleod. Oxford: Berg.

Turner, Peter, et al.

1995 *Indonesia: A travel survival kit.* Hawthorn, Victoria, Australia: Lonely Planet Publications.

Turner, Victor

1969 *The ritual process: Structure and anti-structure.* Ithaca, N.Y.: Cornell University Press.

1979 "Liminal" to "liminoid," in play, flow, and ritual: An essay in comparative symbology. In *Process, performance, and pilgrimage: A study in comparative symbology.* New Delhi: Concept Publishing Company.

Urry, John

1990 *The tourist gaze.* London: Sage Publications.

Valk, Felix A.

1988 Museum voor Volkenkunde, Rotterdam. In *Expressions of belief: Masterpieces of African, Oceanic, and Indonesian art from the Museum voor Volkenkunde, Rotterdam,* ed. S. Grueb. New York: Rizzoli.

Van Brakel, Koos, and David van Duuren

1996 The Georg Tillmann Collection. *A passion for Indonesian art: The Georg Tillmann (1882–1941) Collection at the Tropenmuseum Amsterdam.* Amsterdam: Tropenmuseum.

Van den Abbeele, Georges

1980 Sightseers: The tourist as theorist. *Diacritics* (Winter): 2–14.

1992 *Travel as metaphor from Montaigne to Rousseau.* Minneapolis: University of Minnesota Press.

Van den Berghe, Pierre L.

1992 Tourism and the ethnic division of labor. *Annals of Tourism Research* 19(2):234–249.

1994 *The quest for the other: Ethnic tourism in San Cristobal, Mexico.* Seattle: University of Washington Press.

Van Gennep, Arnold

1960 *The rites of passage.* Chicago: University of Chicago Press.

Veldhuisen-Djajasoebrata, Alit

1988 The Indonesian Collection. In *Expressions of belief: Masterpieces of African, Oceanic, and Indonesian art from the Museum voor Volkenkunde, Rotterdam,* ed. S. Grueb. New York: Rizzoli.

Vergouwen, Jacob C.

1964 *The social organization and customary law of the Toba-Batak of northern Sumatra.* The Hague: Martinus Nijhoff.

Viner, A. C.

1979 The changing Batak. *Journal of the Malysian Branch of the Royal Asiatic Society* 52(2):84–112.

Volkman, Toby A.
1990 Visions and revisions: Toraja culture and the tourist gaze. *American Ethnologist* 17(1):91–110.

Von Brenner, J. F.
1894 *Besuch bei den Kannibalen Sumatras: Erste Durchquerung der Unabhangigen Batak-Lande.* Würzburg: Leo Woerl.

Wasis, Widjiono, ed.
1991 *Mengenal Tanahair: Ensiklopedi Nusantara.* Jakarta: Dian Rakyat.

Welsch, Wolfgang
1996 Aestheticization processes: Phenomena, distinctions, and prospects. *Theory, Culture, and Society* 13(1):1–24.

Wheeler, Tony
1977 *South-east Asia on a shoestring.* South Yarra, Victoria, Australia: Lonely Planet Publications.

Wikan, Unni
1990 *Managing turbulent hearts: A Balinese formula for living.* Chicago: University of Chicago Press.

Witt, Christine A., and Peter L. Wright
1992 Tourist motivation: Life after Maslow. In *Choice and demand in tourism,* ed. P. Johnson and B. Thomas. London: Mansell Publications.

Yiannakis, Andrew, and Heather Gibson
1992 Roles tourists play. *Annals of Tourism Research* 19(2):287–303.

INDEX

Adams, Kathleen, 23, 230n.17, 231n.23, 232n.30, 233n.35
Adams, Vincanne, 233n.37
Ambarita, 9
Anderson, Benedict, 252n.9
Anderson, John, 64, 239n.41
Antique, 3, 150–153, 154–156, 254n.37
Appadurai, Arjun, 39
Arden, Harvey, 242n.26
Armstrong, Robert Plant, 235n.51
Art: artifact and, 153n.22; craft and, 39, 40; evaluations of, 40, 140–142, 235n.51, 253n.17; "masterpiece," 253n.21; Toba Batak perceptions of, 40–41; touristic object and, 39, 40, 140–145, 225. *See also* Style
Authenticity: characteristics of, 37, 234nn.44, 50, 235n.51; discussion of concept, 36–37; fake and, 37, 234n.45; marketplace and, 182; nonexistence of, 37; patina and, 235n.52; style and, 37; touristic objects and, 34, 37, 145, 146–149, 202, 209–210, 219–220, 225; wood carvings and, 34
Author: becoming Batak, 75–77, 240n.10, 247n.50; learning to carve, 102–112; learning Toba Batak language, 70–72; narratives and, 1–14; painting Jesus, 130–132; participant in tourism, 32, 195–198, 204, 212–213, 227n.6; teaching English, 194–195; traveler, 1–4; use of questionnaire, 227n.7. *See also* Tourism, Cultural

Barbier, Jean Paul, 255nn.39, 40
Bargaining, 179–182, 184, 201–206, 211

Basso, Keith, 223n.28, 228n.2, 229nn.8, 10
Bataks: description of, 31–32; disappearing, 141–142
Bataks, Gayo, 232n.33
Bataks, Karo, 234n.34
Bataks, Toba, *adat* and, 10, 106–107, 113, 257n.14; animism and, 84–88, 243nn.32, 36; blacksmiths, 249n.3; cannibalism and, 81–84, 84 fig. 3, 88; cheats, 89–92; cleverness and, 92, 213, 219, 245n.44; complementary schismogenesis and, 33–34; concept of soul, 235n.5; connection with homeland, 57, 58, 223; cooking 239n.3; *datu* (shaman) and, 49, 55, 149, 190, 251n.14; description of, 30–32, 91–93, 95–98; emigration from homeland, 53; ethnic identity, 91–93, 95–97, 170–171, 212, 223n.37, 246nn.48, 49, 247nn.50, 51, 52; family life of, 112–118; folktales, 255n.1; homosexuality and, 17, 227n.5; interactions with travelers, 68, 72–73, 89–90, 164–165; jealousy, 96–97, 247n.53; kinship system, 106–107, 227n.4, 240n.9; land tenure laws, 237n.25; language and, 70–72, 167–168; loss of traditions, 114; migration of, 237n.20; narratives among, 5–7, 14–16, 70, 238n.28; painters, 45–46; Parmalim, 244n.37; perceptions of author, 17; perceptions of Lake Toba, 42–50; perceptions of travelers, 93, 164–165, 171, 174, 245n.47, 256n.11; prehistory, 236n.16; pre-marital relationships, 240n.7; pride of culture, 212; "primitive," 74–75,

Wood carvings: antique, 3, 150–153, 154–156; "authentic," 34, 158, 202; *cankir mewah,* 195–197, 196 fig. 14, 207, 208; changes to, 205–206, 219–220; Christianity and, 114, 203; *cipta baru,* 121, 126–127, 128, 129, 191–201, 206–210, 219; communal property, 124; *debata idup,* 103, 119; energized, 144, 149, 252n.8; fake, 3–4, 119, 135, 150, 213–219, 251n.12; *gorga* decorations, 109, 114, pl. 8, 195, 199, 200, 204, 205, 236n.13, 249n.2; *hasapi,* 96, 199, 205; innovative, 34; loss of antique prototypes, 114, 153–156, 158, 255n.42; narratives and, 254n.36; neotraditional, 115, 158, 250n.9, 253n.24; *orang malu,* 197–199, 204, 207; pendants, 125; photocopies used to create, 123, 132–134, 156–157, 158; plow, 119–127; powder horn, 134; "primitive," 34, 146, 202, 204; promotions and, 203 prototypes for, 121; *pukkor unte,* 190–194, 191 fig. 12, 199, 207; ring box, 126–127, 128 fig. 8; *rumbi,* 119, pl. 10; *sahan,* 109, 119, 120 fig. 6, 190, 199, 201; *sahan* stopper, 134; *sigalegale,* 132–133, 133 fig. 9, 190, 204, 252n.3; *singasinga,* pl.14, 258n.6; *singasinga* lamp, 199–XX, pl. 15, 207, 208; surface finishes, 125–126, 200–201; symmetry of, 111; television and, 200; Toba Batak perceptions of, 115, 153, 255n.41; "traditional," 34, 202; *tunggal panaluan,* 123, 124 fig. 7, 142, 144, 149, 154, 190, 201, 203, 213–219, 251n.14; types of wood used for, 121; Western perceptions of, 136–145, 147–149, 203. *See also* Art; Touristic object

Wood carvers, 250n.10; brokers and, 115, 119, 134, 135, 144, 156; carving *gorga,* 109, 249n.2; competition among, 192, 208, 210; concerns with symmetry, 111; criticism among, 127, 251n.17; difficulties finding wood, 121–122, 250n.7, 251n.13; family life 112–113, 129, 250n.6; father-son relationships, 108–109; innovations and, 109, 126–127, 191–201, 205, 206–210; methods of work, 105–106, 110 fig. 4, 111, 117–118, 125–126, 249n.2, 250n.5; obligations to *hulahula,* 106, 120; photocopies, other visual images and, 123, 128, 132–136, 133 fig. 9; stealing ideas, 192–195, 208–209; teaching and, 102–107, 114; tools of, 104, 105, 107, 110 fig. 4, 249n.3; traveler preferences and, 192–193, 205; tricking travelers, 213–219; women as, 250n.4. *See also* Dolok, Nalom; Partoho; Tanak

Yiannakis, Andrew and Heather Gibson, 229n.10

ABOUT THE AUTHOR

Andrew Causey's early interests focused on the archeology and epigraphy of the Maya peoples of present-day Mexico, Guatemala, and Belize, but it was a tourist trip to Southeast Asia in 1989 that inspired him to shift his research to the contemporary cultures of Indonesia. He received his doctorate in anthropology from the University of Texas at Austin in 1997. Causey has published articles on his Sumatra research in *Museum Anthropology, Indonesia and the Malay World,* and *Crossroads,* and in collected volumes. He is an accomplished artist, having worked as a professional illustrator and cartoonist for many years, and is presently professor of anthropology at Columbia College Chicago.

Production Notes for Causey / *Hard Bargaining in Sumatra*

Cover and interior designed by Rich Hendel
Text and display type in Garamond 3.

Composition by Josie Herr.

Printing and binding by The Maple-Vail Book Manufacturing Group.

Printed on 60 lb. Text White Opaque.